CHOW!
San Francisco
Bay Area

CHOW!
San Francisco
Bay Area

300

**AFFORDABLE PLACES
FOR GREAT MEALS
& GOOD DEALS**

SHARRON WOOD

SASQUATCH BOOKS
SEATTLE

Printed in the United States
Distributed in the United States by Sasquatch Books

First edition
07 06 05 04 03 02 01   5 4 3 2 1

ISBN: 1-57061-283-8
ISSN: 1536-2825

Cover photograph: David Wakely
Cover design: Kate Basart
Interior design: Kate Basart

SPECIAL SALES

Best Places® guidebooks are available at special discounts on bulk purchases for corporate,
club, or organization sales promotions, premiums, and gifts. Special editions, including per-
sonalized covers, excerpts of existing guides, and corporate imprints, can be created in
large quantities for specific needs. For more information, contact your local bookseller or
Special Sales, Best Places Guidebooks, 615 Second Avenue, Suite 260, Seattle, Washington
98104, (800)775-0817.

SASQUATCH BOOKS
615 Second Avenue
Seattle, WA 98104
(206)467-4300
books@SasquatchBooks.com
www.SasquatchBooks.com

Contents

Acknowledgments

Writing a guide to San Francisco restaurants probably seems like so much fun that it shouldn't be classified as work at all. Nevertheless, planning, writing, and editing this guide took many long days and the help of a great many friends. Foremost among them are the contributors to the book, who researched and wrote almost half of its reviews: Miriam Wolf, Kurt Wolff, Karen Solomon, Denise M. Leto, Julie Jares, and Kathleen Dodge. Tara Duggan in particular contributed many reviews and generously shared her vast knowledge of the San Francisco dining scene and food in general. I consider myself fortunate to call these talented writers my colleagues and close friends. Marisa Gierlich, Tania Gutierrez, Kristina Malsberger, Michele Posner, Jonathan Ring, and Maggie Trapp all accompanied me on reviewing expeditions, graciously traipsing across town for Ethiopian food or Korean barbecue when perhaps they would have rather just gone to the corner taqueria for a burrito. Thanks to Kate Rogers at Sasquatch Books for giving me the opportunity to work on a project that allowed me to eat out ten times a week without once feeling decadent. And to editors Laura Gronewold, Cynthia Rubin, and Sharon Vonasch, thank you for shepherding this project from manuscript to published book. Finally, my family—Mom, Dad, Cindi, and Bronson—put things in perspective and reminded me from time to time that there are more important things than a perfect plate of pad Thai.

Contributors

After working as executive editor of the Berkeley Guides division of Fodor's Travel Publications, and as managing editor of a travel website, **SHARRON WOOD** happily became a freelance writer and editor. She has contributed to more than two dozen guides to the San Francisco area, writing about everything from high tea at the Ritz-Carlton to where to shop for feather boas and false eyelashes. Editing and writing much of this book allowed her to indulge her seemingly contradictory passions for sushi and Southern comfort food; when someone figures out how to mix grits and raw fish into a single dish, she'll probably eat it.

KATHLEEN DODGE has scoured the culinary globe, from wasabi-soaked sashimi to tofu-pesto vegan pizzettas, to write reviews for Fodor's UpClose, Berkeley, and Gold Guide series, as well as for Avalon's Moon Handbooks and numerous web sites. When not eating, Kathleen resides in Berkeley, where she tries to bicycle away the calories and cooks up boxed mac and cheese when no one is looking.

TARA DUGGAN received her chef's training at San Francisco's California Culinary Academy. Though she loves to cook, she likes experiencing the Bay Area's amazing restaurant scene even better. Tara is a staff writer for the *San Francisco Chronicle's* Food section.

JULIE JARES has spent the last few years in the dot-com fray as a writer and editor for Sidewalk.com and eHow.com. Her freelance writing and editing projects include Fodor's *UpClose California, The Berkeley Guide to Italy, Los Angeles CityPack,* and *San Francisco CityPack.*

The financial constraints of being a graduate student at UC Berkeley compelled **DENISE M. LETO** to search out the best cheap food in town, and she's been eating well and writing about it ever since. Her work has appeared in numerous Fodor's guidebooks, online, and in the *San Francisco Bay Guardian.* She holds an honorary table at Juan's Place and has been known to eat her weight in Cheese Board pizza.

Rumor has it that **KAREN SOLOMON** will add sugar to water with lemon to save a buck and a half plus tip. When not scrimping for good food she's writing about it for Sidewalk.com and the *San Francisco Bay Guardian;* she also serves as the San Francisco correspondent for Lodging.com.

MIRIAM WOLF was the dining editor of the *San Francisco Bay Guardian* for 10 years. She is currently a freelance writer and editor who lives in San Francisco's very best cheap-eating neighborhood–the Richmond District.

KURT WOLFF is the author of the *Rough Guide to Country Music*. When not busy digging through dusty old record bins, he finds time to write about beer, food, travel, and other life-affirming subject matter for various publications.

What's a Good Deal?

It's no news to any San Franciscan that the city is not what it once was. Sky-high rents, the impossibility of parking, and the mom-and-pop places being taken over by soulless new chains are topics of endless conversation.

In such times, you might think all the city's inexpensive restaurants would just be driven out of business, replaced with la-di-da spots where a bottle of wine costs a day's wages. But we're here to report that, happily, there's life in San Francisco's budget dining scene yet. Some scrappy little establishments have managed to hang on to their leases through the great San Francisco land grab and still serve up heaping plates of food for little more than they charged 10 years ago. And though many newly opened restaurants *do* charge an arm and leg, there are some that serve a full meal for less than others charge for valet parking.

Affordable restaurants come in all stripes, and we've tried to cover as broad a selection as possible. Sometimes we don't mind filling our own water glasses or standing in line in order to get a heaping plate of food for less than eight bucks. And often a Formica wonderland suits us just fine, especially when it serves some of the best barbecue or Vietnamese pho in the city. Other times, how-ever, it's worth digging a little deeper into our pockets to hang out with the beautiful people (or at least the trendy people) in some hip little spot. Or maybe we want a cozy and romantic restaurant where we don't have to look at our dates under fluorescent spotlights.

Chow! San Francisco Bay Area provides 300 honest recommendations on great, inexpensive restaurants in San Francisco, Berkeley, Oakland, and parts of Marin. At each of them, you can put together a dinner for two for $40 or less. At some places you'd be hard-pressed to spend $20, though others are on the higher end of the price range. Breakfast and lunch typically cost a bit less than dinner.

CHOW! TIPS

Some tips to remember: diners, cafes, and even some ethnic restaurants often feature daily specials that include appetizer and main course for one great, low price. At more upscale restaurants, ordering a couple of appetizers instead of an entree may be a good deal. At establishments that offer wine, consider bringing your own bottle and paying a corkage fee, often a better deal than even the cheapest vintage on their list.

MEALS/HOURS

Although a lot of these restaurants serve all three squares, some focus on only one or two meals. We've made a point of telling you which days and meals you'll find a restaurant open. But call ahead for specific hours, as these can change from week to week.

CASHING OUT

Every place listed here accepts cash. A few take checks; some take only local checks. We've indicated which restaurants accept what, but note that the usual ID will probably be required in either case. For those toting plastic, we've listed which credit cards a place accepts: American Express (AE), Diner's Club (DC), Discover (DIS), MasterCard (MC), and Visa (V).

ALCOHOL

For those who want to know, we tell you, using one of the following: full bar, beer and wine, beer only, wine only, no alcohol.

KIDS, PETS, AND OTHER APPENDAGES

As a general rule, where dining is inexpensive, kids are welcome. A few of the places reviewed herein, however, are pubs or bars, which require patrons to be 21 years old. If you're considering one of these spots and want to take along Junior, call ahead. Fido, of course, is generally not welcome, but also note that a few places with sidewalk seating are in fact dog-friendly. Call ahead to be sure.

SMOKING

If you've just arrived in California, perhaps you haven't figured out that smoking is illegal in all restaurants and even bars. The law is occasionally flouted at bars (though violators are subject to a fine if caught by police), but never at restaurants.

DISABILITIES

Those establishments that are wheelchair-accessible are designated by a wheelchair icon at the end of the facts following the review. If you have special needs, however, you may still want to call ahead.

INDEXES AND EATERY INFO

Reviews here are in alphabetical order. When a restaurant has two locations, we list both. For establishments with more than two branches, we list the original or most recommended branch only, but the neighborhood designation indicates where you can find other branches. Each restaurant is indexed in the back of this book by location, type of food served, and other special characteristics, such as outdoor seating, kid-friendliness, late or all-night dining, or live entertainment. With some clever cross-referencing you can find a Middle Eastern spot with live belly dancing in a jiffy.

READER'S REPORT

Please feel free to use the report forms provided in the back of this book (or a copy of one) to let us know what you think. The usefulness of *Chow! San Francisco Bay Area* is dependent upon the hundreds who write to pat us on the back, share a new discovery, or tell us when we screwed up.

Location Index

Pasta Pomodoro
Sapporo-Ya

LAKE MERRITT
Autumn Moon Cafe
Noah's Bagels
Spettro

LAUREL HEIGHTS
Ella's
Pasta Pomodoro
Tortola

LOWER HAIGHT
Axum Cafe
Burger Joint
Hahn's Hibachi
Indian Oven
Kate's Kitchen
Memphis Minnie's Smokehouse
  Bar-B-Que
Pasta Pomodoro
Rosamunde Sausage Grill
Squat and Gobble Cafe
Thep Phanom
Two Jacks Seafood

MARINA
Andalé Taquería
Barney's Gourmet Hamburgers
Bechelli's Restaurant
Bistro Aix
Cafe Marimba
Dragon Well
Fuzio Universal Pasta
Grove Café
Hahn's Hibachi
Home Plate
Left at Albuquerque
Lhasa Moon
Los Hermanos Mexican Food
Malee
Noah's Bagels
Pasta Pomodoro
Pluto's
Yukol Place
Zao Noodle Bar

MISSION DISTRICT
Amira
Angkor Borei
Big Mouth Burgers and Beers
Blue Plate
Bombay Ice Cream and Chaat
Brisas de Acapulco
Burger Joint
Casa Sanchez
Cha Cha Cha
Charanga
Chava's Mexican Restaurant
Dusit Thai
El Nuevo Frutilandia
El Pollo Supremo
Esperpento
Firecracker
Herbivore: The Earthly Grill
Izalco
Katz Bagels
La Palma Mexicatessen
La Rondalla
La Taqueria
Luna Park
Nicaragua
Noah's Bagels
North Beach Pizza
Pakwan Pakistani Indian Restaurant
Panchita's Restaurant
Pancho Villa
Papalote Mexican Grill
Pauline's Pizza
Puerto Alegre
Roosevelt Tamale Parlor
Saigon Saigon
San Miguel
St. Francis Fountain & Candy
Slanted Door
Taqueria Cancun
Taqueria La Cumbre
Ti Couz
Tokyo Go Go
Truly Mediterranean
Yamo Thai Kitchen
Zante Pizza and Indian Cuisine

NOE VALLEY
Alice's Restaurant
Barney's Gourmet Hamburgers
Chloe's
Eric's
Hahn's Hibachi
Lovejoy's Tea Room
Matsuya
Mill Millie's
Pasta Pomodoro
Savor

NORTH BEACH
Bocce Cafe
Café Niebaum-Coppola
Caffè Greco
Caffè Macaroni
Gira Polli
Helmand
Il Pollaio
L'Osteria del Forno
Mama's on Washington Square
Mario's Bohemian Cigar Store
Molinari Delicatessan
Mo's
North Beach Pizza
Pasta Pomodoro
Powell's Place #2
Tommaso's Ristorante Italiano

PACIFIC HEIGHTS
Boulangerie Bay Bread
Chez Nous
Eliza's
Extreme Pizza
Gourmet Carousel
Hard Rock Cafe
Jackson Fillmore
La Mediterranée
Mozzarella di Bufala Pizzeria
Noah's Bagels
Zao Noodle Bar

POLK GULCH
Cordon Bleu
Grubstake
Hahn's Hibachi
Maharani

Mel's Drive-In
Pancho's
Piccadilly Fish and Chips
Swan Oyster Depot

POTRERO HILL
Arturo's Restaurant
Eliza's
Goat Hill Pizza
Just For You

RICHMOND DISTRICT
Angkor Wat
Bill's Place
Brother's Korean Restaurant
Burma Super Star
Cheers Cafe
Cinderella Bakery, Delicatessen and
    Restaurant
Clement Okazu Ya
Coriya Hot Pot City
Extreme Pizza
Fountain Court
Hong Kong Flower Lounge
Jakarta
Khan Toke Thai House
King of Thai Noodle House
La Vie
Le Soleil
Mandalay Restaurant
Mel's Drive-In
Pancho's
Pho Hoa Hiep IV
Pho Tu Do
Q
Taiwan
Thai Cafe
Tommy's Mexican Restaurant
Ton Kiang

RUSSIAN HILL
La Boulange de Polk
Little Thai Restaurant
Mario's Bohemian Cigar Store
Polker's American Café
San Francisco Art Institute Cafe
Za Gourmet Pizza
Zarzuela

SOUTH OF MARKET
asiaSF
Basil Thai
Brainwash Cafe and Laundromat
Caffè Museo
Cha Am
Conard 9th St. Café
Extreme Pizza
Firewood Cafe
Francisco and Molly
Hamburger Mary's
Henry's Hunan
Le Charm
Manora's Thai Cuisine
Mel's Drive-In
Mo's
Mr. Ralph's Café
North Beach Pizza
Primo Patio Cafe
Schnitzelhaus
Specialty's Cafe and Bakery
Taqueria Cancun
Tu Lan
Wa-Ha-Ka
Yank Sing

SUNSET DISTRICT
Café Rain Tree
Cha Am
Crepevine
Einstein's Café
Flipper's Gourmet Burgers
The Ganges
Hahn's Hibachi
Hotei
King of Thai Noodle House
Marnee Thai
Milano Pizzeria
New Eritrea Restaurant and Bar
Noah's Bagels
Park Chow
Pasta Pomodoro
Pho Hoa Hiep IV
Pluto's
Pomelo
Tortola
Zao Noodle Bar

TENDERLOIN
Ba Le
Dottie's True Blue Café
Lalita Thai
Naan 'n' Curry
Pacific Restaurant
Pagolac
Saigon Sandwiches
Shalimar

UNION SQUARE
Armani Cafe
Cafe de la Presse
Firewood Cafe
King of Thai Noodle House
Sears Fine Food
Taqueria El Balazo

UPPER HAIGHT
Asqew Grill
Cha Cha Cha
Citrus Club
Crescent City Cafe
Escape from New York Pizza
Kan Zaman
Massawa Restaurant
North Beach Pizza
Pork Store Café
Sweet Heat
Taqueria El Balazo
Squat and Gobble Cafe
Truly Mediterranean
Zazie's

WESTERN ADDITION
Brother-in-Law's Bar-B-Que
Frankie's Bohemian Cafe
Mozzarella di Bufala Pizzeria

WEST PORTAL
Mozzarella di Bufala Pizzeria

San Francisco Environs

ALBANY
Christopher's Nothing Fancy Cafe
Sam's Log Cabin

DOWNTOWN BERKELEY
Cafe Panini
Cambodiana's
Chaat Café
Crepes-a-Go-Go
Long Life Vegi House

DOWNTOWN OAKLAND
Battambang
Caffe 817
Hahn's Hibachi
Jade Villa
Le Cheval
Ma's Caribbean Cuisine and Roti Shop
Noah's Bagels
Tsing Tao

LARKSPUR
Emporio Rulli

MILL VALLEY
Dipsea Cafe
Gira Polli
Joe's Taco Lounge
Piazza D'Angelo

NORTH BERKELEY
Ajanta
Barney's Gourmet Hamburgers
Cactus Taqueria
Cha Am
Cha-Ya
Cheese Board Pizza
Chester's Bayview Cafe
Fatapple's
Noah's Bagels
Odyssia
Phoenix Next Door
Saul's Restaurant and Delicatessen
Smokey Joe's
Zachary's Chicago Pizza

NORTH OAKLAND
Asmara Restaurant and Bar
Barney's Gourmet Hamburgers
Cactus Taqueria
Crepevine
Flipper's Gourmet Burgers
Isobune

Mama's Royal Cafe
Nan Yang
Oliveto Cafe and Restaurant
Pasta Pomodoro
Pizza Rustica
Red Tractor Cafe
Tropix
Uzen
Zachary's Chicago Pizza

SAUSALITO
à table!
Avatar's
Hamburgers

SOUTH BERKELEY
Barney's Gourmet Hamburgers
Berkeley Thai House
Blue Nile
Cafe Intermezzo
Flint's BBQ
Kirala
La Bayou
La Méditerranée
Le Cheval
Noah's Bagels
Rick and Ann's

TIBURON
Sam's Anchor Café
Sweden House Bakery & Cafe
Waypoint Pizza

WEST BERKELEY–EMERYVILLE
Bette's Oceanview Diner
Breads of India
Café Fanny
Cafe Tululah
Flint's BBQ
Homemade Cafe
Juan's Place
Lois the Pie Queen
Maharani
North Beach Pizza
O Chamé
Picante Cocina Mexicana
Pyramid Brewery and Alehouse
Vik's

Food Type Index

AMERICAN
Asqew Grill
Autumn Moon Cafe
Barking Basset Cafe
Bechelli's Restaurant
Bill's Place
Bistro Burger
Blue
Blue Plate
Brainwash Cafe and Laundromat
Cafe Tululah
Cheers Cafe
Chester's Bayview Cafe
Chloe's
Chow
Conard 9th St. Café
Dipsea Cafe
Doidge's
Ella's
Fatapple's
Fog City Diner
Francisco and Molly
Frankie's Bohemian Cafe
Grubstake
Hard Rock Cafe
Homemade Cafe
Home Plate
It's Tops
Just For You
Kate's Kitchen
Lois the Pie Queen
Luna Park
Mama's on Washington Square
Mama's Royal Cafe
Mel's Drive-In
Miss Millie's
Park Chow
Pluto's
Polker's American Café
Pork Store Café
Powell's Place
Pyramid Brewery and Alehouse
Q
Red Tractor Cafe

Rick and Ann's
Sam's Anchor Cafe
Sam's Log Cabin
Sears Fine Food
St. Francis Fountain & Candy
Squat and Gobble Cafe
Tommy's Joynt

BAGELS
Katz Bagels
Saul's Restaurant and Delicatessen
Noah's Bagels

BAKERY
à table!
Boulangerie Bay Bread
Cinderella Bakery, Delicatessen and
    Restaurant
Citizen Cake
La Boulange de Polk
Rick and Ann's
Savor
Specialty's Cafe and Bakery
Sweden House Bakery & Cafe

BARBECUE
Brother-in-Law's Bar-B-Que
Flint's BBQ
Hahn's Hibachi
Memphis Minnie's Smokehouse
    Bar-B-Que
Powell's Place

BRAZILIAN
Canto do Brasil

BURGERS
Barney's Gourmet Hamburgers
Big Mouth Burgers and Beers
Bill's Place
Bistro Burger
Brainwash Cafe and Laundromat
Burger Joint
Conard 9th St. Café
Fatapple's
Flipper's Gourmet Burgers

Francisco and Molly
Frankie's Bohemian Cafe
Grubstake
Hamburger Mary's
Hamburgers
Homemade Cafe
Hot 'n' Hunky
Joe's Cable Car
Mel's Drive-In
Mo's
Polker's American Café
Pyramid Brewery and Alehouse

CAJUN/CREOLE
Crescent City Cafe
La Bayou
Tropix

CALIFORNIA CUISINE
Bistro Aix
Caffè Museo
Cheers Cafe
Luna Park

CARIBBEAN
Avatar's
Cha Cha Cha
Charanga
Ma's Caribbean Cuisine and Roti Shop
Primo Patio Cafe
Tropix

CENTRAL AMERICAN
Brisas de Acapulco
Charanga
Izalco
Nicaragua
Panchita's Restaurant
San Miguel

CHINESE
Alice's Restaurant
Bow Hon Restaurant
Burma Super Star
Chef Jia's
Citrus Club
Coriya Hot Pot City
Dol Ho
Dragon Well

Eliza's
Eric's
Firecracker
Fountain Court
Gourmet Carousel
Great Eastern
Henry's Hunan
Hing Lung
Hong Kong Flower Lounge
House of Nanking
Jade Villa
Lichee Garden
Long Life Vegi House
Lucky Creation
Meriwa
New Asia
R&G Lounge
Taiwan
Ton Kiang
Tsing Tao
Yank Sing
Zao Noodle Bar

CUBAN
El Nuevo Frutilandia

DELI
Moishe's Pippic
Molinari Delicatessen
Saul's Restaurant and Delicatessen
Tommy's Joynt

DINER
Bechelli's Restaurant
Bette's Oceanview Diner
Bill's Place
Café Rain Tree
Conard 9th St. Café
Dottie's True Blue Café
Fog City Diner
Lois the Pie Queen
Grubstake
Hot 'n' Hunky
It's Tops
Just For You
Mel's Drive-In
Sears Fine Food
St. Francis Fountain & Candy

ECLECTIC
Asqew Grill
Avatar's
Blue Plate
Frjtz
Fuzio Universal Pasta
Luna Park
Pomelo
Q
Savor
Spettro

ETHIOPIAN/ERITREAN
Asmara Restaurant and Bar
Axum Cafe
Blue Nile
Massawa Restaurant
New Eritrea Restaurant and Bar

FISH AND CHIPS
Piccadilly Fish and Chips
Two Jacks Seafood

FRENCH
à table!
Bistro Aix
Boulangerie Bay Bread
Cafe Claude
Cafe de la Presse
Café Fanny
Chez Nous
Crepes-a-Go-Go
Crepevine
Frjtz
La Boulange de Polk
Le Charm
Luna Park
Metropol Café
Ti Couz
Zazie's

GERMAN/EASTERN EUROPEAN
Cafe Prague
Frankie's Bohemian Cafe
Hungarian Sausage Factory
Rosamunde Sausage Grill
Schnitzelhaus

Suppenküche
Tommy's Joynt

GREEK
Odyssia

HAWAIIAN
Tita's Hale 'Aina

HOT DOGS/SAUSAGES
Hungarian Sausage Factory
Rosamunde Sausage Grill

INDIAN
Ajanta
Avatar's
Bombay Ice Cream and Chaat
Breads of India
Chaat Café
The Ganges
Indian Oven
Maharani
Naan 'n' Curry
Pakwan Pakistani Indian Restaurant
Shalimar
Vik's
Zante Pizza and Indian Cuisine

INDONESIAN
Jakarta

IRISH
Autumn Moon Cafe

ITALIAN
Armani Cafe
Bocce Cafe
Café Fanny
Café Niebaum-Coppola
Caffe 817
Caffè delle Stelle
Caffè Greco
Caffè Macaroni
Cheers Cafe
Emporio Rulli
Firewood Cafe
Frjtz
Fuzio Universal Pasta
Gira Polli

Il Pollaio
Jackson Fillmore
L'Osteria del Forno
Luna Park
Mario's Bohemian Cigar Store
Metropol Café
Milano Pizzeria
Molinari Delicatessen
Mozzarella di Bufala Pizzeria
North Beach Pizza
Oliveto Cafe and Restaurant
Pasta Pomodoro
Phoenix Next Door
Piazza D'Angelo
Pizza Rustica
Rose's Cafe
Spettro
Tommaso's Ristorante Italiano

JAPANESE
Cha-Ya
Citrus Club
Clement Okazu Ya
Hotei
Izumiya
Juban
Kirala
Kushi Tsuru
Matsuya
Mifune
Moki's Sushi and Pacific Grill
O Chamé
Sapporo-Ya
Toyko Go Go
Uzen
Zao Noodle Bar

KOREAN
Brother's Korean Restaurant
Hahn's Hibachi

MEDITERRANEAN
Amira
à table!
Cafe deStijl
Caffè Museo
La Mediterranée

Odyssia
Truly Mediterranean

MEXICAN
Andalé Taquería
Arturo's Restaurant
Avatar's
Cactus Taqueria
Cafe Marimba
Casa Sanchez
Chava's Mexican Restaurant
Christopher's Nothing Fancy Cafe
El Pollo Supremo
Francisco and Molly
Joe's Taco Lounge
Juan's Place
La Palma Mexicatessen
La Rondalla
La Taqueria
Left at Albuquerque
Los Hermanos Mexican Food
Mom Is Cooking
Pancho's
Pancho Villa
Papalote Mexican Grill
Picante Cocina Mexicana
Puerto Alegre
Roosevelt Tamale Parlor
Sweet Heat
Taqueria Cancun
Taqueria El Balazo
Taqueria La Cumbre
Tommy's Mexican Restaurant
Tortola
Wa-Ha-Ka

MIDDLE EASTERN
Amira
Chez Nous
Helmand
Kan Zaman
La Mediterranée
Truly Mediterranean

PAN-ASIAN
asiaSF
Citrus Club

Fuzio Universal Pasta
Zao Noodle Bar

PIZZA
Cheese Board Pizza
Escape from New York Pizza
Extreme Pizza
Firewood Cafe
Goat Hill Pizza
Joe's Taco Lounge
Marcello's Pizza
Milano Pizzeria
Mozzarella di Bufala Pizzeria
North Beach Pizza
Pauline's Pizza
Pizza Rustica
Spettro
Vicolo
Waypoint Pizza
Za Gourmet Pizza
Zachary's Chicago Pizza
Zante Pizza and Indian Cuisine

PORTUGUESE
Grubstake

PUB GRUB
Pyramid Brewery and Alehouse

RUSSIAN
Cinderella Bakery, Delicatessen and
    Restaurant

SEAFOOD
Great Eastern
Swan Oyster Depot
Tita's Hale 'Aina
Piccadilly Fish and Chips
Two Jacks Seafood

SOUP/SALAD/SANDWICH
Armani Cafe
à table!
Ba Le
Barking Basset Cafe
Bistro Burger
Brainwash Cafe and Laundromat
Cafe deStijl

Café Fanny
Cafe Intermezzo
Cafe Panini
Cafe Prague
Café Rain Tree
Cafe Tululah
Caffe 817
Caffè Greco
Chester's Bayview Cafe
Chloe's
Conard 9th St. Café
Crepevine
Dipsea Cafe
Einstein's Café
Francisco and Molly
Grove Café
Homemade Cafe
Home Plate
Kate's Kitchen
Katz Bagels
La Boulange de Polk
Mama's on Washington Square
Marina Submarine
Mr. Ralph's Café
Pyramid Brewery and Alehouse
Sam's Log Cabin
San Francisco Art Institute Cafe
Saul's Restaurant and Delicatessen
Savor
Specialty's Cafe and Bakery
Smokey Joe's
Squat and Gobble Cafe
Sweden House Bakery & Cafe

SOUTHERN
Brother-in-Law's Bar-B-Que
Lois the Pie Queen
Pork Store Café
Powell's Place
Q

SPANISH/TAPAS
Barcelona
Chez Nous
Esperpento
Zarzuela

SUSHI

Cha-Ya
Clement Okazu Ya
Isobune
Izumiya
Kirala
Kushi Tsuru
Matsuya
Moki's Sushi and Pacific Grill
Nippon (no-name) Sushi
Tokyo Go Go
Uzen

SWEDISH

Sweden House Bakery & Cafe

TEA ROOM

Frjtz
Lovejoy's Tea Room

THAI

Basil Thai
Berkeley Thai House
Cha Am
Citrus Club
Dusit Thai
Khan Toke Thai House
Khun Phoa
King of Thai Noodle House
Lalita Thai
Little Thai Restaurant
Malee
Manora's Thai Cuisine
Marnee Thai
Thai Cafe
Thai House
Thep Phanom
Yamo Thai Kitchen
Yukol Place

TIBETAN

Lhasa Moon

VEGETARIAN

Ananda Fuara
Cha-Ya
Cheese Board Pizza
The Ganges
Herbivore: The Earthly Grill
Long Life Vegi House
Lucky Creation
Phoenix Next Door
Smokey Joe's

VIETNAMESE/SOUTHEAST ASIAN

Angkor Borei
Angkor Wat
Ba Le
Battambang
Burma Super Star
Cambodiana's
Citrus Club
Cordon Bleu
La Vie
Le Cheval
Le Soleil
Malee
Mandalay Restaurant
Nan Yang
Pacific Restaurant
Pagolac
Pho Hoa Hiep IV
Pho Tu Do
Saigon Saigon
Saigon Sandwiches
Slanted Door
Tu Lan
Zao Noodle Bar

Other Features Index

BREAKFAST/BRUNCH
Ananda Fuara
à table!
Autumn Moon Cafe
Barking Basset Cafe
Bechelli's Restaurant
Bette's Oceanview Diner
Boulangerie Bay Bread
Blue
Brainwash Cafe and Laundromat
Cafe Claude
Cafe de la Presse
Cafe deStijl
Café Fanny
Café Niebaum-Coppola
Cafe Prague
Café Rain Tree
Cafe Tululah
Caffe 817
Chava's Mexican Restaurant
Cheers Cafe
Chester's Bayview Cafe
Chloe's
Citizen Cake
Conard 9th St. Café
Crepes-a-Go-Go
Crepevine
Crescent City Cafe
Dipsea Cafe
Doidge's
Dottie's True Blue Café
Ella's
Fatapple's
Frjtz
Grove Café
Grubstake
Homemade Cafe
Home Plate
It's Tops
Izalco
Just For You
Kate's Kitchen
La Boulange de Polk
Lois the Pie Queen

Mama's on Washington Square
Mama's Royal Cafe
Mel's Drive-In
Meriwa
Miss Millie's
Moishe's Pippic
Mo's
Mr. Ralph's Café
New Asia
Odyssia
Oliveto Cafe and Restaurant
Pakwan Pakistani Indian Restaurant
Panchita's Restaurant
Picante Cocina Mexicana
Pluto's
Polker's American Café
Pork Store Café
Powell's Place
Puerto Alegre
Q
Red Tractor Cafe
Rick and Ann's
Rose's Cafe
Saigon Sandwiches
Sam's Anchor Cafe
Sam's Log Cabin
Saul's Restaurant and Delicatessen
Savor
Sears Fine Food
Specialty's Cafe and Bakery
Smokey Joe's
Squat and Gobble Cafe
Suppenküche
Sweden House Bakery & Cafe
Ti Couz
Tita's Hale 'Aina
Ton Kiang
Yank Sing
Zazie's

KID-FRIENDLY
Ba Le
Barking Basset Cafe
Barney's Gourmet Hamburgers

Bechelli's Restaurant
Big Mouth Burgers and Beers
Blue Nile
Bocce Cafe
Burger Joint
Cactus Taqueria
Chava's Mexican Restaurant
Christopher's Nothing Fancy Cafe
Crepevine
Dipsea Cafe
Einstein's Café
Goat Hill Pizza
Grove Café
Hahn's Hibachi
Hamburgers
Home Plate
Hungarian Sausage Factory
Il Pollaio
Isobune
Joe's Cable Car
Joe's Taco Lounge
Juan's Place
Lois the Pie Queen
Mel's Drive-In
Meriwa
Mifune
Milano Pizzeria
Mom Is Cooking
Mo's
New Asia
New Eritrea Restaurant and Bar
Nicaragua
North Beach Pizza
Pancho Villa
Pho Hoa Hiep IV
Picante Cocina Mexicana
Powell's Place
Pyramid Brewery and Alehouse
Red Tractor Cafe
Savor
Sears Fine Food
St. Francis Fountain & Candy
Spettro
Taqueria La Cumbre
Tommaso's Ristorante Italiano
Vicolo

Vik's
Zachary's Chicago Pizza
Zante Pizza and Indian Cuisine

LATE NIGHT/ALL NIGHT
asiaSF
Barcelona
Brisas de Acapulco
Brother's Korean Restaurant
Coriya Hot Pot City
Escape from New York Pizza
Extreme Pizza
Frjtz
Great Eastern
Grubstake
Hamburger Mary's
Hard Rock Cafe
Hing Lung
It's Tops
Kan Zaman
King of Thai Noodle House
King of Thai Noodle Café
La Rondalla
Marcello's Pizza
Mel's Drive-In
Milano Pizzeria
Mom Is Cooking
Naan 'n' Curry
Odyssia
Pancho Villa
Taqueria Cancun
Taqueria El Balazo
Tommy's Joynt
Truly Mediterranean

LIVE ENTERTAINMENT
Amira
asiaSF
Barcelona
Bocce Cafe
Brainwash Cafe and Laundromat
Cafe Claude
Cafe Prague
Esperpento
Frjtz
Hungarian Sausage Factory
Kan Zaman

La Rondalla
Mario's Bohemian Cigar Store
Odyssia
Puerto Alegre

OUTDOOR DINING
Autumn Moon Cafe
à table!
Barney's Gourmet Hamburgers
Bechelli's Restaurant
Berkeley Thai House
Big Mouth Burgers and Beers
Bill's Place
Bistro Aix
Bistro Burger
Blue
Blue Plate
Bocce Cafe
Cactus Taqueria
Cafe Claude
Cafe de la Presse
Cafe deStijl
Café Fanny
Café Niebaum-Coppola
Cafe Panini
Cafe Prague
Cafe Tululah
Caffè delle Stelle
Caffè Greco
Caffè Museo
Casa Sanchez
Cheers Cafe
Cheese Board Pizza
Chester's Bayview Cafe

Chloe's
Christopher's Nothing Fancy Cafe
Crepevine
Dipsea Cafe
Einstein's Café
Flipper's Gourmet Burgers
Fog City Diner
Francisco and Molly
Frjtz
Fuzio Universal Pasta
Grove Café
Grubstake
Herbivore: The Earthly Grill
La Boulange de Polk
Le Charm
Left at Albuquerque
Molinari Delicatessen
Mom Is Cooking
Odyssia
Pakwan Pakistani Indian Restaurant
Park Chow
Picante Cocina Mexicana
Pluto's
Primo Patio Cafe
Rick and Ann's
Rose's Cafe
Sam's Anchor Cafe
Sam's Log Cabin
San Francisco Art Institute Cafe
Savor
Squat and Gobble Cafe
Sweden House Bakery & Cafe
Tropix

300 GREAT MEALS

Ajanta

1888 SOLANO AVE, BERKELEY   510/526-4373
NORTH BERKELEY   *Indian*

Ajanta is not one of the cheapest Indian restaurants in the Bay Area, but it is one of the best, consistently ranked among the region's best Indian spots. Part of its appeal, no doubt, lies in its policy of presenting specialties from different regions of India each month, allowing intrepid diners to sample dishes beyond the usual curries and tandoori meats. The dining room is simultaneously exotic and serene, with intricate woodwork, golden fabrics, and graceful reproductions of murals found in India's Ajanta cave temples. The *badami murg* (boneless chicken cooked with coconut milk, potatoes, and spices like cardamom and cinnamon) and the lamb rib chops, cooked tandoori style, are a few of the standout dishes usually featured. Prix fixe dinners (around $14 at dinner, $10 at lunch) are a good deal, including appetizer, entree, rice, naan, vegetable, pappadam, and dessert. *AE, DC, DIS, MC, V; local checks only; lunch, dinner every day; beer and wine; www.ajantarestaurant.com.*

Alice's Restaurant

1599 SANCHEZ ST, SAN FRANCISCO   415/282-8999
NOE VALLEY   *Chinese*

Though the words "Alice's Restaurant" conjure up images of Arlo Guthrie and the 1960s for many people, to Noe Valley residents they mean great Chinese food. This bright and cheery corner restaurant serves fabulous and affordable Hunan and Mandarin specialties. The dishes are prepared artistically, with a California Cuisine flair. There are many house specialties: among the best are Alice's spicy eggplant with chicken, shrimp, and chile peppers; the seafood delight, with prawns, scallops, fish, and fresh vegetables; and the Hunan smoked pork, with leeks, cabbage, and red and green chile peppers. The sweet-and-sour dishes and sizzling rice soups are also excellent. The best part is that nothing on the menu is over $10. *MC, V; no checks; lunch, dinner every day; beer and wine.*

Amira

590 VALENCIA ST, SAN FRANCISCO ☎ 415/621-6213
MISSION DISTRICT 🍴 *Middle Eastern*

If it weren't for California's anti-smoking law, you'd feel right at home lighting up a hookah amid the velveteen-pillow decadence of Amira. As it is, a night spent lounging under the fabric-swathed ceiling is like a dreamy visit to a Middle Eastern kasbah. Sink into the ample cushions and feast like a sultan on aromatic dishes like baba ghanouj, hummus, and dolmas brought to the low-lying brass cafe tables scattered throughout the restaurant. Waiters seem to waft silently in and out of the room, leaving you to enjoy such delicacies as Moroccan couscous and the commendable walnut-garlic dip in peace. Flickering candlelight, hypnotic music, and loose-hipped nightly belly-dancing entertainment round out the escapist fantasy. Unless you plan on joining the harem, be sure to order a pot of sweet, thick Turkish coffee toward the end of your evening to ensure that you can pick yourself up off your comfortable spot long enough to stumble away at closing time. *AE, MC, V; no checks; dinner Tues-Sun; beer and wine.*

Ananda Fuara

1298 MARKET ST, SAN FRANCISCO ☎ 415/621-1994
CIVIC CENTER 🍴 *Vegetarian*

At this restaurant dedicated to the teachings of spiritual teacher Sri Chinmoy, ivy cascades down sky blue walls and waitresses in saris smile gently as they take your order. All this plus the flyers advertising meditation retreats can't change the fact that it's actually pretty clamorous here at lunchtime, when Civic Center workers pack in for tasty vegetarian meals. The food is fresh and hearty if not exactly sophisticated. The restaurant's specialty is the "neat-loaf," a big slab of meatless loaf served with mashed potatoes and gravy (you can also get it on a sandwich). A burrito made of whole black beans, brown rice, sour cream, and guacamole is encased in chapati rather than a tortilla—not like any burrito you'll find in the Mission District, but delicious nonetheless. Many of the items can be made for vegans. Drinks include Indian spiced chai, the Balinese Goddess (ice cream, coffee, and whipped cream), and the mango lassi, made of mango, yogurt, and sugar. A small menu of breakfast items—mostly omelets, French toast, and hotcakes—is served until 11AM. The restaurant closes for two weeks in mid-April and two weeks in late August. *Cash only; breakfast, lunch, dinner Mon–Tues and Thurs–Sat, breakfast, lunch Wed; no alcohol; www.anandafuara.citysearch.com.* ⅊

Andalé Taquería

2150 CHESTNUT ST, SAN FRANCISCO 📞 415/749-0506
MARINA 🍴 *Mexican*

In the Mission District, there are dozens of places where you can get a fat, satisfying burrito and a basket of chips for less than five bucks. But unfortunately, you're in the Marina now. There is, however, at least one place here where you can get fresh, tasty Mexican food for prices that, if they wouldn't fly in the Mission, will at least allow you to satisfy your hunger without breaking the bank. A minichain that started in the South Bay more than 10 years ago, Andalé serves up the usual taqueria fare—nachos, enchiladas, tacos, and, of course, the ever-present burrito, stuffed with your choice of mesquite-grilled beef, pork cooked in green sauce, or shrimp. As well as fruity aguas frescas, drinks on the menu include sangria, a variety of Mexican beers, and margaritas so tasty we're almost willing to forgive them for also serving chardonnay (who drinks chardonnay with burritos?). The decor is more attractive than most, with palm fronds cascading from a faux balcony, terra-cotta-colored walls, and black-and-white photos on the walls. The diners here are more attractive than most, too, with sporty men and women stopping by in athletic gear after a pickup game. *AE, MC, V; no checks; lunch, dinner every day; beer, wine, and margaritas only.* ⅊

Angkor Borei

3471 MISSION ST, SAN FRANCISCO 📞 415/550-8417
MISSION DISTRICT 🍴 *Vietnamese/Southeast Asian*

Despite its out-of-the-way location in the Outer Mission, Angkor Borei is one of those small restaurants with a loyal following. In a dining room with pink walls, red carpet, and intricate carvings, this family restaurant serves exquisitely spiced Cambodian fare with surprising refinement and finesse. For an appetizer, try the crispy spring rolls stuffed with a variety of vegetables or the huge lacy crepes folded omelet-style over a juicy vegetable-nut filling. Cold main dishes might include a medley of bean sprouts, chiles, basil, carrot, and julienned cucumbers, assembled over cold noodles and accompanied with a fragrant coconut-milk dipping sauce. For something hot and steamy, dip into the aromatic coconut-milk-laced curry with green Thai basil, lemongrass, Japanese eggplant, and straw mushrooms. A milder yet complex red curry enhances a plate of sautéed shrimp nestled on a bed of spinach. Many vegetarian dishes are available, too. *AE, DC, MC, V; no checks; lunch Mon-Sat, dinner every day; beer and wine.* ♿

Angkor Wat

4217 GEARY BLVD, SAN FRANCISCO 📞 415/221-7887
RICHMOND DISTRICT 🍴 *Vietnamese/Southeast Asian*

One of the city's best and most unusual Asian restaurants, Angkor Wat isn't shy about boasting of the accolades it has received–but it lives up to its reputation every time. Although pushing the envelope of the *Chow!* wallet, this treat is worth every penny. The elegant dining room, peppered with Cambodian art and musical instruments, is the setting for such fine delicacies as *nuom am bang*, a savory, lightly eggy Cambodian crepe wrapped around shrimp and chicken, fresh mint, and pickled cucumber and wearing a bold and tangy lime pineapple sauce. The *baksei laak khlouwn*, a spicy chicken and coconut milk curry steamed and served in a whole coconut, sits on almost every table, satisfied patrons gleefully digging out hunks of cooked coconut meat. And of course, the soup can't be missed; the *samlaw macchau kroeung krahorm* consists of white-meat chicken, fresh shredded pineapple appropriately proportioned and not too sweet, and a tamarind and lemongrass broth bursting with complex flavors. *AE, MC, V; no checks; lunch, dinner Mon-Sat; beer and wine.* ♿

Armani Cafe

1 GRANT AVE, SAN FRANCISCO 📞 415/677-9010
UNION SQUARE 🍴 *Italian*

Everything is as sleek and stylish as you would expect at a restaurant found smack in the middle of all the silk ties and leather jackets sold in the Emporio Armani store. A big oval bar in the center is the most popular place to sit, but a few tables on the second level overlooking the racks of clothing, plus some sidewalk tables set up in fair weather, are also full of well-dressed Financial District types. The food–mostly salads, pizzas, sandwiches, and grilled entrees–is as artfully presented as the fabulous clothing on the surrounding racks. An arugula salad is a little tower of greens with thin slices of Parmesan balanced on top, and an appetizer of prosciutto and fresh seasonal fruits is utterly simple but attractive. Prices are not terribly low for what you get, but for $15 you eat in style. *AE, DC, DIS, MC, V; no checks; lunch every day; beer and wine.* &

Arturo's Restaurant

632 20TH ST, SAN FRANCISCO   📞   415/863-2484
POTRERO HILL 🍴 *Mexican*

In the hinterlands of Potrero Hill, amid the warehouses and delivery trucks, is a slice of Mexican heaven. Admittedly, it doesn't look like much. The dark wood paneling, orange walls, and mirrored beer signs seem to come straight from 1975. But the mostly Mexican clientele come here for burritos, huevos rancheros, and combo platters of tamales, enchiladas, chiles rellenos, and tostadas that give them a taste of home. Forget those California-style black beans dressed up with sprigs of cilantro: here almost-runny refried beans come under a layer of melted cheese. Many order their food to go, but they're missing half the charm of the place. The sole guy who waits tables chats up the regulars and gives advice to the newcomers ("Try it. If you don't like it, you don't pay me"). Our own advice? Order a goblet of one of the sweet and refreshing fruit drinks (*limonada,* mango, and tamarind), available on a rotating basis. *Cash only; lunch Mon–Sat; beer only.*

asiaSF

201 9TH ST, SAN FRANCISCO   📞   415/255-2742
SOUTH OF MARKET 🍴 *Pan-Asian*

No sooner has your sultry waitress seated you at your table than the lights are dimmed and she's prancing across the bar, lip-synching to a disco classic. Only she's a he, but you'd never know. Welcome to asiaSF, where the men have better legs than the women, and everything's delicious—especially the diva wait staff. Japanese-style shoji screens subtly change color throughout the evening in this hip pan-Asian eatery, where some of San Francisco's finest gender illusionists perform nightly. There is no cover for the shows every half hour, but you are required to spend at least $20 a person on drinks and dinner. You're encouraged to share a slew of Asia-influenced dishes such as sake-steamed mussels or smoked duck quesadillas—yet the food, while tasty, comes in skimpy portions. But the best way to blow your wad of cash is on the divine signature cocktails served up in oversize martini glasses. If you want the party to continue well into the night, you can slip downstairs into the subterranean nightclub. Image is everything at asiaSF. *AE, DC, DIS, MC, V; no checks; dinner every day; full bar; www.asiasf.com.*

Asmara Restaurant and Bar

5020 TELEGRAPH AVE, OAKLAND 📞 510/547-5100
NORTH OAKLAND 🍴 *Ethiopian/Eritrean*

Asmara has a split personality: the comfortable restaurant is full of East African kitsch, while the adjacent bar—stark white and brightly lit—is a sterile jolt to the senses. Eritrean expatriates seem to prefer the bar, while locals enjoy the restaurant's African decor. Both groups, however, often get caught up in the communal spirit of the place, sharing their meals with fellow diners and using pieces of spongy injera bread to scoop up tasty *ziggni* (beef marinated in a surprisingly mild berbere sauce made with jalapeño and other chile peppers) and *yegomen alicha* (mustard greens simmered with spices). Make the most of this culinary adventure by getting one of the combination dinners. *MC, V; no checks; lunch Fri-Sun, dinner Tues-Sun; full bar.*

Asqew Grill

1607 HAIGHT ST, SAN FRANCISCO 📞 415/701-9301
3348 STEINER ST, SAN FRANCISCO 📞 415/931-9201
UPPER HAIGHT/MARINA 🍴 *Eclectic*

To say that Asqew Grill serves shish kebabs doesn't quite do it justice: you'll find more than a dozen types of skewered, seasoned meats and vegetables, each with a different global spin, from Thai barbecue chicken to a Japanese-inspired salmon teriyaki. Each skewer comes with a starchy side, from jasmine cilantro rice to citrus couscous (avoid the mashed potatoes, which taste distressingly like the dehydrated kind). The food is served with surprising panache, considering that even with a side of grilled corn or breadsticks, you can eat for about $10. A skewer threaded with chunks of grilled portobello mushroom comes balanced on a triangle of polenta enriched with mascarpone cheese. Surprisingly, even most of the desserts come off the grill—witness the grilled caramel apple or grilled banana split. Best of all, the service here is superfriendly—a far cry from many spots in the Haight, where there seems to be some sort of competition for the honor of surliest counter help. The effect? A friendly neighborhood spot for a warming, hearty meal. *DC, DIS, MC, V; no checks; lunch, dinner every day; beer and wine.* ♿

à table!

1115 BRIDGEWAY, SAUSALITO 📞 415/332-5013
SAUSALITO 🍴 *French*

When owner Anita Jimenez returned from a stint cooking in France, she brought her talents to this little cafe, whose modest appearance belies the superb quality of its food. The items on the small breakfast and lunch menus are simple but perfectly prepared. Scones, available in varieties like raisin cinnamon or lemon ginger, are slightly crispy on the outside, moist and fluffy inside. Served warm, they're nothing like the dry and crumbly things many cafes pass off as the British specialty. More substantial breakfast fare includes a freshly baked croissant filled with eggs, basil, and Swiss cheese. At lunch the popular *pan bagnat,* crusty bread stuffed with spinach, basil, tomato, capers, egg, and goat cheese, shows the cafe's Mediterranean influence, but the Mom's Meatloaf, served with red cabbage slaw, is pure Americana. And when you consider that nothing on the menu is more than $7, you have to think it's one of the best food values in Marin County. The cafe is at its best on warm days; the outdoor seating on the wooden deck, from which you can catch a glimpse of the bay, is more appealing than the four tables crowded into the irregularly shaped interior. *MC, V; no checks; breakfast, lunch Mon–Sat (also open Sun spring–summer); no alcohol; www.atablecafe.com.* ♿

Autumn Moon Cafe

3909 GRAND AVE, OAKLAND 📞 510/595-3200
LAKE MERRITT 🍴 *American*

Though the restaurant shares its name with an ancient Asian festival, the Autumn Moon Cafe doesn't serve Chinese cakes to coincide with the lunar calendar. Rather, the name stems from the childhood roots of chef and co-owner Kerry Hefferman, who grew up on Autumn Moon Drive here in California. Inside this simple, elegant restaurant, you're made to feel as though you're dining in the beautiful turn-of-the-century home of a good friend. Soaring bay windows and colorful tablecloths set the stage inside, and a tree-shaded patio welcomes outside diners in back. The only thing this restaurant does have in common with the thousand-year-old autumn moon festival is the promise of a bountiful harvest. Its reputation for inventive twists on classic American comfort food—witness the oatmeal brûlée—is well deserved. Entrees like char-grilled lamb steak with potato fritters are a testament to Kerry's Irish heritage, while co-owner and award-winning filmmaker Wendy Levy's influence is evident in the homemade matzo ball soup and vintage movie posters lining the walls. *AE, MC, V; no checks; breakfast, lunch Wed–Sun, dinner every day; full bar; www.autumnmooncafe.citysearch.com.*

Avatar's

2656 BRIDGEWAY, SAUSALITO 📞 415/332-8083
SAUSALITO 🍴 *Eclectic*

We thought we had seen every permutation of fusion cuisine possible–and then we visited Avatar's, a refined spot where beautiful black-and-white photos and classical music set a serene mood. Indian, Mexican, and even Caribbean cuisines all meld in the unusual dishes on the menu. Standout items include the curried lamb Punjabi tostada, which was nothing like anything we had tasted before. Spicy ground lamb covered a thick, dense round of paratha (whole-wheat Indian bread) and was topped with an artful swirl of sweet and creamy yogurt and tamarind sauces. Punjabi enchiladas, made with a cross-cultural mix of marinated meats, corn tortillas, cheese, basmati rice, and fruit chutney, strike some as just plain weird; purists may prefer items like the crispy vegetable samosas or chicken curry. Avatar's is a friendly family operation; even though founder Avatar Ubhi himself passed away in 1999, his charming brother is still there to seat you, and his wife works in the open kitchen. *MC, V; no checks; lunch, dinner Mon–Sat; beer and wine.*

Axum Cafe

698 HAIGHT ST, SAN FRANCISCO 📞 415/252-7912
LOWER HAIGHT 🍴 *Ethiopian*

Tacky fringed light fixtures and mustard yellow walls that look as if they were painted in 1972 hardly encourage high expectations at this dimly lit little spot. But the huge platters of sautéed beef and puréed vegetables served with spongy injera flat bread are a very pleasant surprise, as is the astonishingly tiny bill. If possible, come with a crowd. Not only is it more fun to order a $10 pitcher of beer and dig into a communal platter of food, here you even get a price break. A vegetarian sampler platter costs $10 for two, $18 for four. Specialties include the fiery *zighine,* bits of beef sautéed in tomato, onion, olive oil, and Ethiopian spices, and *tibsie,* made of large, tender chunks of lamb. One of the best of the many vegetarian choices is the *alicha atet,* chickpeas puréed with red onions and spices. You don't need a lot of money to eat here, but you do need a bit of time: the small staff is stretched to the limit during the nightly dinner rush. *AE, MC, V; no checks; lunch Sat-Sun, dinner every day; beer and wine; axumcafe@msn.com.* &

Ba Le

511 JONES ST, SAN FRANCISCO 📞 415/474-7270
TENDERLOIN ⑪ *Vietnamese*

At first sight it may look more like an oddly stocked grocery store than a sit-down restaurant, but Ba Le is a wonderful destination for a quick and satisfying lunch or midafternoon meal. The handful of tables are in the back, behind the cases of Sprite and shelves stuffed with packaged soups, sauces, cakes, and nuts. To call the decor "nothing fancy" is a grand understatement, but once you're settled in, the atmosphere is actually quite homey and friendly, as are the folks who run the place. The food is tasty and cheap—the best combination. You can order from the take-out counter up front, or from the excellent sandwich bar (meat and marinated veggies on a crusty roll for two bucks), but ask for a menu and you'll find they also have table service, dishing up plenty of noodle plates and big bowls of hot soup. It's hard to go wrong with the grilled pork, but if you want something more adventurous, try the tomato-snail or the duck-bamboo noodle soup. A thick, strong Vietnamese coffee is a worthy accompaniment, and, for a sweet treat, pick up a cup of house-made tapioca pudding on the way out. *Cash only; lunch every day; no alcohol.*

Barcelona

7 SPRING ST *(off California between Kearny and Montgomery Sts),* SAN FRANCISCO 📞 415/989-1976
FINANCIAL DISTRICT ⑪ *Spanish*

Get to know "the margarita king" and you'll have a night to remember. That's the self-applied title of owner Giovanni, whose restaurant serves some of the only tapas available downtown. And Giovanni is the consummate host, seemingly always there, and always with a welcoming smile. After 5PM the restaurant, decorated in lively, rich colors and dark wood accents, fills up with happy-hour revelers spilling out of the surrounding office towers. They clamor toward the bar for Giovanni's margaritas and the generous spread of complimentary appetizers. The regular menu is chock-full of Spanish and

Catalan treats, many based on centuries-old recipes. Don't miss the *pimientos de piquillo* (beef-stuffed peppers with goat cheese) or the *gambas al ajillo* (shrimp with garlic and olive oil) appetizers. The paella is a specialty and is made with a wide selection of seafood and meats. On Friday and Saturday nights, the main dining room is turned into a dance floor at 10PM, and live flamenco performances on Wednesday, Friday, and Saturday nights set a boisterous party atmosphere. *AE, DC, DIS, MC, V; no checks; lunch Mon-Fri, dinner every day; full bar; gigi@barcelona-restaurant.com.* &

Barking Basset Cafe

803 CORTLAND AVE, SAN FRANCISCO   📞   415/648-2146
BERNAL HEIGHTS   🍴   *American*

This is the sort of cozy, casual restaurant that every neighborhood should be so lucky to have. Walls painted in buttery yellow and sage green and curtains of the same color recall memories of grandma's kitchen. Perhaps best known for its breakfasts, Barking Basset serves luscious, rich pancakes made with cottage cheese in the batter. Ordering them with crème fraîche and seasonal berries almost seems to be gilding the lily. But the lunch and dinner items on the small but diverse menu are equally tempting. Burgers are made from Niman Ranch beef, and a skirt steak sandwich comes dressed with a Gorgonzola vinaigrette. Also look for ambitious and well-executed daily specials, like a fillet of swordfish with a tart caper relish. Desserts couldn't be homier: when was the last time you saw chocolate pudding on a menu? The servers are friendly and familiar with the Bernal Heights residents who stop in several times a week. *AE, MC, V; checks OK; breakfast, lunch Wed-Mon, dinner Thurs-Sat; beer and wine.*

Barney's Gourmet Hamburgers

4138 24TH ST, SAN FRANCISCO *(and branches)*   📞   415/282-7770
NOE VALLEY/MARINA/NORTH BERKELEY/NORTH OAKLAND/SOUTH BERKELEY
🍴   *Burgers*

When your friends have dragged you to one too many restaurants where the "chicken" is made of wheat gluten or the "meat loaf" is actually tofu, pay them back with a visit to Barney's. Satisfying slabs of ground beef come in their unadulterated state or buried underneath mounds of toppings: sautéed mushrooms, avocado, bacon, spinach—even sesame-ginger sauce and bean sprouts. The baskets of fries are absurdly large—a half basket easily serves two—and you can stand a spoon up in the dreamy milk shakes. Of course, this *is* San Francisco, so you *could* order a veggie burger, a salad, or perhaps a portobello burger, a whole portobello mushroom flame-broiled and served on a sesame bun. The interior of each location is fairly generic, so consider getting your food to go. Or, on rare warm days, brave the wait for one of the tables on the leafy patio. *MC, V; local checks only; lunch, dinner every day; beer and wine.* &

Basil Thai

1175 FOLSOM ST, SAN FRANCISCO 📞 415/552-8999
SOUTH OF MARKET 🍴 *Thai*

In the heart of SoMa's after-hours scene, this is probably the hippest Thai restaurant in the city. The music is cool and the waiters are dressed like they're ready to go hit a club. Indeed, the restaurant often doesn't get crowded until club-goers arrive late in the evening, and it has a full bar to get things started off right. The decor features glass block walls warmed up with large, leafy bamboo plants, rattan chairs, and antique Thai posters. All that style aside, the food itself is excellent. To start, try the grilled marinated calamari skewers served with a sweet-and-sour tamarind sauce, or the turnip cakes sautéed with bean sprouts and egg and served with a red chile sauce. The list of main dishes includes scallops with tempura long beans and black bean sauce, drunken tofu (in a wine and chile sauce), and grilled lamb in a kaffir-infused curry. Entree prices are a little higher than at most neighborhood Thai restaurants ($8.50 to $14), but the creative choices, delicate preparation, and pleasing atmosphere make it worthwhile. *AE, MC, V; no checks; lunch Mon–Fri, dinner every day; full bar; arum@basilthai.com; www.basilthai.com.* &

Battambang

850 BROADWAY, OAKLAND 📞 510/839-8815
DOWNTOWN OAKLAND 🍴 *Vietnamese/Southeast Asian*

An evening at this low-key Cambodian eatery is all about the smells. Once you step inside, you're engulfed in an aromatic cloud of sweet and spicy scents. Just when you're ready to order, the waiter will whisk a pungent plate to the patrons sitting next to you, and you'll consider changing your mind because what they ordered just *smells* so good. Wrap your tongue around such difficult-to-pronounce specialties as *kari dong kchei* and you'll be rewarded with a subtle melange of green beans, yams, coconut meat, and chicken swimming in a thick red curry. If it's a rainy night and you're facing the street, it's easy to imagine you're tucked into a cozy New York dining spot, but otherwise the decor seems to have been lifted from the lobby of a cheap hotel, with lots of nondescript lamps lining the walls. Brightly colored paintings of Cambodian dancers do little to add a Southeast Asian flavor to the room, but the real reason to visit is such savory specialties such as *trorb ktiss*, in which grilled eggplant rubs shoulders with roasted peanuts in a lemongrass curry sauce. Other dishes regularly make use of healthy doses of green papaya, fresh mint, shredded ginger, and bamboo shoots. *AE, MC, V; no checks; lunch Mon–Sat, dinner every day; beer and wine.*

Bechelli's Restaurant

2346 CHESTNUT ST, SAN FRANCISCO 📞 415/346-1801
MARINA 🍴 *Diner*

The sign in the window boasts that Bechelli's has been around since 1977, though from the look of things this diner could have opened in 1957. Green leatherette stools wrap around the Formica counter, and art deco-ish light fixtures illuminate the battered booths. It feels like nothing has been changed in decades, which is precisely the way the regulars like it. Marina residents, some of whom stop by almost every day, know that the breakfast items, served all day, are better than most of the lunch items—burgers, hot dogs, grilled sandwiches, corned beef hash, and the like—though no one seems to have any complaints about the milk shakes. The French toast, made from thick slices of sweet French bread, is a favorite. Service can be indifferent, but the restaurant's authentic old-fashioned style is sure to charm. *DC, MC, V; no checks; breakfast, lunch every day; no alcohol.* ♿

Berkeley Thai House

2511 CHANNING WAY, BERKELEY 📞 510/843-7352
SOUTH BERKELEY 🍴 *Thai*

Just around the corner from the hoopla of Telegraph Avenue, where street hawkers line the way up to the UC Berkeley campus, this comfortable Thai joint is a definite improvement on the fast-food restaurants that fill the area. Well-worn wood floors and Thai knickknacks add to the homey atmosphere, while efficient service means you can get out in a hurry if you need to. Students and faculty are much in evidence here; in fact, the Berkeley Thai House is a favorite among large groups looking to fill up after class. In warm weather, the front deck, well screened from the street by flowering plants, is popular at lunch. Menu favorites include *tofu tod* (deep-fried tofu with spicy peanut sauce), basil chicken steeped in a rich and mildly spicy broth, spicy roast duck, and pineapple prawns. *MC, V; no checks; lunch Mon–Sat, dinner every day; beer and wine.*

Bette's Oceanview Diner

1807-A 4TH ST, BERKELEY 📞 510/644-3230
WEST BERKELEY 🍴 *Diner*

We're not sure how Bette's got its name—there's no view of anything at all here. It's just as well, though, because if Bette's were any more popular we might never get in at all. Folks are willing to wait (and wait, and wait) for one of the enormous, soufflé-like pancakes with fresh berries, eggs scrambled with prosciutto and Parmesan, and excellent huevos rancheros with black beans. Muffins and scones served on the side with many of these dishes are so large and packed with fruits or nuts that they're almost a meal by themselves. Red vinyl booths, a black-and-white tile floor, and a counter with chrome stools set the scene with art deco flair that's simultaneously hip and comforting. For shorter waits on weekends (by which we mean less than an hour), come alone or in a pair and be willing to sit at the counter. If you're too hungry to wait, pop into Bette's-to-Go (BTG) next door for a prebreakfast snack. *MC, V; local checks only; breakfast, lunch every day; beer and wine.* ♿

Big Mouth Burgers and Beers

3392 24TH ST, SAN FRANCISCO 📞 415/821-4821
MISSION DISTRICT 🍴 *Burgers*

You better be hungry if you hope to make a dent in one of Big Mouth's burgers, a whopping half pound of Mountain Natural Foods beef that's considerably larger than the bun it comes on. Served with your choice of spreads (including spicy chipotle mayonnaise and sun-dried tomato aioli), it's hot, juicy, and satisfying, just as a burger should be. Fries are of equally prodigious proportions: thick, 6-inch-long slabs of potato that are crisp on the outside, tender inside. Milk shakes are made with Mitchell's ice cream, produced by San Francisco's favorite ice cream shop, though it's tough to make room for a shake when eating here. The restaurant's interior is cheerful but undistinguished, with colorful sponge-painted walls and wooden tables and chairs. And although service is not particularly speedy for a burger spot, consider it the price you pay for having your burger cooked just the way you like it. *Cash only; lunch, dinner every day; beer only.* &

Bill's Place

2315 CLEMENT ST, SAN FRANCISCO 📞 415/221-5262
RICHMOND DISTRICT 🍴 *American*

Man (and woman) cannot live by salad alone. Sometimes there must be burgers. And if you're looking for an honest burger in the Richmond District, you'll want to know about Bill's Place. Here you'll find meaty, hefty, juicy burgers made with fresh ground chuck. Have your burger plain, or try one of Bill's "Celebrity Burgers," like the Carol Doda Burger (with two fried eggs looking like, well . . .) or the Herb Caen, Red Skelton, or Paul Kantner. Vegetarians can get any of the combination burgers with a veggie patty instead of ground chuck. The fries here are okay, but you're better off spending your extra calories on a rich and decadent milk shake or malted to wash down your chunk of cow. Inside, the decor is generic diner; what sets the atmosphere here apart from the rest is a secluded and charming patio complete with fishpond out back. *Cash only; lunch, dinner every day; no alcohol.* &

Bistro Aix

3340 STEINER ST, SAN FRANCISCO 📞 415/202-0100
MARINA 🍴 *French*

French-trained chef and owner Jonathan Beard is the person to thank for this charming Marina district bistro with its creamy lime-green walls decorated with black-and-white photos of Italy and France. Part of the bistro's draw is the $13.95 early-bird fixed-price dinners served Sunday through Thursday from 6 to 8PM (at other times entrees go for about $9 to $17). Diners choose from three entrees, such as grilled top sirloin with roasted garlic, linguine with clams and tomatoes, or a juicy roasted chicken with a crusty golden skin. The main menu features cracker-crust pizza with goat cheese and grilled eggplant or wild mushrooms and truffle oil, sirloin burgers on focaccia, ahi tuna with black-trumpet mushrooms, and an excellent orrechiette with spinach, pancetta, and a peppery tomato sauce. The wine list is reasonably priced and primarily Californian, sprinkled with European varietals. Desserts can be staggeringly rich, including the warm chocolate fondant cake with chocolate sauce. The dining room is small and sometimes cramped and noisy, so head for the heated back garden patio; it's romantically lit at night. *AE, MC, V; no checks; dinner every day; beer and wine.* ♿

Bistro Burger

333 BUSH ST, SAN FRANCISCO *(entrance on Trinity St between Bush and Sutter Sts)* 📞 415/434-3754
343 SANSOME ST, SAN FRANCISCO *(entrance on Leidesdorff St between California and Sacramento Sts)*
📞 415/989-7566
FINANCIAL DISTRICT 🍴 *Burgers*

On an alley surrounded by high rises, Bistro Burger may not be the best place to be during an earthquake. But at all other times, it's prime real estate for scrumptious burgers prepared with high-quality Niman Ranch beef, if you're prepared to wait in the daunting lunch line. Neither branch offers much in the way of charm, but both boast outdoor dining on pedestrian-only alleys, and the burgers in all their incarnations are first-rate. Try an artery-clogging staple like the bacon cheeseburger, or opt for fancier grub à la the Paris burger, topped with Brie and sautéed mushrooms, or the bacon cheeseburger royale, with Brie, Gorgonzola, or aged cheddar. Other tempting plates include the Thai peanut chicken sandwich and the chicken Capri, made with prosciutto and Gruyère cheese. Passing up a burger in favor of a salad here seems almost sacrilegious, but if willpower reigns, the albacore tuna salad and the Chinese chicken salad are worthy alternatives. Substitute turkey, grilled chicken, or a garden patty for any burger. Expect speedy service after you've placed your order. *AE, DC, MC, V; no checks; lunch Mon–Fri; no alcohol.*

Blue

2337 MARKET ST, SAN FRANCISCO 📞 415/863-2583
CASTRO 🍴 *American*

When Blue opened in 1999, it proved that new San Francisco restaurants don't have to serve exotic fusion cuisine and charge sky-high prices. Instead, Blue re-creates dishes your grandma might have made and serves them at prices that, even if your grandma couldn't fathom, are at least extremely reasonable by San Francisco's standards. The menu includes a piping hot chicken potpie and grilled steak served with crunchy shoestring potatoes and barbecue sauce. The small menu expands to include a few brunch items like an egg-stuffed croissant on Saturday and Sunday, when the restaurant opens at 11AM. (Here's a tip: Castro dwellers seem to be late sleepers. Come between 11 and 12 for that rare luxury–a wait-free brunch.) Though the food isn't up to the standards of some other American and California Cuisine newcomers like Blue Plate and Luna Park (see reviews), it *is* a few bucks cheaper, and it has one of the best-looking (mostly gay male) clienteles in the city. The tiny restaurant's industrial look—with unadorned blue-gray walls and lots of reflective surfaces—belies the comforting quality of its dishes, as does the ear-splitting noise level. *MC, V; no checks; lunch Sat-Sun, dinner every day, brunch Sat-Sun; full bar.*

Blue Nile

2525 TELEGRAPH AVE, BERKELEY   📞 510/540-6777
SOUTH BERKELEY   🍴 *Ethiopian*

Strings of bamboo beads separate the tables at this intimate two-level Ethiopian restaurant, creating the feeling that each table is the scene of a clandestine tête-à-tête. Groups of students and local families hunker under bamboo matting surrounded by a happy jumble of plants, pepper-shaped Christmas lights, Ethiopian textiles and hand-woven baskets, and posters of the homeland. Blue Nile's cuisine, consistently voted the best Ethiopian food this side of the Bay Bridge in the local weeklies, includes both meaty and veggie dishes, all scooped up by injera, the spongelike, unleavened bread that replaces silverware. Most choices consist of lamb, beef, chicken, or legumes, all seasoned with Blue Nile's special combination of Ethiopian spices, plus veggies, bread, and rice. Perennial favorites include *ye siga wat,* steak strips cooked in a blend of fiery spices, and *yekik wat,* a mild but flavorful split pea purée. If you can't decide, go for the combo plate and mix and match your own entrees. Top off your meal with a taste of Ethiopian honey wine, which, despite the name, has only a hint of sweetness. *MC, V; no checks; lunch Tues-Sat, dinner Tues-Sun; beer and wine.* ♿

Blue Plate

3218 MISSION ST, SAN FRANCISCO   📞 415/282-6777
MISSION DISTRICT   🍴 *Eclectic*

If you didn't know it was here, you might never notice this trendy restaurant, located in what looks like a former taqueria. Though it strains at the budget constrictions put forth by this book, it's great for a reasonably priced splurge.

With flower vases made of hominy cans and a skateboard attached to the wall, the decor is both stylish and welcoming, and the funky enclosed porch and heated patio in back make it feel even more like someone's home. The kitchen staff is young and inclined toward the experimental, and though not everything works out exactly as planned, they're continually working out the kinks and playing with ingredients usually found at much higher-end restaurants. The menu changes often, but look for interesting salads, like a plate of tender Asian greens with crispy chickpeas, *ricotta salata* (a firm, salty type of ricotta), and hard-cooked egg. If you order the delicious *bresaola* (aged, salted beef) with grapefruit, radicchio, and shaved Parmigiano for $6, it's not going to be huge, but just right for a first course. Dinners are more substantial, like pork chops with spätzle and sweet peppers. A simple roast chicken might come with tomatoes skewered on cinnamon sticks, rainbow chard, and crispy red potatoes. Desserts can be old-fashioned, like banana cream pie, or more contemporary, like flourless chocolate cake. *AE, MC, V; no checks; dinner Tues–Sat; beer and wine.*

Bocce Cafe

478 GREEN ST, SAN FRANCISCO 📞 415/981-2044
NORTH BEACH 🍴 *Italian*

Duck through the wrought-iron gates, head down the arbor-covered pathway, and step into Bocce's vast interior to enjoy one of the city's most festive and casual Italian restaurants. Raucous with plants, braided garlic, and massive mirrors encrusted in sculpted roses, Bocce entertains large groups, young families, and the odd after-work dot-commer. A glass wall overlooks the cheery patio, a green oasis that centers on a large fig tree; white lights drape the vine-covered beams that border the area. A happy break from trendy food, Bocce's menu is comfortably familiar: choose from salads, antipasti, pizza, pasta, and such house specialties as veal Parmesan. Whether you're looking for a quick but hearty dinner with the kids or a leisurely meal with close associates or friends, this boisterous eatery fits the bill. Friday and Saturday evenings you can dine to the strains of live jazz; on Wednesday, Thursday, and Sunday evenings, a pianist entertains the crowd. *AE, DC, DIS, MC, V; no checks; lunch, dinner every day; full bar; www.boccecafe.com.*

Bombay Ice Cream and Chaat

552 VALENCIA ST, SAN FRANCISCO 📞 415/431-1103
MISSION DISTRICT 🍴 *Indian*

The food here isn't pretty, but it's cheap and satisfying. This combination snack shop/ice cream parlor started as an offshoot of the Indian general store next door but has gained a following for its dirt-cheap, served-in-a-hurry plates of spicy Indian food and its exotic ice cream flavors. The small menu consists of items like samosas, chicken curry, and *aloo tikki* (potato fritters), sold individually or in combo plates that go for a mere $3.50 to $5. True, one dish is barely distinguishable from another, and combo plates faintly resemble a brown puddle surrounding a pile of white rice. But the chicken is so tender it's falling off the bone, the samosas are full of big chunks of meat, potato, and peas, and the whole affair is spicy enough that you might want to order a mango lassi or glass of sugarcane juice to wash it down. The ice creams, homemade by owner Bharti Parmar, are worthy of a stop in their own right. Though flavors like cardamom and *kesar pista* (saffron-pistachio) can be a bit overwhelming, we're very fond of the fig, with sweet and chewy little bits of the fruit studding the velvety ice cream. The shop is spacious but has only two tables and is entirely lacking in atmosphere; most get their food to go. *Cash only; lunch, dinner Tues–Sun; no alcohol.*

Boulangerie Bay Bread

2325 PINE ST, SAN FRANCISCO 📞 415/440-0356
PACIFIC HEIGHTS 🍴 *Bakery*

French expats and other fans of French food swoon over this bakery, where a line forms out the door most mornings for the breads, pastries, and deli items. For about 800 bucks less than a flight to Paris, you can stock your picnic basket with oodles of ooh-la-la items. Consider the *croque monsieur* (ham sandwich topped with grated, melted Gruyère), the *pan bagnat* (a baguette stuffed with tuna and vegetables), a miniature quiche, or one of several types of *tarte*, a buttery brioche dough topped with cheese, meat, or vegetables. And it's hard to imagine anyone resisting dessert items like glistening fruit tarts or a *pain au chocolat*, a rectangle of flaky pastry stuffed with two slivers of bitter chocolate. Unfortunately, items are available to go only, but Alta Plaza and Lafayette Parks are each only about four blocks away. If you're unfamiliar with the area, ask one of the charming French folks behind the counter for directions. *No credit cards; checks OK; breakfast, lunch Tues–Sun; no alcohol.* ♿

Bow Hon Restaurant

850 GRANT AVE, SAN FRANCISCO 📞 415/362-0601
CHINATOWN 🍴 *Chinese*

Up and down this restaurant-laden block in Chinatown, touts stand outside the restaurants enticing passing tourists inside for dinner. The ladies at Bow Hon need none of that, because the tables are filled with local Chinese diners eating authentic fare. And if you hadn't already figured out that this place doesn't depend on tourists, refer to the first page of the menu, which is entirely in Cantonese. Turn the pages to read the bilingual version of the menu, just slightly shorter than a Tolstoy novel. You'll find all the usual suspects—pot stickers, sweet and sour pork, and cashew chicken—but the house specialty is clay pot dishes, served piping hot in earthenware pots. The "Bow Hon Special" is a combo of bean curd, meaty mushrooms, thin-sliced pork, and cabbage in a savory broth. The truly adventurous can opt for exotic choices like frog with Chinese mushrooms or fish balls with lettuce. The decor is as nondescript as your usual Chinese hole-in-the-wall, and the service, though friendly, is sometimes erratic. But for Chinese food fans who want the real deal, this is the place. *Cash only; lunch, dinner every day; no alcohol.*

Brainwash Cafe and Laundromat

1122 FOLSOM ST, SAN FRANCISCO 📞 415/861-3663
SOUTH OF MARKET 🍴 *Soup/Salad/Sandwich*

Multitasking reaches new heights at Brainwash, the combination restaurant/Laundromat where you can get one set of clothes clean and another dirty slurping a bowl of soup or eating a plate of pasta. Add to that the ATM machine, the pinball machine, and the Internet terminal in Brainwash's industrial-looking space, and you could pretty much make a full day of it here. The menu is creative and the food good. Try the fish tacos, made of seasoned shredded snapper stuffed inside tortillas with cabbage, red onion, and feta. Burgers, sandwiches, and salads all satisfy, including the extremely popular Brainwash Salad, a mountain of greens and steamed potatoes, boiled egg, and feta dressed with a tangy lemon mustard dressing. A tip: Unless you particularly enjoy the scent of fabric softener with your meal, you might not want to sit at the tables closest to the washing machines. Spoken word, comedy, and open mike nights provide entertainment almost nightly while your clothes do the sudsy tango. *MC, V; no checks; breakfast, lunch every day; dinner Mon–Fri; beer and wine; www.brain-wash.com.*

Breads of India

2448 SACRAMENTO ST, BERKELEY   📞   510/848-7684
WEST BERKELEY   🍴   *Indian*

Off the beaten path, this tiny storefront draws legions of adoring fans who huddle on the sidewalk for a chance to enjoy delicacies from the daily changing menu. Colorful Indian wall hangings, painted blue elephants, and heavy red curtains add a splash of color to an otherwise ordinary space, while the aromas wafting from the kitchen provide the rest of the sensory experience. The brief menu, which always includes a couple of vegetarian choices, explains in loving detail the origin and composition of each dish and recommends a bread accompaniment. As the name of the restaurant suggests, bread is more than an afterthought here; the delectable naan, paratha, kulcha, and chapati are handmade in-house and feature different spices to complement the day's entrees. Favorites that appear frequently include tandoori chicken and *kerala kootu* (zucchini, tomatoes, cashews, ginger, and tamarind). The tasty mango lassi (a thick yogurt drink) cools the palate and slakes the thirst. The small size and huge popularity of Breads of India mean that after a 30- to 60-minute wait, you may end up sharing a table with new friends; come late or early if you want a table all to yourself. *Cash only; lunch Mon–Sat, dinner every day; no alcohol.* ♿

Brisas de Acapulco

3137 MISSION ST, SAN FRANCISCO   📞   415/826-1496
MISSION DISTRICT   🍴   *Central American*

Among the mishmash of Mexican restaurants in the Mission District, this one stands out by offering dishes with a Salvadoran influence. Its friendly, no-frills, family-style approach is evident from the minute you walk in. And although the staff speaks little English, they are quick to point to their menu favorites. Specialties are seafood (in particular, the excellent shrimp dishes) and *sopa de pollo,* a hearty chicken soup that shouldn't be missed. If you're really hungry, order the Combinacion Brisas de Acapulco, which comes with snapper fillets, squid, shrimp, and clams. The *bistec salvadoreo,* a grilled steak in an onion-tomato sauce, is another highlight. Late-night hours, especially on weekends, make this a popular spot to fill up on enchiladas when the bars in the Mission start winding down. *Cash only; lunch, dinner every day; beer and wine.*

Upscale Markets, Bargain Dining

Food to go from the local grocery doesn't have to mean headcheese sandwiches and Jell-O salad. Many upscale markets and groceries sell the makings of substantial and flavorful meals, and, when compared to eating out, it's great food at a great bargain.

When you're ready for a quick meal, REAL FOOD COMPANY (3939 24th St, 415/282-9500; 2140 Polk St, 415/673-7420; 1023 Stanyan St, 415/564-2800; 3060 Fillmore St, 415/567-6900) will suffice with a simple curried tofu sandwich, grilled vegetable wrap, or adequate sushi roll or burrito. But if you're really ready to dine, consider one of the following for a better selection. BI-RITE's (3639 18th St; 415/241-9773) roasted vegetable pizza, roasted chicken, and house-made pasta salads and raviolis are the perfect picnic if you're heading to nearby Dolores Park. Treat yourself to something from the small but perfect assortment of imported chocolates and locally produced chocolate-covered fruits. At WHOLE FOODS MARKET (1765 California St; 415/674-0500 ext. 219), the array of choices is even bigger. The expansive organic salad and soup bar would suffice, but in truth it's just a teaser. Poached salmon, roasted turkey, or rare grilled beef are served to go, and the selection of side dishes will blow you away with fresh herbs, fragrant oils, and subtle accents. Ingredients like beets, sweet potato, and roasted portobello mushrooms show up in imaginative appetizers and entrees, and classics like pasta salad and red potato salad are light and fresh. At the high end of the bargain hunter's budget, seared tuna with olive tapenade, goat cheese tarts, and skewered chicken are excellent and priced far below what you'd pay in a restaurant. Finally, gourmet do-it-yourselfers will melt over MOLLY STONE'S MARKET's (2435 California St; 415/567-4902) offerings of just about everything, including a wall of international cheeses. Smoked fish is flown in daily from the East Coast. The bakery is a little lacking, but the prepared foods are simply dazzling. Choose from orzo and feta salad, succulent roasted game hens, and hearts of palm temperately spiced and drizzled with good olive oil. Whatever your taste, taking out will feel more like dining in.

Brother-in-Law's Bar-B-Que

705 DIVISADERO ST, SAN FRANCISCO   📞 415/931-7427
WESTERN ADDITION   🍴 *Barbecue*

When the wind is right, you'll smell the tantalizing barbecue smoke and the tangy sauce from blocks away. The chicken, available hot or not-so-hot, is excellent—moist white or dark meat sealed with a kiss of tangy homemade sauce. And the pork ribs, especially the short ends, are sure to make you salivate. It's the beef brisket, though—so tender it can be eaten with a fork—that's the pièce de résistance. As legendary as the barbecue are the side dishes: corn bread muffins, salty greens, house-made baked beans, and, if there's room, sweet potato pie for dessert. This is soul food that sticks to your ribs. Most people get their food to go, but if you just can't wait to get home, there are two tables near the counter. *DC, MC, V; no checks; lunch, dinner Tues-Sun; no alcohol.*

Brother's Korean Restaurant

4128 GEARY BLVD, SAN FRANCISCO   📞 415/387-7991
RICHMOND DISTRICT   🍴 *Korean*

It's not much to look at—just a wood-paneled room with overhead ceiling fans and bright lights—but the folks who line up for dinner here aren't too concerned about aesthetics. They've come for a taste of home, and the many Korean expatriates who dine here are a testament to the great food. You can grill your own meal at your table or, if you're not feeling so ambitious, have the kitchen do it for you. Either way, the marinated beef and pork are succulent and delicious, best when rolled into a lettuce leaf and eaten with your hands. The kitchen also offers other authentic Korean fare, from beef soups to pan-fried fish to tempura, served with side dishes like rice and the Korean staple *kimchee* (pickled cabbage). Be forewarned, though, that many of the dishes are so spicy you might think the barbecue smoke in the air is coming from your mouth. *MC, V; no checks; lunch, dinner every day; beer and wine.*

Burger Joint

807 VALENCIA ST, SAN FRANCISCO 📞 415/824-3494
700 HAIGHT ST, SAN FRANCISCO 📞 415/864-3833
MISSION DISTRICT/LOWER HAIGHT 🍴 *Burgers*

The name pretty much tells you everything you need to know about this spot. The menu does include a chicken breast sandwich and a hot dog—but it's not like anyone is expected to actually order those things. That's because the burgers here are everything they should be—including being made out of locally renowned Niman Ranch beef. This is the sort of food that's made to go with a root beer float, so it's mighty convenient that it's just about the only other thing on the small menu. Unfortunately, the fries—limp and stubby things that aren't the least bit crispy—don't live up to the standard set by the burgers. The restaurant has a certain slick retro charm, with big red vinyl booths and matching chairs surrounding aqua-colored Formica tables. Black-and-white cartoon-style murals adorn the walls. *Cash only; lunch, dinner every day; no alcohol.* ♿

Burma Super Star

309 CLEMENT ST, SAN FRANCISCO 📞 415/387-2147
RICHMOND DISTRICT 🍴 *Vietnamese/Southeast Asian*

The wood paneling on the walls makes this place look ancient, but the menu of Chinese and Burmese dishes is just the thing for the jaded diner craving something new. You may not even notice the sparseness of the decor (just tables and chairs) after a bite of the first zingy dish. *La pat doke* (tea leaf salad), tossed at your table, is a potent mix of imported Burmese tea leaves, lettuce, tomato, fried garlic, crispy yellow peas, and spicy chile sauce. Neighboring India and China meet in a bowl of *baya kyaw samusa doke,* a savory curried soup broth enveloping chunks of Burmese samosas. This soup alone could serve as a meal, and at only $5.50 for an enormous bowl, it's a real bargain-seeker's treat, as are most menu items. The rest of the dishes are pretty good, but few are as stellar. The curried chicken with *platha,* like an exotic India-inspired Yorkshire pudding, is slow cooked and Mom-inspired. But the bold *chin mong kyaw,* a pan-fried selection of "soured" vegetables, is, as they say, an acquired taste. *DC, MC, V; no checks; lunch, dinner Tues–Sun; beer and wine.* ♿

Cactus Taqueria

5525 COLLEGE AVE, OAKLAND 📞 510/547-1305
1881 SOLANO AVE, BERKELEY 📞 510/528-1881
NORTH OAKLAND/NORTH BERKELEY 🍴 *Mexican*

Often voted the best burrito spot in the East Bay, Cactus Taqueria usually has a line of hungry burrito lovers spilling out the door. Several things make eating here worth the wait. First is the tender, tasty Niman Ranch beef, infused with a tangy lime marinade and served in items like the carne asada burrito. But another plus is the wide choice of menu items, including red and green chicken mole and salads. Fresh and fruity aguas frescas, in flavors like watermelon, lime, and tamarind, go well with almost everything on the menu (as do the many varieties of Mexican and domestic beers in the cooler). A colorfully painted dining room with an exposed beam ceiling is pleasant, but an outdoor patio is the place to be on even remotely sunny days. *V; checks OK; lunch, dinner every day; beer and wine.* ♿

Cafe Claude

7 CLAUDE LN, SAN FRANCISCO 📞 415/392-3515
FINANCIAL DISTRICT 🍴 *French*

Take a turn down tiny Claude Lane and it's as if you've accidentally encountered a little Parisian alleyway. The lane is anchored by Cafe Claude, where tables are set out with umbrellas, servers are alternately flirty and haughty, and everyone loves it as they sit and sip espresso and listen to the man playing the accordion in the corner. Authentic French cafe fare includes steamed mussels, cheese plates, and salads (the niçoise is terrific); baguette sandwiches are a popular choice at lunch. The daily pizza, which comes with toppings from eggplant to artichoke hearts, is usually a good choice. At dinner on Thursday through Saturday, a hip crowd files in to hear live jazz by local trios and enjoy such plates as beef braised in red wine with mushrooms and the soup du jour. *MC, V; no checks; lunch Mon–Sat, dinner Tues–Sat; beer and wine; www.cafeclaude.com.*

Cafe de la Presse

352 GRANT AVE, SAN FRANCISCO ☎ 415/249-0900
UNION SQUARE 🍴 *French*

Parisian transplants congregate at this combination newsstand/cafe/restaurant across from the French consulate to pick up a copy of *Le Monde* or *Le Figaro* and read it over a café au lait and perhaps a croissant. Tourists who are staying at the Hotel Triton next door or have wandered in from Chinatown (the Chinatown gate is right outside) are also often seen scribbling postcards with a cup of tea and a scone in hand. And at lunch and dinner the tables are filled with locals indulging in simple but satisfying French cuisine. It would be easy enough to top $20 or $30 for dinner (start with a half dozen oysters on the half shell, for example, or finish with an after-dinner *Calvados,* a French apple brandy). But most of the menu items are around $10 or less, including a very French goat cheese salad, a *croque madame* (a grilled ham and cheese sandwich with a whole egg on top), and even a cassoulet of mushrooms and crab. Crème caramel makes a traditional finale. The attached dining room is quieter but more expensive; if the weather's nice, try to snag one of the sidewalk tables. *AE, DC, MC, V; no checks; breakfast, lunch, dinner every day; full bar; cafedelapresse@usa.com; www.bsfweb.com/cafedelapresse.htm.*

Cafe deStijl

1 UNION ST, SAN FRANCISCO ☎ 415/291-0808
FINANCIAL DISTRICT 🍴 *Soup/Salad/Sandwich*

As you would expect of a cafe named after a 20th-century style of art, Cafe deStijl has a sleek urban look that appeals to the architects and multimedia types who work in the surrounding buildings. Exposed brick walls, a concrete floor, and industrial-looking metal shelving behind the counter set the scene; owner/designer Nilus de Matran has even lavished attention on such details as the poured concrete tables and whimsical pottery on which your meals are served. Luckily, the food tastes as good as the cafe looks. A small menu featuring salads, grilled chicken sandwiches, and lemon chicken kebabs is augmented by Mediterranean-influenced daily specials, including pasta salads and spanakopita. Look for specials like the baked sea bass, simply prepared but flaky and perfectly fresh; served with risotto and salad, it's a steal at only $8.50. Breakfast items such as fruit and granola and waffles are equally delicious. *No credit cards; checks OK; breakfast, lunch Mon–Sat; beer and wine.* ♿

Café Fanny

1603 SAN PABLO AVE, BERKELEY   📞 510/524-5447
WEST BERKELEY 🍴 *French*

Alice Waters's tiny corner cafe can handle fewer than a dozen stand-up customers at once, but that doesn't deter anyone. On sunny Saturday mornings
the adjacent parking lot fills with the overflow, with the luckier customers
snaring a seat at one of the few tiny outdoor tables. They don't come for the
view—the cafe faces busy San Pablo Avenue—but for a simple, inexpensive
breakfast or lunch in the inimitable Waters style. Named after Waters's daugh-
ter, this popular spot recalls the beloved neighborhood cafe of Paris, but
Fanny's food is better. Breakfast on crunchy Café Fanny granola—so popular it's
packaged and sold at gourmet and specialty food stores—or buckwheat crepes
with ham and Gruyère, and sip a café au lait from a big bowl. The morning
meal is served until 11AM and all day on Sunday. For lunch, order one of the
ultrafresh sandwiches, often featuring seasonal grilled vegetables on crusty
bread slathered with pesto, or perhaps a simply perfect goat cheese salad,
made, of course, with the freshest local produce and cheese. *MC, V; checks OK;
breakfast, lunch every day; beer and wine; cafefann@lmi.net; www.cafefanny.citysearch.com.*

Cafe Intermezzo

2442 TELEGRAPH AVE, BERKELEY   📞 510/849-4592
SOUTH BERKELEY 🍴 *Soup/Salad/Sandwich*

The two best features at Cafe Intermezzo—a long-standing Berkeley institution—are its amazingly delicious and cheap salads and its amazingly well
pierced staff. The two combine to make this the quintessential Berkeley cafe,
and there is always a line waiting to order. You can't go wrong by choosing the
tossed salad—a vegetarian monstrosity that will provide you with enough
roughage for the month. This is no iceberg lettuce and tomato wedge concoction, but a jumbo bowl overflowing with fresh mixed greens, sprouts, flavorful
tomatoes, and the world's best croutons. Poppy seed is the most popular dressing, but the super-cheesy blue cheese also comes highly recommended, and all
the dressings are homemade. Every salad comes with a hearty hunk of Intermezzo's fresh-from-the-oven honey-wheat bread. If you haven't eaten for
weeks—or want to make breakfast, lunch, and dinner out of your meal—then
try the chef's salad, with chunks of cheese, egg, and sliced meats, or one of the
sandwich-and-salad combos. Finding a seat can be competitive, but it's worth

trying to grab a spot near the window to watch the urban carnival of students, tourists, musicians, and panhandlers on Telegraph Avenue. *Cash only; lunch, dinner every day; no alcohol.*

Cafe Marimba

2317 CHESTNUT ST, SAN FRANCISCO 📞 415/776-1506
MARINA 🍴 *Mexican*

This exuberant little restaurant sandwiched between shops in the Marina district is easy to miss, despite its vibrant sunset-purple facade and the seemingly endless stream of people who squeeze through its lime-green doors every evening. Step inside and you'll be bowled over by a profusion of more screaming colors—pink, turquoise, orange—despite a clientele that dresses primarily in black. The secret to eating at Marimba, which packs more people into a small space than a yuppie-express Muni bus, is to make a reservation for early in the evening so you won't have to wait long for a table. The quite reasonably priced fare—entrees start at around $8—is real Mexican food, not an overpriced version of Taco Bell. The restaurant has a changing repertoire of more than 50 salsas; the nightly selections might include roasted corn, avocado-tomatillo, or tomato with smoked chiles. Sample some of these with chips, then move on to the spicy snapper tacos with pineapple salsa, or grilled chicken spiced with mild, smoky achiote seed. Even the more common fare has a twist: the seafood comes with a choice of five sauces, including garlic, caramelized onions, and fresh jalapeño sauces or a combination of capers, olives, tomatoes, and jalapeños. *AE, MC, V; no checks; lunch Tues-Sun, dinner every day; full bar.* ♿

Cafe Niebaum-Coppola

916 KEARNY ST, SAN FRANCISCO 📞 415/291-1700
NORTH BEACH 🍴 *Italian*

Film director Francis Ford Coppola brought all the amenities of his hugely popular Napa Valley winery to the city and nestled them stylishly at the foot of the landmark Sentinel Building in North Beach. It may sound at first like a bit of a marketing ploy (and, in fact, it is), but once you sit down to eat you'll be convinced your stop was worthwhile. Coppola is known in these parts for his gourmet savvy, and it is reflected in the casual country Italian dishes served here—many are reportedly made from the director's favorite recipes. The pastas, pizzas, and panini are excellent, great for a light lunch or dinner. A large selection of Italian pastries is available early in the day, and the entire menu can be served outside on the sidewalk, underneath blissfully powerful heat lamps. As you might expect, there are some 100 wines on the list, many available by the glass. You can also taste a flight of four wines at the stylish wine bar. A few complaints: sometimes the best tables are cordoned off for VIPs, and service ranges from friendly to downright frosty. *AE, DC, MC, V; checks OK; breakfast, lunch, dinner every day; full bar; cafe-sf@ffcnotes.com; www.cafecoppola.com.* &

Cafe Panini

2115 ALLSTON WAY, BERKELEY   📞 510/849-0405
DOWNTOWN BERKELEY   🍴 *Soup/Salad/Sandwich*

Tucked away off the street on an ivy-covered patio called Trumpetvine Court, unpretentious Cafe Panini serves up delectable sandwiches to a mellow crowd of UC Berkeley students and local office denizens. The spare interior, though cheery enough with brick accents and faux terra-cotta tile, reflects the fact that the emphasis here is on food rather than atmosphere. The daily changing menu features such sandwich choices as sun-dried tomatoes with mushrooms, pesto, basil, and melted mozzarella, and roast leg of lamb with rosemary, tomatoes, spinach, chutney, and curry mayonnaise, all on crispy toasted focaccia. One soup and salad are offered each day. Order at the counter and grab a table inside; on warm days, tables outdoors in the courtyard offer a welcome respite from bustling downtown Berkeley. The outside tables share space with the courtyard's main occupant, the popular beer garden Jupiter, which may entice you into an after-lunch pint among grad students. *No credit cards; checks OK; lunch Mon-Fri; no alcohol.* &

Cafe Prague

584 PACIFIC AVE, SAN FRANCISCO   📞 415/433-3811
FINANCIAL DISTRICT   🍴 *Soup/Salad/Sandwich*

Despite Cafe Prague's proximity to the Financial District, where office workers dash in and out of cafes in a mad rush in search of another caffeine fix, this is the type of spot where people arrive midmorning and are still working on their novel come lunchtime. The vibe is exceedingly hip Euro-bohemian, with murals on the walls, faux fur curtains at the front windows, and copies of Prague newspapers for all to read—all who read Czech, that is. Live music on weekends and poetry readings on Sunday nights add to the boho flair. The food is mostly organic salads, focaccia and baguette sandwiches, and the like, all tasty and prepared with the freshest ingredients. A house specialty is homemade granola, studded with pieces of dried fruit. At dinnertime, the menu broadens to include a few Eastern European specialties, like sauerbraten with dumplings. As at any cafe in Europe, many of those sitting at the sidewalks enjoy a cigarette with their espresso—if you're bothered by smoke, don't sit close to the front. *No credit cards; checks OK; breakfast, lunch, dinner every day; beer and wine.* ♿

Cafe Rain Tree

654 IRVING ST, SAN FRANCISCO 📞 415/665-3633
SUNSET DISTRICT 🍽 *Diner*

We've never seen more than 10 people in this overlooked comfort-food haven, but surely that's due only to intense competition from other restaurants in this busy corridor, not lack of quality. In fact, we expect you'll be quite pleased by both the attentive wait staff and the simple, satisfying diner fare. Delicious banana pancakes and waffles served with thick-cut bacon are menu highlights, as are the crisp fish and chips, hearty hamburgers served a dozen different ways, and hefty sandwiches, including the Monte Cristo cooked, as the menu proudly proclaims, "in a lot of butter." The accompanying salads, french fries, and coleslaw are better than you would expect from a place with such a sticky layer of grease on the tables, and all meals are a good value, with most breakfasts around five dollars, and dinner specials like meat loaf and pork chops around ten. *MC, V; no checks; breakfast, lunch, dinner every day; no alcohol.*

Cafe Tululah

2512 SAN PABLO AVE, BERKELEY 📞 510/548-4697
WEST BERKELEY 🍽 *American*

From the sunny wooden sign to the warm yellow-and-brick interior, this favorite breakfast eatery in a newly hip row of shops radiates casual friendliness. An open counter area at the back of the generous space is ideal for solo diners or those who want to grab a quick bite on the run. Grand Hollywood divas gaze down from black-and-white photos upon a neighborhood crowd enjoying such breakfast offerings as glazed asparagus omelets, homemade French toast, and Tululah Potatoes, an appealing mixture of red, russet, and sweet potatoes. The lunch crowd chows down on grilled portobello mushroom sandwiches on house-baked bread and innovative soups and salads. This women-owned establishment is committed to serving nutritious meals made with the freshest ingredients, so if you're tempted to indulge in that stack of blueberry pancakes, this is the place to do it. On sunny days, the herb-surrounded garden patio with its handmade tables makes a relaxing setting. *MC, V; local checks only; breakfast, lunch every day; beer and wine; tululah@earthlink.net.* &

Caffe 817

817 WASHINGTON ST, OAKLAND 📞 510/271-7965
DOWNTOWN OAKLAND 🍽 *Soup/Salad/Sandwich*

Visit the downtown Oakland farmers' market on Friday morning, then rest your weary bag-laden arms at Caffe 817. This tiny restaurant bears the stamp of its design-conscious owner, Alessandro Rossi, an electrical engineer who saw potential in the high-ceilinged space and hired local craftspeople to fashion its avant-garde furnishings. Despite its ambitious decor, the cafe has modest ambitions: cappuccino and pastries are mainstays in the morning, and Italian sandwiches, simple salads, and fresh soups and stews are on the midday menu. The sandwich fillings are what you might call contemporary Italian-American: roast beef with arugula, grilled mozzarella with artichokes, prosciutto with herb butter and pears. But the cranberry bean soup with rice is a classic Tuscan dish. If all this good fare inspires you to make your own Italian classics at home, head next door to G. B. Ratto International Grocers, a favorite East Bay source for arborio rice, olive oil, beans, and other imported foodstuffs. *No credit cards; checks OK; breakfast, lunch Mon–Sat; beer and wine.*

Caffè delle Stelle

395 HAYES ST, SAN FRANCISCO 📞 415/252-1110
HAYES VALLEY 🍽 *Italian*

In an area rife with "flavor of the month" restaurants popping up every week, Caffè delle Stelle has been consistently attracting symphony and opera crowds for more than a decade. Its success hinges on the hearty Italian fare and relaxed atmosphere. Starched white tablecloths, hanging lanterns, vintage Campari posters, antique kitchen implements, and artfully stacked bottles of olive oil and cans of tomatoes set a scene that is playful yet dignified. The weekly handwritten menus offer great seasonal specialties and reasonably-priced wine

selections. But any time of the year, you can savor the pumpkin ravioli smothered in sage-butter or the gnocchi, which comes topped with a divine honey
cream sauce. Balmy summer evenings bring sidewalk seating. One taste of the
garlicky bruschetta, and you'll feel like you've come home to *nonna*. Everything
is homemade, and the tiramisu has a reputation for being some of the Bay
Area's best. *AE, DC, DIS, MC, V; no checks; lunch Mon-Sat, dinner every day; beer and
wine; www.caffedelle.citysearch.com.*

Caffè Greco

423 COLUMBUS AVE, SAN FRANCISCO   415/397-6261
NORTH BEACH   *Italian*

In San Francisco's most Italian neighborhood, Caffè Greco is the city's most
beloved Italian cafe. Each morning small groups of Italian men congregate for
conversation over cups of dark espresso. Later in the day, snag one of the
choicest tables along the wall of windows overlooking Columbus Avenue and
order lunch or dinner. Though the dishes are limited mostly to warm, fragrant
focaccia sandwiches (try the prosciutto, mozzarella, and roasted bell pepper)
and a few salads, all the better to save room for desserts like chocolate Kahlúa
cake, gelato, or, of course, tiramisu. Though it can be crowded in the evenings
with couples making eyes at each other over cups of cappuccino, afternoons
provide plenty of peace and quiet for reading and writing: Italian newspapers
like the *Corriere della Sera* await those whose Italian is up to the challenge. *Cash
only; breakfast, lunch, dinner every day; beer and wine.*

Caffè Macaroni

59 COLUMBUS AVE, SAN FRANCISCO   415/956-9737
NORTH BEACH   *Italian*

Don't let the funky little facade or silly name fool you—Caffè Macaroni is one of
the best southern Italian restaurants in the city. It's so bloody small you can't
help but feel special, as if you've been invited to dine in some stranger's kitchen
in Rome. (And if you think the main dining room is tiny, check out the one
upstairs!) The diminutive kitchen churns out a surprising variety of antipasti
and pastas. The menu changes daily; look for items like outstanding pork
medallions in a fennel sauce. Gnocchi fans will find happiness here as well. The
polenta with mushrooms makes a good starter, and there's a wide selection of
reasonably priced Italian wines. You'll adore the jovial and vivacious Italian

waiters, too. Lunch is served at the more informal cafe across the street. Prices are on the high end for this book, but you won't find better Italian food for the price. *Cash only; dinner Mon-Sat; beer and wine.*

Caffè Museo

MUSEUM OF MODERN ART, 151 3RD ST, SAN FRANCISCO   📞   415/357-4500
SOUTH OF MARKET   🍽   *Mediterranean*

Unlike many museum restaurants that sell bland, overpriced food in a sterile cafeteria setting, Caffè Museo dishes up flavorful Cal/Mediterranean fare in a stylish setting that hints at the brilliant design of the rest of SFMOMA. From the wooden trays that echo the wooden walls to the staff clad in Asian-looking gray tunics, it seems every detail has been attended to. And that's before you even get to the food. The small menu of salads, sandwiches, and pizzas rarely disappoints. A mop of peppery arugula in the roasted chicken sandwich peeks out from between slices of soft focaccia, and a puckery apricot and blueberry tart isn't tender but is extremely flavorful. Or opt for a bakery item like a jam-filled scone or peanut butter cookie. Because of the museum's location, the restaurant attracts droves of dot-commers at lunchtime, as well as the out-of-town museum-goers you would expect. Tables can be hard to come by, but helpful, exceptionally friendly staffers will help you stake out a place once you've placed your order. *AE, MC, V; no checks; lunch Thurs-Tues, dinner Thurs; beer and wine.* ♿

Cambodiana's

2156 UNIVERSITY AVE, BERKELEY   📞   510/843-4630
DOWNTOWN BERKELEY   🍽   *Vietnamese/Southeast Asian*

There aren't many Cambodian restaurants in Cambodia, where wayfarers rely on teahouses and noodle shops, and traditional dishes may be sampled only in private homes. It took a forward-thinking Assyrian priest—Father Nazarin—to convince the Bay Area immigrant community that a Cambodian restaurant could be a hot property. Cambodiana's is the best of the bunch. Owner Sidney Sok Ke and his wife Carol Bopha Ke, the restaurant's talented chef, have assembled a menu organized around six regional sauces (based, respectively, on tamarind, ginger, lemongrass, lamb juice, curry, and anchovy), each designed to complement delectable renditions of chicken, salmon, rabbit, lamb, prawns, quail, beef, and trout. Try the deboned quail stuffed with ground pork, shrimp, and garlic or the wonderful grilled lamb chops marinated in a mixture of garlic, lemongrass, galangal, paprika, and soy sauce. The country-style smoky eggplant, roasted and tossed with pork, shrimp, green onion, and garlic, also wins raves. The place is usually packed, so make reservations, especially for weekend evenings. *AE, DC, MC, V; checks OK; lunch Mon-Fri, dinner every day; beer and wine.*

Canto do Brasil

41 FRANKLIN ST, SAN FRANCISCO 📞 415/626-8727
HAYES VALLEY 🍴 *Brazilian*

This festive restaurant with the bright blue and yellow facade is a perfect place to take an evening-long Brazilian holiday. Potted plants and colorful paintings on the walls set a warm, tropical mood, and the friendly waitresses make you wonder if all Brazilians are so charming. (This location is certainly more festive than the Mission District space it vacated a few years ago, now taken over by the wildly popular Delfina.) The festivities usually start with a *caipirinha,* the traditional Brazilian cocktail of lime, sugar, and cachaça, a rumlike liquor. Next, traditionalists will want to go for the *feijoada completa*—Brazil's special stew of sausage, ham, black beans, and garlic—available Friday through Sunday only. But any day of the week is a good day for the *pernil recheado,* a roast leg of pork cooked with vegetables in a red wine sauce. Seafood specials can be a bit pricey, but most entrees, including red snapper in coconut milk, are about $10 to $11. Its proximity to the symphony hall and opera house are a plus, but if you're on your way to a performance give yourself plenty of time; service is not super-speedy. *AE, MC, V; no checks; lunch Mon-Sat, dinner every day; full bar; www.cantodobrasil.com.*

Casa Sanchez

2778 24TH ST, SAN FRANCISCO 📞 415/282-2400
MISSION DISTRICT 🍴 *Mexican*

First established in 1924 as a *tortilleria* (tortilla factory), this place eventually evolved into a taqueria. Today, the house-made thick, hand-cut chips and fresh salsas have become so popular that they're for sale throughout the Bay Area. Though the rest of the food is nothing special, the reason to visit in person is to grab a beer and taco, load up at the all-you-can-eat chips and salsa bar, and catch a bit of the Mission's sunshine on the mural-bedecked patio. Be sure to ask to see the tattoo book, filled with blurry snapshots of various body parts tattooed with the Casa Sanchez logo: a little sombreroed man riding an ear of corn. In 1998, the owners promised those willing to get themselves tattooed with this symbol a lifetime of free burritos. Around 40 people have taken the plunge, though apparently only a handful of them show up regularly for free food. (Interested parties must go through a strict screening process.) *AE, DC, DIS, MC, V; no checks; breakfast, lunch every day; beer only.*

Cha Am

1543 SHATTUCK AVE, BERKELEY *(and branches)* 📞 510/848-9664
NORTH BERKELEY/FINANCIAL DISTRICT/SOUTH OF MARKET/SUNSET DISTRICT
🍴 *Thai*

Proudly perched above Shattuck Avenue in an area nicknamed the Gourmet Ghetto, Cha Am reigns supreme in the Thai food category. It's been raking in awards for over a decade, and its popularity has spawned a cookbook and funded an expansion into a larger room. The most romantic area to sit in is the front greenhouse portion of the restaurant. But unless requesting that seating, you're more likely to be relegated to one of the back rooms, where the walls are a soft shade of lemongrass, and paper lanterns and a mural are the only nods to decor. The real reason to come, however, is for the food, such as an aromatic salmon curry or a complex-tasting coconut-prawn soup. While the luau-shirted waiters tend to thrust the daily specials menu at you in a somewhat aggressive fashion, that won't detract from the pleasure of feasting on some of the best Thai food the Bay Area has to offer. A word to the uninitiated: those aren't finger bowls—it's your drinking water. *AE, MC, V; no checks; lunch, dinner every day; beer and wine.*

Chaat Café

1902 UNIVERSITY AVE, BERKELEY 📞 510/845-1431
DOWNTOWN BERKELEY 🍴 *Indian*

Step inside this cavernous storefront and you may think someone decided to set up a temporary restaurant in a store or office space: High ceilings dwarf rows of simple tables, and the whole place has an odd, fly-by-night feel. Although the space may be awkward, the service underwhelming, and the decor nonexistent save for a row of black-and-white glamour shots of Indian film stars, Berkeleyites of all stripes seek out this ultracasual address for its cheap and excellent *chaat*, or Indian snacks. Order at the counter in back, grab some silverware, and prepare to be pleasantly surprised. Outstanding dishes include *papri chaat*, a refreshing yogurt dish reminiscent of Greek tzatziki, with potatoes, garbanzo beans, and a lentil dumpling; and the perpetually sold-out *aloo tikki*, zesty potato patties with green chile and onions, whose sharpness is offset by sweet chutney. At three bucks a pop, you may decide to share a few and forgo the entrees altogether. If you do venture there, the tasty wraps—Indian versions of falafel wrapped in naan—are a fine bet. *MC, V; no checks; lunch, dinner every day; beer and wine.* &

Cha Cha Cha

1801 HAIGHT ST, SAN FRANCISCO ☎ 415/386-5758
2327 MISSION ST, SAN FRANCISCO ☎ 415/648-0504
UPPER HAIGHT/MISSION DISTRICT 🍽 *Caribbean*

When you arrive to find there's a 90-minute wait for a table and they don't take reservations, you may wonder why anyone chooses to eat here. But add your name to the waiting list, pack yourself into the impossibly tiny bar area, and order a pitcher of the signature sangria and you, too, will discover Cha Cha Cha's charms—eventually. It has little to do with the kitschy, over-the-top faux-tropical decor and more to do with the flavorful Caribbean-style tapas. The chicken paillard consists of strips of chicken breast swimming in a creamy mustard sauce served in a miniature cast iron skillet, and the heap of fried potatoes come with a spicy aioli that will have you contemplating a second pitcher of sangria. Jerk chicken, pork quesadillas, fried plantains, and garlicky shrimp are all favorites. The second branch in the Mission has lackluster decor and falls short of the original's festive atmosphere, but the waits can be considerably shorter, especially on weeknights. *MC, V; no checks; lunch, dinner every day; beer and wine.* &

Charanga

2351 MISSION ST, SAN FRANCISCO ☎ 415/282-1813
MISSION DISTRICT 🍽 *Caribbean*

A few years ago chef Gabriela Salas left her post at the popular restaurant Cha Cha Cha (see review) after nine years to open her own tapas place, named after a style of Latin music. And many people eagerly followed her to this new outpost tucked behind an unassuming Mission Street facade. She has provided San Franciscans with one of the few—and one of the best—restaurants in town serving cuisine from Costa Rica and the Caribbean. Salas's spicy vegetable empanaditas are out of this world, served with a yogurt-pineapple-mint salsa that quickly cools the palate. The ceviche is another good selection, as are the mussels and the sautéed mushrooms. Charanga is relatively nondescript, but bring a large group, order a few pitchers of sangria, and you'll soon be creating your own atmosphere. *DC, DIS, MC, V; no checks; dinner Tues-Sat; full bar.*

Chava's Mexican Restaurant

3248 18TH ST, SAN FRANCISCO   📞   415/552-9387
MISSION DISTRICT   🍴   *Mexican*

Tired of waiting in line at yet another Mission taqueria? Want to immerse yourself in a down-home Mexican-American atmosphere? Try Chava's, an eternally busy but always inviting restaurant that's been serving up huge plates of steaming enchiladas, chiles rellenos, tacos, and burritos to local crowds for many years now. On Sunday mornings the room is full of nicely dressed Latino families digging into bowls of *menudo* (beef tripe soup, served only on weekends) or plates of huevos rancheros after church. Weekdays it's packed with hungry workers looking for a hearty lunch in a colorful, bustling environment. One major draw is the fresh, homemade corn tortillas, which are far thicker and tastier than anything you'll find at Safeway. The soups are also excellent: if *menudo* isn't your style, the big bowl of chicken soup, with lots of veggies and meat on the bone, is a knockout, even if you're not fighting a cold. Wash it all down with a glass of *horchata* (the rice milk is sweet and soothing after a spicy meal) or a bottle of orange soda. *Cash only; breakfast, lunch, dinner every day; no alcohol.*

Cha-Ya

1686 SHATTUCK AVE, BERKELEY   📞   510/981-1213
NORTH BERKELEY   🍴   *Japanese*

A low-key vegetarian gem tucked along the southern edge of Berkeley's Gourmet Ghetto, Cha-Ya takes Japanese cuisine to a level of sophistication unmatched this side of San Francisco. Behind the small orange counter, chef/owner Atsushi Katsumata uses the freshest ingredients available to create singular udon and soba noodle dishes, sushi, and a mean miso soup. Young couples slurp noodles with mushrooms and bamboo shoots or seasonal vegetables (including lotus root) and tofu, while visiting-scholar types struggle to choose from among more than a dozen sushi options, including *kampyo* (seasoned gourd) and *yamagobo* (pickled burdock). What better to accompany vegetarian sushi than organic wine or sake? And be sure to save room for the surprisingly good vegan ice cream with green-tea sauce. With a mere four tables and nine seats at the counter, Cha-Ya is consistently packed, so arrive early or late, or prepare to idle on the sidewalk with other hungry patrons. *MC, V; no checks; dinner Tues-Sun; beer and wine.* &

Cheers Cafe

127 CLEMENT ST, SAN FRANCISCO 📞 415/387-6966
RICHMOND DISTRICT 🍴 *California Cuisine*

Cheers is a mainstay for the weekend brunch crowd, but don't overlook it for a weekday afternoon lunch or even a nice dinner. Of course, what makes it so popular are the brunch specials. Bargain-priced omelets, delicate waffles, decadent French toast, and crusty rolls are what keep people waiting outside every Sunday morning. The simple elegance of the interior makes it the perfect spot for bringing your mom, your out-of-town friends, or your new sweetheart. The back patio is more rustic, but it's a pleasant spot to enjoy a latte and two-egg special or one of Cheers's sandwiches at lunch. The crowds thin out for dinner, which is a shame, because the patio makes Cheers a real find on those rare warm evenings. The evening menu features pastas, thin-crusted pizzas, and grills, some with fusion-style Asian overtones. *AE, MC, V; no checks; breakfast, lunch Mon-Fri, dinner Tues-Sun, brunch Sat-Sun; beer and wine; www.cheersrestaurant.com.* &

Cheese Board Pizza

1512 SHATTUCK AVE, BERKELEY 📞 510/549-3055
NORTH BERKELEY 🍴 *Pizza*

When you see a line snaking down the sidewalk in front of the "Closed" sign on the door, you know Cheese Board Pizza is about to open for business. Two doors down from its parent cheese shop, one of Berkeley's oldest collectives serves the town's most revered pies. Only one kind of pizza—available by the slice, the half, or the full pie—is offered each day, and it's always vegetarian, always has a thin, crispy sourdough crust, and is always made with the freshest ingredients available. It might be tomatoes, fresh basil, garlic, and fontina or the Cheese Board's classic potatoes, fresh rosemary, and Gruyère, but it hardly matters. Patrons, and that includes everyone in Berkeley at one time or another, rarely glance at the flavor of the day before snagging a spot in line.

Those lucky enough to get one of the few indoor tables may chow down to live music, if anyone is moved to play the piano, though the few outdoor tables have the better view: Berkeley on parade. *No credit cards; checks OK; lunch Mon–Sat, dinner Tues–Sat; beer and wine; www.cheeseboardcollective.com.*

Chef Jia's

925 KEARNY ST, SAN FRANCISCO   📞 415/398-1626
CHINATOWN 🍴 *Chinese*

There's never a line at Chef Jia's, but don't let that fool you. Slaves to convention may line up outside the door of its legendary neighbor, House of Nanking (see review), but those seeking a quick meal will do far better wrapping their chopsticks around Chef Jia's chunks of sticky, spicy honey chile chicken than waiting for a table next door with a growling stomach and a deteriorating mood. The waitress might not say anything more than "Spicy?" to you, and the card tables and butcher-paper menus leave a little to be desired, but when it comes to quick service and tasty food, you can't beat this hole-in-the-wall. Subtlety is not Chef Jia's specialty, and no one would call the sauces delicate or nuanced: most of the dishes are sort of like a Chinese version of mac and cheese, the color unnaturally bright and the flavor unbelievably potent. But when the mood hits, there is nothing more satisfying than a cheap-as-hell plate of spicy green beans piled high with fried tofu and washed down with a Tsing Tao beer. *Cash only; lunch, dinner every day; beer and wine.*

Chester's Bayview Cafe

1508-B WALNUT AVE, BERKELEY   📞 510/849-9995
NORTH BERKELEY 🍴 *American*

Breakfast on the upper patio of Chester's is hands-down the best way to escape the Sunday blues. Bougainvillea spills over the deck railing, and you'll be bathed in sunlight and taking in a calming bay view as you sink your teeth into a tomato pesto omelet. After a few bites, Monday will seem miles away. Best of all, they're extremely generous here with the coffee refills—just like your favorite greasy spoon, only the food is a heck of a lot better. It is Berkeley, after all, so you can choose between the Tofu Vegan Scrambler (organic tofu with fresh spinach, mushrooms, and garlic) and the Minnesota Omelet (chicken breast with artichoke hearts, bell peppers, and jack cheese). If a regular cup of joe isn't doing the trick, then you can add a shot of hazelnut syrup to a latte or have it made with organic soy milk. Inside, the setting is reminiscent of a ski chalet, only the snow has been supplanted by bayside fog. Service is friendly and efficient. *MC, V; no checks; breakfast, lunch every day; no alcohol.*

Chez Nous

1911 FILLMORE ST, SAN FRANCISCO   415/441-8044
PACIFIC HEIGHTS   *French*

Tapas restaurants took San Francisco's Mission District by storm in the 1990s, and the Bay Area has been in love with "small plates" ever since. This restaurant serves only small plates, but chef Laurence Jossel's tapas are a wonderful mix of French, Middle Eastern, and Spanish dishes. It's a good thing the plates are small, since almost every dish is irresistible—like two perfect grilled lamb chops with lavender salt for dipping, or smoky, tender squid on a bed of shaved fennel, orange segments, and greens. If you and a friend share an order of grilled quail with chanterelle mushrooms, sautéed greens with pine nuts, a salad, and an artisan cheese plate, you can get out of the place for around $35. It's so popular that you might have to wait a while for a seat at one of the narrow tables (they don't accept reservations), but luckily you can pass the time at the small wine bar. *MC, V; no checks; lunch Wed–Sun, dinner Tues–Sun; beer and wine.*

Chloe's

1399 CHURCH ST, SAN FRANCISCO   415/648-4116
NOE VALLEY   *American*

This cute-as-a-button breakfast spot usually has a line out the door from 9AM on—most weekdays included. The reason for the wait is simple: you just can't get such a good breakfast in San Francisco without a fight. In warm weather, seating does extend out to a few sidewalk tables, where customers can sometimes observe the friendly firefighters two or three doors down doing ladder exercises. The menu includes a list of scrambled egg choices, all of which are served with crisp home fries and toast (ask for the dense walnut bread). Creative daily specials include things like the New Mexico scramble, which is folded with cream cheese and mild green chiles. Sweeter offerings include stacks of buttermilk pancakes, but the real house special is French toast made of luscious slices of croissant. What's incongruous is the (so-called) bacon, which is some kind of suspicious, low-fat variety. You can also choose from a list of sandwiches and salads. *No credit cards; checks OK; breakfast, lunch every day; beer and wine.*

Chow

215 CHURCH ST, SAN FRANCISCO   📞 415/552-2469
CASTRO 🍽 *American*

Chow, the first of Tony Gulisano's no-frills cafes serving bargain-priced food, regularly has Castro dwellers lining up. The warm, 80-seat dining room, with a long mahogany bar stretching the length of it, offers a casual and relaxed atmosphere—a good match for the inexpensive food. This no-reservations restaurant is known for its robust wood-fired pizzas with such toppings as fennel sausage and red onions or a roast-chicken pie with pancetta. Vegetarians can easily find their way around the menu, with offerings like pasta with peppers and eggplant, grilled portobello mushrooms and polenta, or noodles with tofu and pesto. The desserts tend toward such classics as strawberry shortcake and a pie of the day. An impressive beer list includes several Belgian options and six microbrews on tap. A small list of wines by the glass is also available. A sister restaurant, Park Chow (see review), is located near Golden Gate Park. *MC, V; no checks; lunch, dinner every day; beer and wine.*   ♿

Christopher's Nothing Fancy Cafe

1019 SAN PABLO AVE, ALBANY   📞 510/526-1185
ALBANY 🍽 *Mexican*

Don't let the name fool you: Christopher's idea of nothing fancy is Mexican food made from scratch using the freshest ingredients, with bonuses like fat-free beans, whole wheat tortillas, and some organic produce. Favorites include grilled chicken fajitas, steak strip chimichangas, and shrimp quesadillas wrapped in chipotle tortillas; also keep your eyes peeled for seasonal specials. The atmosphere is quite casual—order at the front, stock up on salsa, and choose a wooden table, each adorned with a different Mexican image. Tile mosaics add splashes of color to an already colorful space. On chilly evenings, a blaze crackles in the towering fireplace in the corner. On warm afternoons, the picnic-style dining area tucked out back, surrounded by jasmine and herbs, is a pleasant refuge. Christopher's attracts a loyal crowd of locals, especially families with young children, who appreciate a healthy fast-food alternative. *AE, DIS, MC, V; checks OK; lunch Mon–Sat, dinner every day; beer and wine.*   ♿

Cinderella Bakery, Delicatessen and Restaurant

436 BALBOA ST, SAN FRANCISCO 📞 415/751-9690
RICHMOND DISTRICT 🍴 *Russian*

The servers here actually praise you for your voracious appetite, just like any good Russian grandmother would. And it's not difficult to eat a lot here, because everything is so good. The heavy beef stroganoff with kasha on the side is old-country awesome, as are the chicken Kiev and the remarkable borscht with dill and sour cream. The sour cherry *vareniki* are tart-and-savory dumplings and taste best with—you guessed it—sour cream on the side. Sour cream is the operative word here, and it is a welcome accompaniment. That's the way your babushka would have it, as she would have baked everything from scratch, like they do here. And we mean everything, including the breads (and thankfully, not a crust of sourdough in sight), the savory cabbage and meat-stuffed piroshki, and the caramelized onion and mushroom *viziga*. And of course, you won't be leaving without one of the awesome strudels, butter cookies, fruit pastries, or other freshly baked desserts. *MC, V; checks OK; breakfast, lunch, dinner Tues-Sun; beer only.* ♿

Citizen Cake

399 GROVE ST, SAN FRANCISCO 📞 415/861-2228
HAYES VALLEY 🍴 *Bakery*

When you're looking to impress with dessert, this chic little bakery takes the cake. In fact, owner/baker Elizabeth Falkner has become something of a minor celebrity for her extravagant concoctions. Locals love the place as much for its hip, modern feel as for its magnificent baked goods. At lunch, folks who work in the area line up for the salads, fresh-baked bread, and excellent sandwiches, and before the symphony you'll see well-dressed folks there for the pretheater menu. Ordering dessert, whether a perfectly velvety slice of pound cake or a warm cookie and a glass of milk, seems a moral imperative when dining here. In fact, cake and pastries only are available every afternoon, 2:30PM to 5:30PM. *AE, MC, V; local checks only; breakfast Tues-Sun, lunch Tues-Fri, dinner Tues-Sun; no alcohol; www.citizencake.com.*

Citrus Club

1790 HAIGHT ST, SAN FRANCISCO 📞 415/387-6366
UPPER HAIGHT 🍴 *Pan-Asian*

A great place to eat and a great place to drink, this Haight Street hangout is a superb value for solid noodle dishes in a sophisticated ambience. For lunch, a fantastic bowl of noodle soup is more than enough, and the rich coconut tofu soup and the light and fruity vegetable noodle soup feature a tangle of hearty rice noodles, fresh vegetables in abundance, and broth blanketed with the scent of ginger, lemongrass, and onion. Soups are the menu's best offerings, but a dinner entree will not disappoint if it's the spicy lime and coconut noodles, or the hot, wok-tossed spicy lemon and coconut chicken. Linger over your meal with a cold or hot sake from the good selection, or the tangy and unusual sake martini. Bottles of French wine for less than $20 are an excellent deal and can be enjoyed with snacks and appetizers like cool and minty Vietnamese spring rolls, a simple beef satay, or the popular edamame (boiled, salted soybeans). *MC, V; no checks; lunch, dinner every day; beer and wine.* ♿

Clement Okazu Ya

914 CLEMENT ST, SAN FRANCISCO 📞 415/668-1638
RICHMOND DISTRICT 🍴 *Japanese*

It often seems that going out for Japanese food is the best way to bust your dining budget, which is why neighborhood spots like Clement Okazu Ya are so welcome. Bowls of donburi are a bargain $5, as is shrimp tempura with udon noodles. Sushi prices, too, are more than reasonable. Extremely generous sushi lunch specials that come with miso soup are less than $8, and at dinner even ahi tuna steaks and swordfish go for about $10. Unfortunately, the nondescript decor isn't helped by the small TV in the corner, and at lunch the place can be mighty quiet. But in the evenings the place has a casual, friendly neighborhood vibe—especially on Mondays and Thursdays, when beers go for an incredible 99 cents. *MC, V; no checks; lunch, dinner Wed-Mon; beer and wine.*

Conard 9th St. Café

160 9TH ST, SAN FRANCISCO 📞 415/487-1706
SOUTH OF MARKET 🍴 *American*

A black-and-white checkered linoleum floor, huge wooden booths, and old-fashioned fixtures set the stage for comfort food sold at comforting prices. In fact, looking around the restaurant or at the old equipment in the open kitchen, you'd think this could still be 1955–until the cell phones start ringing, that is. The bulk of the menu is soups, salads, sandwiches, and burgers. A big chicken breast sandwich is laden with roasted bell peppers, avocado, and jack cheese and comes with baby salad greens or a pasta salad. The truly famished might be able to finish off one of the blackboard specials, like a slab of meat loaf and mashed potatoes rich with butter. Breakfast items are the usual eggs and toast, pancakes, and fruit and granola. Service is typically speedy, accommodating the folks rushing back to their desks at one of the offices that have sprung up in the neighborhood. *Cash only; breakfast, lunch Mon–Fri; no alcohol.*

Cordon Bleu

1574 CALIFORNIA ST, SAN FRANCISCO 📞 415/673-5637
POLK GULCH 🍴 *Vietnamese/Southeast Asian*

"Dive" is a generous word to describe this Vietnamese hole-in-the-wall with three tables and about 10 stools perched above a battered Formica counter. Sitting at the counter, you can feel the heat of the grill that's searing thin strips of beef and the restaurant's signature "Five Spiced Roast Chicken," both dishes slightly sweet, slightly tangy, and served just a shade past well done. These two types of meat, plus a thick, fried imperial roll, a mountain of white rice topped with meat sauce, and a coleslawlike salad, represent the sum total of the items you can order here, available in five prodigious combo plates. Huge portions and a certain seedy charm are what attract local regulars and those on their way to a movie at the Lumiere Theatre next door. Waits during dinner can be long, when it seems everyone in the neighborhood is stopping by to get their supper here, to go. And with the low, low prices (only one combo costs more than $6), they can stop by almost every day. *Cash only; lunch Tues–Sat, dinner Tues–Sun; no alcohol.*

Coriya Hot Pot City

852 CLEMENT ST, SAN FRANCISCO ☎ 415/387-7888
RICHMOND DISTRICT 🍴 *Chinese*

The bustling Coriya Hot Pot City is one of the most popular of the Richmond District's all-you-can-eat, cook-it-yourself Taiwanese buffets. Coriya combines the joy of going out to eat (no dishes to wash) with the fun of cooking. There's no menu here—just big piles of food in its raw state, plus grills and hot pots built right into your table. The secret ingredient here is your own creativity. Stack your plate high with raw beef, lamb, pork, poultry, or seafood (with all that meat lying around, it's not an ideal place for vegetarians); choose a sauce; get some vegetables; and take it all back to your table to grill or boil for soup. Follow the written tips or make up your own combinations. As you can imagine, with the cooking appliances right on your table, the decor and accoutrements here are basic rather than fancy, but it's comfortable enough. Coriya is open until midnight during the week, and 1AM on weekends, and during the late-night hours it's a hot spot for young Asians on dates or in groups. *MC, V; no checks; lunch, dinner every day; beer and wine.* ♿

Crepes-a-Go-Go

2165 UNION ST, SAN FRANCISCO ☎ 415/928-1919
2125 UNIVERSITY AVE, BERKELEY ☎ 510/841-7722
COW HOLLOW/DOWNTOWN BERKELEY 🍴 *French*

The staff at this cheery little five-table restaurant is full of Gallic charm, calling all the women "mademoiselle" and chatting up diners—in French, if they understand it. The staff is admittedly more authentically French than the crepes—here savory crepes are made with wheat flour rather than the traditional buckwheat and are a tad sweet—but they're good nonetheless, just slightly crisp on the outside and tender within. Design your own, perhaps with avocado, tomato, cheese, and smoked turkey, or opt for a simpler combo of egg and cheese or even apple and cheese, the better to save room for a decadent dessert crepe. Choose one with maple syrup, fresh strawberries and kiwi, ricotta cheese and jam, or Nutella, the lusciously thick chocolate hazelnut paste. And if you'd just like a sweet snack, you can pop in and get a dessert crepe to go; they'll wrap it in paper so you can enjoy it as you walk down Union Street. The Berkeley branch is a little more bare-bones—Formica-topped tables and floor, paper plates and plastic cups—but serves the same great crepes. *No credit cards (Cow Hollow); AE, MC, V (Berkeley); local checks only; breakfast, lunch, dinner every day; no alcohol.*

Crepevine

5600 COLLEGE AVE, OAKLAND 📞 510/658-2026

624 IRVING ST, SAN FRANCISCO 📞 415/681-5858

NORTH OAKLAND/SUNSET DISTRICT 🍴 *Soup/Salad/Sandwich*

When Edible Complex, the favorite cafe of many Rockridge residents, closed last year, many feared its space would go to some bland corporate chain. Instead, most were thrilled when Crepevine arrived to fill the cheap eats void. There's no bad table at this spacious restaurant. Choose from a sunny table next to the floor-to-ceiling windows; a table on the heated patio out front; or a table on the upper level, looking down on the dozens of happy diners below. In a bit of culinary cross-pollination, crepes come in varieties like the Greek (with spinach, black olives, feta, and cucumber) and Italian (with artichoke hearts, mozzarella, roasted red pepper, and eggplant), all served with home fries cooked with plenty of rosemary. Other choices include a variety of sandwiches and salads, but save room for dessert. Next to a display case of cakes and pastries are jars of tasty but unusual cookies; try the banana chunk. *Cash only; breakfast, lunch, dinner every day; beer and wine.* ♿

Crescent City Cafe

1418 HAIGHT ST, SAN FRANCISCO 📞 415/863-1374

UPPER HAIGHT 🍴 *Cajun/Creole*

Walk past the blue-tiled facade and it's as if you've stepped into the heart of New Orleans. This postage stamp-size place—just four tables and about a dozen stools around an L-shaped bar—is like a little slice of Creole comfort, complete with jazz filling the air at all times. When you want spicy, come here and order the gumbo or the jambalaya, each rich, hearty, and fiery hot. The Southern fried chicken with mashed potatoes and corn bread is rib-sticking good, and there are some mighty fine blackened fish dishes. On weekends, neighborhood folks line up for the huge buckwheat pancakes, Southern-style biscuits and gravy, and Creole omelets with grits. Service is good and prompt, if just a bit frazzled. But it's worth getting shuffled out the door to save yourself the airfare to the Big Easy. *MC, V; no checks; breakfast, lunch Mon-Fri, dinner every day, brunch Sat-Sun; beer and wine.*

Dipsea Cafe

200 SHORELINE HWY, MILL VALLEY 📞 415/381-0298
MILL VALLEY 🍽 *American*

Named after the trail that leads from Mill Valley over Mount Tamalpais to the ocean, this sunny, spacious cafe couldn't be any cuter if it tried. Blond wood floors and tables, blue-and-white checked tablecloths, coat pegs shaped like cows and chickens, and trompe l'oeil murals of farmhouse and barnyard scenes somehow manage to be cheery rather than cloying. Maybe it's the friendly service or the generously sized windows that put us in a good mood when we come here. No, it's definitely the food. Breakfast is the specialty: unusual seasonal dishes like dill potato pancakes and bay scallop omelets complement the broad menu of morning fare. The perennially popular Dipsea Special is perfect for the indecisive diner: an egg, bacon, sausage, home fries, and two fluffy buttermilk pancakes that taste buttery even without a dollop of the stuff. Lunch dishes are mostly burgers, sandwiches, and salads, but, again, seasonal specials like the crusty chicken potpie are worth a try. And if you've actually tackled the Dipsea Trail this morning, you'll be ready for a smoothie like the Waterdew, made of honeydew, watermelon, strawberries, and frozen yogurt. Kids are welcome and catered to with a kids' menu and crayons, but their patience will surely be tested if you arrive on a sunny weekend, when the wait can stretch to more than an hour. *AE, DIS, MC, V; no checks; breakfast, lunch every day; beer and wine.* ♿

Doidge's

2217 UNION ST, SAN FRANCISCO 📞 415/921-2149
COW HOLLOW 🍽 *American*

Those who like their breakfast places just a little more upscale than Kate's Kitchen (see review) often name Doidge's as their favorite. This tiny spot open since 1971 prides itself on using the freshest ingredients, which means you'd do well to order your omelet stuffed with fresh veggies or avocado, or perhaps get a bowl of seasonal fruit with your creamy bowl of steel-cut oats. An open-faced frittata with sausage, spinach, melted cheese, and tomato is a work of art and served with peppery potatoes. The main dining room is a bit cutesy, with floral curtains and tables that could have come from your grandma's dining room. The best seats in the house are at the old wooden counter, where you can watch the cooks flip omelets and cook up the crispiest of bacon. Sadly, Doidge's closes at 12:30PM Monday through Thursday, at 1:30PM on Fridays, and at 2:30PM on weekends, so get here early. The upside? Doidge's is one of the few breakfast places in the city that takes reservations. Call well in advance for a Sunday morning spot. *MC, V; no checks; breakfast, lunch every day; beer and wine.*

Dim Sum Dining

Hugely popular in Hong Kong and Canton, dim sum is also one of the best things going in Bay Area Chinese cuisine. Meaning "heart's delight" in Cantonese, it's a morning or afternoon tea served with delicately prepared sweet and savory snacks.

In a proper dim sum experience, the tea itself is as important as the food. When you first get to your table, a waiter will ask for your drink order, and you can request flower-scented jasmine, smoky oolong, or earthy poner, among other choices.

In larger dim sum teahouses, servers roll carts or carry trays full of fresh, hot dishes, bringing their offerings by your table for a look. Simply choose what you like, but try to resist taking too many items at once or the food might get cold. Prices usually start at around $2 per plate (the servers tick off your orders one by one on the bill). Since most plates come with three or four pieces of the same item, it's a good idea to go with a group to try as many different dishes as possible.

Most items are announced first in Cantonese, so it doesn't hurt to learn a few common names such as *siu mai*, small round pork dumplings, or *ha gao*, translucent shrimp dumplings. Besides the more familiar pot stickers and egg rolls, the usual dim sum suspects include barbecue pork buns, foil-wrapped chicken, stir-fried greens, delicate egg custard tarts, wide rice noodles stuffed with shrimp or meat, hearty sticky rice steamed in a lotus leaf, and crisp but chewy sesame balls filled with sweet bean paste.

The higher the prices, the lighter and more creative the dim sum tends to be. But you can also find delicious food at the more modest dim sum halls as well as at small Chinese bakeries, where items are sold for as little as three for a dollar.

Since most dim sum dishes are made with shrimp, pork, or pork fat, it's not the best meal for vegetarians or those keeping kosher. More upscale dim sum restaurants, however, usually have some vegetarian options, and Chinatown's KOWLOON (909 Grant Ave; 415/362-9888) serves all-vegetarian dim sum made with mushrooms, taro root, cabbage, and water chestnuts.

Dol Ho

808 PACIFIC AVE, SAN FRANCISCO 📞 415/392-2828
CHINATOWN 🍴 *Chinese*

Some contend the mark of authenticity and quality at an ethnic restaurant is when people of that ethnicity are filling the place. Given that benchmark, Dol Ho must be one of the best places in town for dim sum. And it is. Despite not having the polish and, well, cleanliness of the city's more popular dim sum parlors, this place serves up dim sum that's quite fresh and delicious. What's more, it's considerably cheaper than you'll find almost anywhere else. The trays of shrimp and pork dumplings, fried eggplant, custard tarts, and other delights roll out from the kitchen every few minutes; as at all dim sum restaurants, just point at what you want when it passes. *Cash only; dim sum every day 7AM–5PM; beer and wine.*

Dottie's True Blue Café

522 JONES ST, SAN FRANCISCO 📞 415/885-2767
TENDERLOIN 🍴 *Diner*

Don't let the dicey neighborhood deter you from venturing to one of the best breakfast cafes in the city. Though Dottie's serves lunch, it's the all-day, all-American morning fare everyone lines up for, such as hefty portions of French toast, cornmeal pancakes, bacon and eggs, and omelets that look especially appealing against the blue-and-white checkerboard tablecloths. Because it's all made from scratch they don't mind taking special orders, and they do wonders with bean cakes that double as meatless sausage patties. The clincher, though, is the fantastic fresh-baked breads, muffins, or scones that accompany your order. It's a great place to start your day, and the kind of diner you wish were just around the corner from home. *DIS, MC, V; no checks; breakfast, lunch Thurs–Mon; beer and wine.* ♿

Dragon Well

2142 CHESTNUT ST, SAN FRANCISCO 📞 415/474-6888
MARINA 🍴 *Chinese*

Everything at Dragon Well is artful, from the attractive, spare, high-ceilinged interior to the beautifully presented dinner entrees arranged on rectangular lacquer trays. Even the cushy linen napkins and hefty chopsticks are a cut above your average Chinese restaurant. Open since 1998, Dragon Well specializes in fresh, healthy Chinese cuisine. Along with old Chinese standbys like a fiery kung pao chicken and a spicy Mongolian beef, you'll find slightly more delicate choices: the cool and crispy vegetarian salad is a beautifully composed plate of shredded carrots and lettuce and fried tofu topped with crushed peanuts, and the steamed Hawaiian butterfish is flavored with rice wine and sesame oil. Refreshing iced tea comes with a lychee floating in it. Since prices are only minimally higher here than at your average Chinese hole-in-the-wall, and the servers attentive and downright charming, it's hard to think of a reason not to come here when you're hankering for Chinese food. *MC, V; no checks; lunch, dinner Tues–Sun; beer and wine; www.dragonwell.com.* &

Dusit Thai

3221 MISSION ST, SAN FRANCISCO 📞 415/826-4639
MISSION DISTRICT 🍴 *Thai*

Dusit Thai may be small and hidden between many other businesses in an out-of-the-way corner of the Mission District, but this friendly neighborhood restaurant is solid and very reliable. The *tom yum koong* (shrimp and mushroom soup) makes a knockout starter, the punch of the hot spices working in harmony with the spirited lemongrass and tangy tomato. It's not an anomaly either, as main dishes involving typical Thai ingredients like peanut sauce, garlic, coconut milk, and basil are fresh and flavorful. The stuffed squid—filled with ground pork and mushrooms, cut into chunks, and covered in sweet plum sauce—makes for an interesting side trip, but you may ultimately be more satisfied with the roast duck curry or the basil beef. Dusit isn't necessarily a place to go out of your way for . . . but then again, why not? You'll find nothing fancy here—just one big white-walled room—but it's a good bet you'll walk away happy and vowing to return. *DIS, MC, V; no checks; lunch Mon and Wed–Fri, dinner Wed–Mon; beer and wine.*

Einstein's Café

1336 9TH AVE, SAN FRANCISCO 📞 415/665-4840
SUNSET DISTRICT 🍴 *Soup/Salad/Sandwich*

Who knows if the complex theories of the restaurant's namesake scribbled on the chalkboard are correct, but the concept of the place is sheer genius. For around five bucks, diners can treat themselves to wholesome, healthy lunches and dinners of humongous salads with homemade dressing, mammoth sandwiches on freshly baked bread, and soups hearty enough for a meal. The menu features everything from peanut butter sandwiches to vegetable soups to treats like real lemonade and made-from-scratch brownies. Although the food is pretty standard, it's well prepared and served in generous portions—and it's a healthy alternative to the Burger King across the street for about the same price. Not only will your stomach be satisfied, but your social conscience will be, too: all of Einstein's employees are inner-city youth employed by the nonprofit Youth Industry program, designed to get them working and learning a marketable skill. How's that for a satisfying meal? *Cash only; lunch, dinner every day; no alcohol.*

Eliza's

1457 18TH ST, SAN FRANCISCO   📞   415/648-9999
2877 CALIFORNIA ST, SAN FRANCISCO   📞   415/621-4819
POTRERO HILL/PACIFIC HEIGHTS   🍴   *Chinese*

Eliza's is not only one of our favorite Chinese restaurants in San Francisco, it's one of our favorite San Francisco restaurants period. Where else can you get such fresh, high-quality cuisine in an artistic setting for under $8 a dish? You'll love the decor—oodles of gorgeous handblown glassware, orchids, and tasteful neon lighting create a soothing, sophisticated ambience despite the crowded dining room. The menu offers a large array of classic Hunan and Mandarin dishes, all served on beautiful Italian plates. Start with the assorted appetizer dish, which is practically a meal in itself. Two other recommended dishes are the kung pao chicken—a marvelous mixture of tender chicken, peanuts, chile peppers, hot sauce, and fresh vegetables—and the vegetable mu shu with sweet plum sauce. Regardless of what you order you're likely to be impressed, and the $6 lunch specials are a steal. The only drawback is the line out the door that often forms around 7PM, and they don't take reservations. *MC, V; no checks; lunch, dinner every day; beer and wine.* ♿

Ella's

500 PRESIDIO AVE, SAN FRANCISCO   📞   415/441-5669
LAUREL HEIGHTS   🍴   *American*

Brave the crowds milling about outside waiting for a table at brunch and you'll understand what all the hullabaloo is about. House-baked breads and pastries are the stars on the weekly changing menu, which takes advantage of the Bay

Area's seasonal bounty. Brunch might feature a substantial stack of fluffy pancakes and such innovative scrambles as pork, black beans, tomatillo sauce, and jack cheese. Ella's is known and loved for its scrumptious brunches, but lunch and dinner are also worth a trip (and don't require the wait that brunch does). Lunch fare includes upscale takes on burgers, salads, and sandwiches, while dinner offers up American classics such as chicken potpie and beef stew (dinner entrees run about $11 to $17). Two large dining areas mirror one another, each featuring fresh flower-laden counter space for solo diners and those in a hurry, an open kitchen, and banquette-lined walls. More fresh flowers brighten up each table, and heavy curtains add an elegance beyond the usual breakfast joint. Closely spaced tables and tiled floors combine with the perpetual crowd to give the joint a permanent buzz, but somehow the noise level stays this side of a shout. The casually stylish Laurel Heights crowd includes couples of all stripes, a heavy dose of yuppies, elderly matrons, and the occasional young family. *AE, MC, V; local checks only; breakfast, lunch, dinner Mon–Fri, brunch Sat–Sun; full bar; feedback@ellassanfrancisco.com; www.ellassanfrancisco.com.* &

El Nuevo Frutilandia

3077 24TH ST, SAN FRANCISCO 📞 415/648-2958
MISSION DISTRICT 🍴 *Cuban*

With budget-friendly appetizers like fritters filled with meat and plantains for less than $2 and dinners with soup, rice, and beans for less than $10, this friendly spot is one of San Francisco's best bets for Cuban and Puerto Rican food. Cuban sandwiches come with a variety of meats and cheese and slathered in mustard, but more interesting are the daily specials, like Saturday's *lechón horneado,* roast pork served with rice with pigeon peas and yucca. A wide-ranging menu that's got everything from ceviche to flank steak in a creole sauce to french fries means that some items are more successful than others. But wash it down with a tamarind fruit shake or an India de Puerto Rico beer, and you'll not likely want to quibble. Service is attentive, though not necessarily fast; the menu warns that some dishes take at least 20 minutes to prepare and urges patrons to "be patient and enjoy [their] stay at Frutilandia." *MC, V; no checks; lunch, dinner Tues–Sun; beer and wine.*

El Pollo Supremo

3036 16TH ST, SAN FRANCISCO   📞   415/431-7977
2801 FOLSOM ST, SAN FRANCISCO   📞   415/550-1193
MISSION DISTRICT   🍴   *Mexican*

The two locations of this Mission District restaurant are in fairly seedy neighborhoods a block or so from the Mission's two BART stations, and with counter service and plastic booths, they could be mistaken for fast-food joints. But the employees are all much friendlier than those you would find at KFC, and the chicken is delicious: marinated Mexican-style and then thrown on the grill, it comes out crisp, tender, and spicy. Prices are amazingly low. A quarter chicken with tortillas and salsa is $2.99, and a Supreme Family Pack, with eight pieces, rice, beans, tortillas, and salsa, is $11.76 and easily feeds three. You can order extras like fried plantains, fried yucca, or *moro* rice (mixed with black beans) on the side for under $2. Perfectly multicultural, the restaurant also serves cole slaw, potato salad, macaroni salad, and corn on the cob for around a dollar. The only thing to watch out for is the salsa, which sometimes tastes a little off. *AE, DIS, MC, V; no checks; lunch, dinner every day; no alcohol.*

Emporio Rulli

470 MAGNOLIA AVE, LARKSPUR   📞   415/924-7478
LARKSPUR   🍴   *Italian*

The rich aroma of full-bodied espresso wafts through the air. Gleaming glass display cases, set off by marble and polished wood, show off tantalizing Italian delicacies. This authentic Italian experience was created by Gary Rulli, who was apprenticed to master pastry chefs in Milan and Turin. Most famous for its signature Panettone Milanese, a holiday bread studded with fruit and nuts, Emporio Rulli is nonetheless a perfect place to stop by for lunch on your way to or from Larkspur's ferry terminal. The menu consists of panini like the *tonnata,* a grilled tuna sandwich with red onions sauteed in wine, marinated olives, and capers, all drizzled with a balsamic vinaigrette. At less than $5 a pop, you'll have plenty of money left over for one of the desserts for which Emporio Rulli is justly famous: consider a slice of *sbrisolona,* a buttery almond cake, or one of several types of cookies. *MC, V; local checks only; breakfast, lunch Tues-Sun; wine only;* emprulli@aol.com; www.rulli.com. ♿

Eric's

1500 CHURCH ST, SAN FRANCISCO 📞 415/282-0919
NOE VALLEY 🍴 *Chinese*

The service is oh-so-efficient at this small corner restaurant brightened with potted plants and blooming orchids. And while no one seems really hurried, the orchestration is actually essential to help expedite the feeding of Eric's Hunan and Mandarin specialties to the crowds lined up out the door. The mango beef and chicken are very good and come in sizable portions. Other excellent bets are Eric's soups, tiger prawns, and the five-taste chicken, battered and fried and served in a sweet-and-sour sauce. There are also some great vegetarian selections, including asparagus with black-bean sauce. And Eric's prices are incredibly reasonable—part of the reason this small spot packs 'em in. *MC, V; no checks; lunch, dinner every day; beer and wine.*

Escape from New York Pizza

1737 HAIGHT ST, SAN FRANCISCO *(and branches)* 📞 415/668-5577
UPPER HAIGHT/CASTRO/FINANCIAL DISTRICT 🍴 *Pizza*

The pierced and the penniless who hang out on Haight Street know that it takes less than four bucks to get a slice of pizza and a soda at this Upper Haight institution—less than three bucks if you've got one of the coupons frequently published in the *SF Weekly* and the *Bay Guardian*. Tasty slices include the greasy-but-good "You Say Potato," with thin slices of roasted potato and whole cloves of garlic on top of a layer of pesto, and "The Gourmet," with fresh spinach, sundried tomato, artichoke hearts, and feta. The decor consists mainly of autographed photos on the walls—from Metallica to Rosie O'Donnell. Service is fairly surly, and the college rock station playing on the stereo is a bit loud, but regulars, who are apt to stop by in the wee hours after a stint at the nearby bars, would say that it's all part of the place's charm. *AE, MC, V; local checks only; lunch, dinner every day; no alcohol.*

Esperpento

3295 22ND ST, SAN FRANCISCO 📞 415/282-8867
MISSION DISTRICT 🍴 *Spanish*

When you ask Esperpento fans to name their favorite dish, nine times out of
ten they will heartily proclaim, "The sangria!" And therein lies the danger:
Esperpento serves sangria so good that it threatens to erase all memory of the
dining experience. Which is too bad, because the kitchen dishes out an amazing selection of tapas. Although you can order entrees such as paella for two,
it's far more fun to get a slew of these small plates to pass around the table.
Before you start practicing your tabletop flamenco, be sure to indulge in the
spicy potatoes and chicken croquettes; just make sure your loved ones share
dishes like the spicy garlic shrimp, because you'll be able to smell one another
from a block away. Smack dab in the Mission District, casual, jovial Esperpento
benefits from the occasional mariachi band that strolls in from the street, an
addition that perfectly matches the flamboyant and colorful decor. One word
of warning: the noise can be deafening during peak hours. This is the place for
a festive gathering with friends rather than an intimate tête-à-tête. *AE, DIS, MC,
V; no checks; lunch, dinner every day; beer and wine; www.esperpento.citysearch.com.*

Extreme Pizza

1052 FOLSOM ST, SAN FRANCISCO *(and branches)* 📞 415/701-9000
SOUTH OF MARKET/COW HOLLOW/PACIFIC HEIGHTS/RICHMOND DISTRICT 🍴 *Pizza*

Despite the extremely silly name of this pizza place, we're extremely fond of
their pizzas and subs. Each day a few different pies are available by the slice;
look for the Rodeo, a meaty wedge with sausage, salami, cheddar, and mozzarella. Or order an entire pizza, thin or deep-dish. As well as all the usual toppings, there are at least a couple of original concoctions, like the cheeseless
"White Out" with mushrooms, red onion, tomatoes, roasted red pepper, and
fresh basil. Though the salads are not particularly impressive, they are plenty
fresh and conveniently come in sizes small enough to go perfectly with a slice,
and desserts like homey carrot cake and Rice Krispie treats are worth saving
room for. Pictures of snowboarders and skateboarders on the walls are a nod to
the "extreme" theme, but the crowd here probably spends more time at
Banana Republic than on the slopes. *AE, MC, V; no checks; lunch, dinner every day;
beer and wine; contactus@extremepizza.com; www.extremepizza.com.* ♿

Fatapple's

1346 MARTIN LUTHER KING JR. WAY, BERKELEY 📞 510/526-2260
NORTH BERKELEY 🍽 *Burgers*

The Berkeley branch of Fatapple's is surprisingly popular, given there are probably more vegetarians per capita in Berkeley than anywhere else in the country. Fatapple's makes its burgers with exceptionally lean, high-quality ground beef and serves them on house-made multigrain rolls with a variety of toppings, including five very good cheeses (ask for the creamy crumbled blue). The soups, such as the rich beef barley or creamy corn chowder, are usually winners, as is the delicious spinach salad tossed with feta, walnuts, red onions, marinated black beans, and a tart vinaigrette. Standout desserts include the flaky olallieberry or pecan pie, thick jumbo milk shakes served in icy stainless-steel mixer containers, and cheese puffs (ethereal pastry pillows stuffed with baker's cheese and dusted with powdered sugar). Fatapple's is also famous for its all-American breakfasts: fluffy egg dishes, waffles, pancakes, and the like. *MC, V; no checks; breakfast, lunch, dinner every day; beer and wine.*

Firecracker

1007½ VALENCIA ST, SAN FRANCISCO 📞 415/642-3470
MISSION DISTRICT 🍽 *Chinese*

Does your chi need readjusting? Has your yin gotten into a scuffle with your yang? Then seek inner peace amid the sumptuous red decor and namesake firecrackers of this intimate family-run eatery in the Mission. Ducking behind a red velvet drape, you enter into the warm glow of the small dining room, where a multitude of soft red lights plays off the chandelier swaying from the ceiling. If you have to wait for a table, there's a curved bar with beautifully illuminated stools where you can study the menu with a glass of wine. Both the room and the cuisine are infused with fiery light, and you can rest assured that you won't find any heavy, syrupy sauces or wilted vegetables set before you. Peanuts and jicama at each table serve as a predinner challenge for your chopstick skills, while the menu offers a well-rounded selection of traditional favorites and spicy Northern Chinese specialties. Five-spice duck and mango shrimp are popular choices. *MC, V; no checks; dinner Tues–Sun; beer and wine; www.firecracker.citysearch.com.*

Firewood Cafe

4248 18TH ST, SAN FRANCISCO *(and branches)* 📞 415/252-0999
CASTRO/SOUTH OF MARKET/UNION SQUARE 🍴 *Italian*

Just because the proprietors here are willing to save you money doesn't mean they don't bother to decorate: the 18th Street branch of Firewood Cafe has a handsome, comfortable dining room with enormous streetside picture windows. So what's the catch? No table service. Order at the counter and then retire to your seat. You'll quickly forget about the self-service once you sink your teeth into the succulent roast chicken and roasted new potatoes. Or try one of Firewood's gourmet pizzas. Salads here are large, fresh, and worthy of a higher-end restaurant. The wine list is well edited and priced. By meal's end, if you haven't already gotten over the fact that there's no wait staff, you surely will when you walk out with your tip money in your pocket. *MC, V; no checks; lunch, dinner every day; beer and wine; kaivance@aol.com; www.firewoodcafecas.citysearch.com.*

Flint's BBQ

6609 SHATTUCK AVE, BERKELEY 📞 510/652-9605
3114 SAN PABLO AVE, OAKLAND 📞 510/595-0524
SOUTH BERKELEY/WEST BERKELEY–EMERYVILLE 🍴 *Barbecue*

Flint's is nearly legendary among Bay Area barbecue fans. It's not because of the atmosphere: there's not even any seating at this smoky-smelling little take-out shack. And it's certainly not because of the service: surly staffers are made even more intimidating by the meat cleavers they wield for chopping up slabs of meat. But what meat it is! A rich, dark, smoky sauce is slathered on your choice of beef ribs, pork ribs, beef links, sliced beef, or chicken, each more tender than the next. Order the meat in a monster sandwich, or get a dinner plate with a dollop of undistinguished potato salad and a couple of slices of Wonder bread (extra slices are five cents each, which is less than you'll pay if you ask for extra bags or plates). Or do what a lot of the regulars do and order an entire beef or pork slab to take home to the family. At this point the only problem will be resisting the call of the 'cue until you get it home to the table. *Cash only; lunch, dinner every day; no alcohol.*

Flipper's Gourmet Burgers

482 HAYES ST, SAN FRANCISCO *(and branches)* 📞 415/552-8880
HAYES VALLEY/NORTH OAKLAND/SUNSET DISTRICT 🍴 *Burgers*

Flipper's isn't often mentioned in discussions about the best burgers in the city, but it should be. This little-known minichain, with two restaurants in San Francisco and one in Oakland, serves a mighty fine slab of ground chuck—a whopping one-half pound of it, to be exact. Of course, the burgers are available with a wide variety of toppings, like melted feta or grilled onions or avocado, but much more popular is the plain cheeseburger, served with one slice of cheddar and one of jack. The interior of the restaurant has almost zero ambience and the echoey acoustics of Grand Central Terminal, but no matter, because there's a large patio with about a dozen umbrella-shaded tables. The popular weekend breakfast consists of the usual dishes. *Cash only; breakfast, lunch, dinner every day; no alcohol.*

Fog City Diner

1300 BATTERY ST, SAN FRANCISCO 📞 415/982-2000
FINANCIAL DISTRICT 🍴 *Diner*

The polished brass, dark wood, mirrored bar, and enormous booths at Fog City Diner make the restaurant sleeker and more sophisticated than any other diner we've seen. Ditto for the menu, which takes the usual diner fare (gourmet chili dogs, sandwiches, salads, and damn good onion rings) to a higher level. The kitchen also offers a frequently changing menu of savory "small plates" ($4–$10) such as crab cakes, Asian-style prawns, and quesadillas with chile peppers and almonds. "Large plates" ($11–$24) are available as well, usually putting an inventive, sometimes Asian-inspired, twist on American favorites: look for creamy macaroni and cheese made with Gouda, fresh fish of the day prepared a variety of ways, or thick pork chops marinated in a ginger-soy marinade. Desserts tend toward the decadently gooey, like the chocolate peanut butter chunk pie or their signature banana split, which can easily feed a threesome. At lunch local businessfolk are here for button-down lunches, but at dinner expect festive (and loud) crowds. Make reservations well in advance. *DC, DIS, MC, V; no checks; lunch, dinner every day; full bar; www.fogcitydiner.cc.* ♿

Fountain Court

354 CLEMENT ST, SAN FRANCISCO   📞   415/668-1100
RICHMOND DISTRICT   🍽   *Chinese*

The great thing about the Richmond District having so many Chinese restaurants is that they often have to specialize to make their mark. Fountain Court focuses on the food of Shanghai—one regional cuisine you don't find very often—though it offers plenty of Chinese standards for the less adventurous. And adventurous you may very well have to be if you decide to dive into exotic seafood options like sea cucumbers in shrimp roe sauce. With braising—a cooking technique that's popular in Shanghai—the sea creatures become extremely yielding, almost gelatinous. Let's face it: they're downright weird if you're not used to it, but you don't have to go that far. Savory Shanghai spareribs sit on a bed of spinach that soaks up a tangy, orange-hued braising liquid. Stir-fried pea sprouts and chicken in a spicy orange sauce are among the lighter options. The friendly servers will happily guide you through the menu's exotica, and the decor is cheerful and somewhat formal: an elevated seating area is lit up with rows of bare lightbulbs like something from the set of *A Chorus Line. AE, MC, V; no checks; lunch, dinner every day; beer and wine; fc@pacbell.net; www.222.to/fountaincourt.*

Francisco and Molly

83 NATOMA ST, SAN FRANCISCO   📞   415/975-5700
SOUTH OF MARKET   🍽   *Soup/Salad/Sandwich*

A stone's throw from jam-packed Mr. Ralph's (see review), this spot affectionately nicknamed "Mr. Ralph's Annex" opened in 1999. It shares the same owners and staff but serves an entirely different—though equally delicious—menu of burritos, burgers, sandwiches, and salads. The sizable burritos, accompanied by house-made chips, come vegetarian or carnivore-friendly, while burgers range from a basic cheeseburger to the less traditional blue cheese version. A salmon BLT vies for your attention, as does the Caribbean chicken, a sandwich heaped with Caribbean barbecue sauce, pineapple, caramelized onions, and lettuce. The two spacious rooms in Francisco and Molly (nicknames for owners François and Robin) are blessed with lovely brick walls, high ceilings, large windows, and plenty of light, but the restaurant also shows signs of a decorator's handiwork: potted plants, artwork, and seasonal touches. At press time, the construction zone right outside was silent, but be warned that the noise level could escalate in the coming months. *MC, V; no checks; breakfast, lunch Mon-Fri; no alcohol.* &

Frankie's Bohemian Cafe

1862 DIVISADERO ST, SAN FRANCISCO 📞 415/921-4725
WESTERN ADDITION 🍴 *American*

Friendly bartenders pull pints of Guinness and Red Hook for a raucous crowd of thirtysomethings at night, but Frankie's is also a great place for lunch or dinner, with or without a pint of your favorite brew. Most people just come for the burgers, served in several different varieties like the unusual Gilroy burger, made with grilled minced garlic, basil, and feta. But in addition to pasta, salads, and grilled meats, the kitchen specializes in *brambory,* a Czech specialty of shredded potato and zucchini baked into a crisp pancake before being topped with anything from vegetables to barbecued shrimp to grilled swordfish. Deep red walls covered in knickknacks like deer antlers and a battered-looking wooden bar give the place a kind of rustic charm, which diminishes somewhat when the dinnertime crowd segues into the nighttime crowd, here to enjoy beer, wine, and a little low-key flirting. *AE, MC, V; no checks; lunch, dinner every day; beer and wine.*

Frjtz

579 HAYES ST, SAN FRANCISCO 📞 415/864-7654
HAYES VALLEY 🍴 *Eclectic*

It seems the proprietors must have been suffering from some serious indecision when they dreamt up this hip new spot they describe as a "Belgian Fries, Crepes, and Art Teahouse." Some come for sandwiches like the Michelangelo, a huge, sloppy mix of roasted bell pepper, grilled eggplant, and Gorgonzola on focaccia. Others would rather snack their way through the afternoon with a hot order of french fries, served Belgian-style wrapped in a paper cone (but with some very un-Belgian condiments, like jalapeño, Vidalia onion, and cilantro ketchups or spicy yogurt peanut sauce). Crepes come in both sweet and savory varieties, from smoked salmon with sour cream to lemon and sugar. And in case you're bamboozled by the Italian-influenced sandwiches, Belgian fries, and French crepes, perhaps you'd like to relax with a proper pot of English Breakfast tea? The relaxed atmosphere and shady back patio make this a lovely place to while away the afternoon, and on Saturday nights from 8PM to midnight DJs spin drum 'n' bass and trance music while patrons drink Belgian beer and wine. *AE, MC, V; no checks; breakfast, lunch, dinner Mon–Fri, brunch, dinner Sat–Sun; beer and wine; frjtz@frjtzfries.com; www.frjtzfries.com.* &

Fuzio Universal Pasta

2175 CHESTNUT ST, SAN FRANCISCO *(and branches)* ☎ 415/673-8804
MARINA/CASTRO/FINANCIAL DISTRICT 🍴 *Eclectic*

A few years ago the newest fusion food trend was to bundle up everything from Thai chicken to salmon teriyaki in a tortilla or other flatbread and call it a wrap. A lot of the "wraps" restaurants have now closed up shop, replaced with places like Fuzio, which are applying the same cross-cultural strategy to pasta and other types of noodles. Yes, it's a chain, so many people wouldn't set their trendy San Franciscan toes across the threshold. But at Fuzio the ambience is surprisingly warm, many of the dishes are quite tasty, and the prices are good. At the Chestnut Street location, where a few lunch specials like fusilli primavera go for an extremely reasonable six bucks, the high-ceilinged room is stylish and cheerful, with plenty of counter seating overlooking both the street and the open kitchen. The Italian-influenced dishes are typically better than the Asian ones: vegetable pad Thai is dressed with a peppery sauce that overpowers the delicate sprouts, carrots, and tofu in the dish, but the pesto penne salad is more successful, with warm pasta enhanced by the piquant bite of arugula and feta cheese. *AE, DIS, MC, V; no checks; lunch, dinner every day; full bar; www.fuzio.com.* &

The Ganges

775 FREDERICK ST, SAN FRANCISCO ☎ 415/661-7290
SUNSET DISTRICT 🍴 *Indian*

San Francisco isn't really an Indian food kind of town, but this longtime off-the-beaten-path choice is inconsistently good. What sets this place apart is that there's always an empty table, friendly service, an outdated fancy decor, and rock-bottom prices: a complete meal, from pappadam to mango ice cream, is under $15. The menu is confusing and overwhelming; just order special combination number one. Regulars are eating the *chili pakoda,* a stuffed, deep-fried pepper appetizer that's not nearly as spicy as the menu suggests. The classic samosa is a fair bet, and the *kelana bhajia,* a savory mashed banana fritter, is also a great way to start. The dahl and saffron rice are always good, though they tend to lean a little heavy on the nutmeg. The wide array of curries is a gamble, but the stuffed banana is unique and delicious, as is the *unehiea,* a coconut-based dish of beans, sweet potatoes, eggplant, and peanut. For dessert, you'll beg for more of the excellent homemade ice creams of mango, pistachio, and cardamom. *MC, V; no checks; dinner Tues–Sat; beer and wine.*

Gira Polli

659 UNION ST, SAN FRANCISCO 📞 415/434-4472
590 EAST BLITHEDALE AVE, MILL VALLEY 📞 415/383-6040
NORTH BEACH/MILL VALLEY 🍴 *Italian*

The menus at Gira Polli brags, "No one does polli better," and we're inclined to agree–though Il Pollaio (see review), around the corner, also does a fine job with the birds. Glistening chickens come out of the wood-burning rotisseries with flecks of rosemary clinging to the skin and go perfectly with simple side dishes like Palermo potatoes, seasonal vegetables, and a sourdough roll. Best of all, the almost shockingly reasonable prices ($6 to $7 for a quarter of a bird, $9 for a half, including sides) means that if you're lucky enough to live in the area you can stop by to pick up dinner-to-go whenever the mood strikes. The risotto and pastas–like rigatoni with ricotta, mozzarella, tomatoes, and basil–are respectable, but really beside the point here. Though they do most of their business in takeout, the tiny dining room is also cozy, with funky light fixtures casting a warm, rosy glow on your dinner companion. *AE, MC, V; no checks; dinner every day; beer and wine.*

Goat Hill Pizza

300 CONNECTICUT ST, SAN FRANCISCO 📞 415/641-1440
POTRERO HILL 🍴 *Pizza*

In a quickly changing neighborhood where it seems every other restaurant is a newcomer, longtime favorite Goat Hill Pizza is refreshingly low-key. Red-and-white-checked tablecloths in the sunny dining room set the scene for some of the best pizza in the city, served on a great sourdough crust that's equal parts crispy and chewy. A top choice is the Greek Gourmet special, a slightly salty, slightly tangy pie topped with feta cheese, green olives, red onions, and fresh tomatoes. Basic pastas like spaghetti and lasagne are also on the menu, as is knockout garlic bread, served with cheese or without. But all most diners order is pizza, perhaps a dinner salad, and a bottle of beer or glass of house wine. Monday night the restaurant is packed with locals for "Neighborhood Night," when all-you-can-eat pizza and salad is a mere $8.50. Service is extraordinarily friendly, if slightly harried on weekend nights. *AE, MC, V; no checks; lunch, dinner every day; beer and wine.* &

Gourmet Carousel

1559 FRANKLIN ST, SAN FRANCISCO 📞 415/771-2044
PACIFIC HEIGHTS 🍴 *Chinese*

This oddly located restaurant is packed during both lunch and dinner—despite the fact it's on the pedestrian-unfriendly corner of Franklin and Pine. That's because San Franciscans know great Chinese food when they eat it. And best of all, the fresh-tasting dishes here are cheap, cheap, cheap. At lunch chow fun and chow mein dishes are $3.50 to $4 and rice plates so big they could easily serve two are $2.75 to $4; dinner prices are a couple dollars more. For such low prices you might expect unidentified glop on a plate, but the dishes here are stellar. Fresh mushroom chicken over rice is full of big, whole mushrooms, stems of bright-green broccoli, and water chestnuts; crispy medallions of ginger are a pleasantly pungent surprise. Another standout is the pot stickers, not too greasy and served a generous eight to a plate. The low-ceilinged, carpeted room is fairly nondescript and service is brusque. *MC, V; no checks; lunch Tues–Sat, dinner Tues–Sun; beer and wine.*

Great Eastern

649 JACKSON ST, SAN FRANCISCO 📞 415/986-2500
CHINATOWN 🍴 *Chinese*

This venerable Chinatown restaurant is famous for its hard-to-find seafood, yanked fresh from the myriad fish tanks that line the back wall. If it swims, hops, slithers, or crawls, it's probably on the menu. Frogs, sea bass, soft-shell turtles, abalone, sea conch, steelhead, and lord only knows what else are served sizzling on large, round, family-style tables. Check the neon board in back for the day's catch, which is sold by the pound. Some advice: Unless you're savvy at translating an authentic Hong Kong menu, order one of the set dinners (the crab version is fantastic) or point to another table and say, "I want that." (Don't expect much help from the overworked servers.) The crystal chandeliers and glimmering emerald-and-black furnishings make an attempt at elegance, but it's the gaudy fish tanks filled with edible creatures that capture everyone's eye. *AE, MC, V; no checks; lunch, dinner every day; beer and wine.* &

Grove Café

2250 CHESTNUT ST, SAN FRANCISCO   415/474-4843
MARINA   *Soup/Salad/Sandwich*

Possibly the prettiest cafe in town, the Grove is decorated in comfortable Arts and Crafts style, from the wooden paneling on the walls to mica lamps hanging from the ceiling. And best of all, during fair weather, the floor-to-ceiling windows along two walls are thrown open, making the breezy tables indoors as appealing as those on the sidewalk. Maybe that's why this is the favorite spot of young Marina district moms and their babies in strollers on sunny weekdays. The cafe fare, mostly salads and sandwiches, is fresh and tasty, if occasionally lacking in a little zing. Vegetarian chili is heavy on the vegetables, with chunks of tomato, carrot, zucchini, and corn, and the Thai noodle salad is topped with snow peas, red bell peppers, and scallions. Lavender lemonade or honey vanilla cream soda is a refreshing accompaniment. Bakery items like orange raisin scones and peach oat bars make a great breakfast or afternoon snack. *MC, V; no checks; breakfast, lunch, dinner every day; beer and wine.* &

Grubstake

1525 PINE ST, SAN FRANCISCO   415/673-8268
POLK GULCH   *Diner*

A mix of crusty old-timers and bedraggled drag queens eats at this rustic diner, unique because half the tiny restaurant is housed in an old railcar that chugged between San Francisco and Oakland almost a hundred years ago. The diner's authentic old-fashioned charm (notice the antique marbled glass of the railcar) is one reason to visit; another is its very late hours. As the 4AM closing time approaches, crowds from the nearby Polk Gulch bars straggle in before heading home. You'll notice that we didn't mention the food, which, unfortunately, often comes up short. Old-fashioned appetizers like fried mozzarella served with marinara sauce are exactly what you would expect, while burgers taste like the beef has been frozen and are a bit of a disappointment. Breakfast items and the surprising menu of Portuguese dishes are a better bet, as are homey desserts like rice pudding. Another plus: since this is more of a late-night hangout than a brunch spot, you can usually waltz right in on weekend mornings (they open at 10AM on Saturday and Sunday). *Cash only; lunch, dinner every day; brunch Sat-Sun; beer and wine; fao@jps.net; www.sfgrubstake.com.*

Hahn's Hibachi

525 HAIGHT ST, SAN FRANCISCO *(and branches)* 📞 415/864-3721
LOWER HAIGHT/MARINA/NOE VALLEY/POLK GULCH/SUNSET DISTRICT/
DOWNTOWN OAKLAND 🍴 *Korean*

If you stop to count Hahn's Hibachi's six Bay Area branches, you could call this Korean barbecue spot a chain restaurant. But never mind that—and ditto for the faux-industrial wood-and-steel interior—because Hahn's knows a thing or two about grilled meat. That's the main order of business on the menu, be it thinly sliced pork or beef, marinated chicken breasts, racks of ribs, or kebabs of shrimp. The popular barbecue plates come with rice, salad, and tangy-spicy *kimchee* (pickled cabbage), and most only cost between six and eight bucks. For those craving even more meat there's the Pile O' Pork and the Meat Mountain—very scary. Korean plates like Beboppin' Bibimpop and *chopchae* are a great way to go, too, combining barbecued meat with eggs, noodles, and veggies. Vegetarians have a few options here, too, including tofu kebabs and Vegetable Bibimpop (veggies and a fried egg over rice). In a curious culinary twist, the Haight Street location boasts an additional menu of soul food dishes by "Chef Rene" that includes pork chops, fried chicken, and a surf-and-turf platter combining Hahn's grilled steak with Rene's Southern fried shrimp. *MC, V; no checks; lunch, dinner every day; beer and wine.* ♿

Hamburgers

737 BRIDGEWAY, SAUSALITO 📞 415/332-9471
SAUSALITO 🍴 *Burgers*

Though this little sliver of a restaurant may not seem much to get excited about, its location in the midst of Sausalito's most overpriced and tourist-clogged restaurants makes it a real find. While everyone else is paying $30 or more for a mediocre meal with a view of the bay, you can spend less than $7 for a fine hamburger, hot dog, steak sandwich, or even chicken sausage sandwich. Though the buns could perhaps have a better texture, the burgers themselves are very good and served fresh off the grill. Even the Sausalito locals come to this place in droves (though many call ahead to place their order, thus avoiding the perpetual line out the door on sunny days and weekends). Though there are a few seats in the tiny restaurant, smart diners take their burgers outside; park benches are directly across the street, and additional benches on the opposite side of the park offer a better view of San Francisco and the Bay Bridge than you'll get at any of those hoity-toity restaurants. On cold and blustery days, you can enjoy your burger from the dark and cozy Paterson's Bar, next door. Order at the bar and they'll fetch your plate, tacking about a buck onto the price. *Cash only; lunch every day; no alcohol.*

Hard Rock Cafe

1699 VAN NESS AVE, SAN FRANCISCO 📞 415/885-1699
PACIFIC HEIGHTS 🍽 *American*

This San Francisco link in the Hard Rock chain is exactly what you would expect it to be: a loud, cavernous room filled with rock-and-roll memorabilia, tourists, and a line for T-shirts. You'll have to speak up to be heard over the blaring rock music, but that's just part of the Hard Rock experience. Despite the often annoying ambience, the food is actually pretty good (not healthy, exactly, but good)—and who knows when you're going to have to entertain your nieces from Des Moines. The highlight of the menu is the juicy chicken sandwich, best accompanied with a side of crispy onion rings. Other diner-style menu items include fajitas, baby back ribs, grilled fish, salads, sandwiches, and (of course) the all-American burger. Perhaps Hard Rock's strongest point is that it's one of the few restaurants in the city that caters to children and teens. Otherwise, in a city with so many incredible restaurants, it's hard to justify a meal here. *AE, DC, DIS, MC, V; no checks; lunch, dinner every day; full bar; www.hardrock.com.* ♿

Helmand

430 BROADWAY, SAN FRANCISCO 📞 415/362-0641
NORTH BEACH 🍽 *Middle Eastern*

An oasis of good taste on Broadway's tacky topless strip, Helmand serves delicious renditions of Afghan cuisine in an elegant, carpeted room lit by brass chandeliers. The restaurant's light and variously spiced house-made yogurts, a staple of Afghani cooking, dress several favorite appetizers, including *mantwo* (a house-made dumpling filled with sautéed onions and beef, topped with a carrot, yellow split pea, and beef sauce, and served on yogurt) and *kaddo borawni* (sweet baby pumpkin that's pan-fried, then baked, and served with a piquant yogurt-garlic sauce). Other fine choices include *sabzi challow* (a wonderfully seasoned mixture of spinach with lamb) and *koufta challow* (light, moderately spicy meatballs with sun-dried tomatoes, peppers, and peas), each served with a ramekin of flavorful fresh cilantro sauce and aromatic white or brown rice. Servers are personable, if sometimes slightly scattered, and the wine list is well chosen and well priced. Parking is scarce in this neighborhood, so take advantage of the validated parking at the lot down the block. *AE, MC, V; no checks; dinner Tues–Sun; full bar.* ♿

Henry's Hunan

110 NATOMA ST, SAN FRANCISCO *(and branches)* 📞 415/546-4999
FINANCIAL DISTRICT/SOUTH OF MARKET 🍴 *Chinese*

Like your Chinese dishes hot and spicy? Henry's won't let you down in the heat-seeking department. In fact, those who tend toward the mild side of life should make their preference clear to the server when they order; otherwise they may be soaking their misery in white rice and water for the rest of the meal. Vegetarians, too, should know that Henry's uses chicken stock in its cooking (but no MSG), including the vegetable dishes as well. Again, if this is a problem, discuss the matter with your server and adaptations can ususally be made. The place can get packed, so figure in at least a 15- or 20-minute wait at peak mealtimes (add your name to a list at the hostess station). The restaurant has a brisk and businesslike feel—the room is modern and spacious, the service swift. The portions are enormous—two could easily share if you start with an appetizer—but the quality is spotty. The entrees with smoked ham, though, are packed with flavor, and the chicken-garlic rice plate and sautéed string beans are also good choices. *AE, DIS, MC, V; no checks; lunch, dinner Mon–Sat; beer and wine.* ♿

Herbivore: The Earthly Grill

983 VALENCIA ST, SAN FRANCISCO 📞 415/826-5657
MISSION DISTRICT 🍴 *Vegetarian*

If you think vegan food means a plate full of tofu and bean sprouts, you haven't been to Herbivore. Dishes include a wide array of sandwiches, salads, and entrees like pasta with charbroiled veggies. Pad Thai comes with a flavorful peanut sauce, and veggie burgers are served on a plate heaped with a green salad and herbed home fries (ask for a side of tahini for dipping). And if a glass of carrot, apple, and ginger juice won't hit the spot, you can also order an organically farmed merlot or a refreshing organic light Belgian ale (organic produce is used whenever possible). All these heart-healthy dishes are served cheerfully, even enthusiastically, in a sleek, airy, high-ceilinged room, where the only distraction is the occasional whirring of the vegetable juicer. On sunny days a few lucky diners get the three tables on the leafy patio out back. *MC, V; no checks; lunch, dinner every day; beer and wine.* &

Hing Lung

674 BROADWAY, SAN FRANCISCO   📞 415/398-8838
CHINATOWN 🍴 *Chinese*

Vegetarians are unlikely to get past the entrance of this restaurant, where crispy-skinned poultry hangs in the front window. That would be a shame, though, because the authentic Chinese dishes here are a real treat. The house specialty is a vast array of hearty porridges, topped with everything from the innocuous (tofu) to the hair-raising (pork liver). But the wide-ranging menu also dabbles in rice plates, noodle plates, and a variety of wonton soups. Service is extremely friendly–they might bring you a fork when they see you struggling with your chopsticks and slippery rice noodles–though don't expect all the servers to be able to explain the dishes in English. The interior of the restaurant is as charmless as most budget restaurants in Chinatown, though if you're sitting near the front you might catch a glimpse of the cooks laboring in the oddly placed glassed-in kitchen. *MC, V; no checks; breakfast, lunch, dinner every day; no alcohol.*

Homemade Cafe

2454 SACRAMENTO ST, BERKELEY   📞 510/845-1940
WEST BERKELEY 🍴 *American*

Favored by pierced West Berkeley hipsters, UC Berkeley students, and local businessfolks alike, the Homemade Cafe dishes up fantastic breakfast fare in a low-key setting. Serve yourself refills of coffee and water as you pore over the menu; don't overlook the seasonal specials and house-made muffins and breads listed on the chalkboard. Tattooed waitresses bustle about delivering densely stuffed, fluffy omelets, stacks of light buttermilk pancakes, blintzes, and the cafe's signature Home Fry Heaven, a divine concoction of home fries, cheese, sour cream, and guacamole or pesto that must be tasted to be believed. On weekend mornings, bring the paper and be prepared for a lengthy wait, or pull up a seat at the counter, where you have front-row seats to the show the fry cooks put on. The Homemade is known and loved for its breakfast offerings, but lunch, which consists of an extensive choice of hearty soups, salads, and sandwiches, is also satisfying. *No credit cards; local checks only; breakfast, lunch every day; beer and wine.* &

Home Plate

2274 LOMBARD ST, SAN FRANCISCO ☎ 415/922-4663
MARINA 🍴 *American*

Once you discover this humble little restaurant's scrumptious breakfasts, you'll be ready to trek across town for the food any day. No matter that it's hard to park, no matter that you might sit on the sidewalk for half an hour with your name on a waiting list: it's worth the effort. You know it's a good sign when you're immediately presented with a plate of tasty, tiny scones. On the menu, the choices range from fluffy pancakes and waffles (made from scratch) to giant omelets to homemade granola to what might well be the best eggs Benedict in town. There's just something about the smoked ham (or turkey) and that creamy hollandaise. Ask them to add avocado for an extra-decadent delight— and don't forget that side of potato-carrot pancakes with apple compote. Though breakfast is the main draw, the array of sandwiches, salads, pasta, and chicken dishes served at lunch is worth exploring. On weekends, arrive early or wait until midafternoon to avoid the crowds. *MC, V; no checks; breakfast, lunch every day; no alcohol.*

Hong Kong Flower Lounge

5322 GEARY BLVD, SAN FRANCISCO ☎ 415/668-8998
RICHMOND DISTRICT 🍴 *Chinese*

In 1987 Alice Wong, whose family owns four Flower Lounges in and around Hong Kong, expanded their empire to California with restaurants in Millbrae, then San Francisco and Palo Alto. Here in the city, Hong Kong chefs continue to produce cuisine according to the stringent standards of their home city. A vast dining room with gaudy red and green decor can be a little off-putting, but not so much that it mars the pleasure of a dim sum brunch here. Barbecue pork buns are an ethereal puff of dough surrounding a center of rich, saucy pork, and the deep-fried taro root and meat dumpling is a similarly delicious blend of starch and protein. The mango pudding is a cool and refreshing way to end the meal–even if you've never been wild about Chinese desserts. Dim sum, served at lunch only, is a better value than dinner entrees, which can creep up into the stratosphere when they include ingredients like whole abalone and lobster. Still, there are some reasonably priced choices no matter what time you come. *AE, DC, DIS, MC, V; no checks; lunch, dinner every day; full bar.*

Hotei

1290 9TH AVE, SAN FRANCISCO 📞 415/753-6045
SUNSET DISTRICT 🍴 *Japanese*

From the same owners of one of the city's most popular sushi houses, Ebisu, comes this noodle spot, serving exquisite examples of some of the best in Japanese cookery. The decor is stunning, making this a nice date place, though families will feel welcome as well. Heavy tables and chairs and a twinkling waterfall balance lush plants hung high on the wall and climbing toward the ceiling. Green tea arrives while you look over the menu featuring light plates like *onigiri*, balls of rice stuffed with dried fish flakes, salmon, or pickled-plum, or *hiyashi wakame* salad, the most delectable way to enjoy seaweed this side of the Pacific. Cool weather calls for warming *oden* stew, an autumn Japanese favorite of mild daikon radish, *kombu* (seaweed), and fish cake in a subtle dark broth. Homemade pork *gyoza* (dumplings) are perfectly seared and steamed, while the novel vegetarian *gyoza* with a yam and vegetable filling is equally satisfying. Hopefully you've saved room for noodles, either the warm blanket of *cha-shu* ramen with pork in a miso broth, the tempura soba, or the rich beef and vegetable udon, all served in large, beautiful pottery bowls. *AE, DC, MC, V; no checks; lunch, dinner Wed-Mon; beer and wine.* ♿

Hot 'n' Hunky

4039 18TH ST, SAN FRANCISCO 📞 415/621-6365
CASTRO 🍴 *Burgers*

Hot and hunky describes the clientele as aptly as it does the burgers, and the two sweethearts sharing a cherry Coke cheek to cheek at this old-fashioned burger joint are more likely than not to be of the same sex. No one can order "I want to hold your ham" with a straight face, and therein lies the beauty of Hot 'n' Hunky: it's kitschy, it's fun, and it serves damn good burgers. The "Macho

Man" offers three-quarters of a pound of sizzling beef on a bun, while the "Ms. Piggy" adds cheddar cheese and bacon to the mix. Watching your girlish figure? Then steer clear of the chunky fries and thick shakes and go for the veggie burger. Formica tables and vintage furniture lend retro charm to this tiny diner, but the gleaming jukebox is more liable to be pumping '70s disco than a Buddy Holly tune. *Cash only; lunch, dinner every day; no alcohol.*

House of Nanking

919 KEARNY ST, SAN FRANCISCO 📞 415/421-1429
CHINATOWN 🍴 *Chinese*

The dinnertime waiting line outside this tiny, greasy, wildly popular hole-in-the-wall starts at 5:30PM; by 6PM, you may face an hour wait for a cramped, crowded, itsy-bitsy table with a plastic menu that lists only half of the best dishes served here. Lunchtime crowds make midday eating just as problematic. Here's a solution: arrive for a late lunch or a very early dinner (between 2:30 and 5PM) and walk right in. When owner-chef-headwaiter Peter Fang can give you his full attention, he'll be glad to tell you about the day's unlisted specials: perhaps succulent chicken or duck dumplings, an exotic shrimp-and-green-onion pancake with peanut sauce, or tempura-like sesame-battered Nanking scallops in a spicy garlic sauce. Or just take a look at what the diners sandwiched around you are eating and point to what looks good (it's hard to go wrong in this place). Nanking, Fang's hometown, is at the inland end of the Shanghai Railroad, making it an exchange point for foods from Sichuan, Peking, Guangdong, and the local coast; Fang is famous for concocting wily revisions of many traditional dishes. While the food is usually very good and the prices are some of the most reasonable in the city, the service is downright terrible (you may not get your beer until 10 minutes after you've started eating). *Cash only; lunch Mon–Sat, dinner every day; beer and wine.*

Hungarian Sausage Factory

419 CORTLAND AVE, SAN FRANCISCO 📞 415/648-2847
BERNAL HEIGHTS 🍴 *German/Eastern European*

Partly because of its location in friendly Bernal Heights, this might be one of the coziest restaurants you'll find in San Francisco. One room has the kitchen and front counter, while the other has just enough room for a handful of tables and a few musicians—and you can find some kind of live music most nights, whether jazz or Eastern European. The owner is likely to be around and will share a smoke with customers outside in between courses and music sets. The food is not all about sausages, as the name implies, but it's all simple and hearty. Start with a cucumber salad, a warming soup, or a savory crepe. For dinner, homemade *kolbasz* (sausage) is served with sauerkraut and salad, and the classic pork cutlet is served with cabbage and parsley potatoes. Wash it down with Hungarian wine or beer, and top it off with a flambéed chocolate and walnut crepe. Note: This restaurant is on the upper end of the cheap eats range (entrees peak around $14), but the service is casual enough that you can just order a salad and a crepe if you like. *MC, V; no checks; dinner Tues-Sun; beer and wine.*

Il Pollaio

555 COLUMBUS AVE, SAN FRANCISCO   415/362-7727
NORTH BEACH   *Italian*

Big servings of chicken are unbelievably cheap in this easily overlooked spot in the heart of North Beach. And what chicken it is: delicately seasoned with Italian herbs and cooked to juicy, crisp-skinned perfection in front of your eyes. For about $10 you can get an entire half chicken (four pieces), a salad or substantial side of fries, and even a glass of wine—enough for dinner and tomorrow's lunch as well. Other items on the small menu include half a rabbit and a big slab of rib-eye steak—more expensive than the chicken, but good deals in their own right. The decor is pretty minimal—just a few Italian knickknacks on the walls—but the real entertainment is watching the old Italian guys who come here every day, drinking Cinzano and shooting the breeze with the friendly Castellucci family, who run the place. Perhaps because of the astonishing prices, this place does a big business in takeout as well. *MC, V; no checks; lunch, dinner Mon-Sat; wine only.*

Indian Oven

233 FILLMORE ST, SAN FRANCISCO   415/626-1628
LOWER HAIGHT   *Indian*

In the culturally diverse Lower Haight, you can find the gamut of ethnic restaurants, including one very good and very authentic Indian spot. Indian Oven, a good-looking eatery with an especially attractive upstairs dining room, is by many accounts the best Northern Indian restaurant in town. Roll up your sleeves and order the appetizer sampler plate: samosas (vegetable puffs stuffed with peas and potatoes), pakoras (deep-fried fritters filled with your choice of meat or vegetables), and pappadam crackers. The entrees are mostly outstanding, including a delicious *jheenga masala*—prawns sauteed in a spicy tomato sauce. The tandoori chicken and the chicken and lamb skewers are also good. When you've got to have your curry fix, there are few better places. *AE, DC, DIS, MC, V; no checks; dinner every day; beer and wine; www.indianovensf.com.*

Isobune

1737 POST ST, SAN FRANCISCO   📞   415/563-1030

5897 COLLEGE AVE, OAKLAND   📞   510/601-1424

JAPANTOWN/NORTH OAKLAND   🍴   *Sushi*

There are several sushi spots in the Bay Area where, instead of ordering off a menu, you pluck your plates of sushi off a never-ending parade of little wooden boats, but Isobune was the first and is still the best. As you sit elbow to elbow with other sushi lovers, you can take your pick of all the usual sushi choices—including eel, tuna, yellowtail, and salmon roe—and a few more uncommon ones, like rolls stuffed with enoki mushrooms and the *shiro torigai* (white cockle clams). Sushi is never dirt cheap, but prices are more than reasonable here, with plates going for anywhere from $1.50 (for *tamago*, bits of omelet on top of rice) to $3.25 (for *ama ebi*, sweet shrimp). Though you serve yourself, the helpful staff will help you figure out what's what, describing, for example, how to tell the salmon from the smoked salmon. Several take-out boxes are also available, most for $8 to $12. *MC, V; no checks; lunch, dinner every day; beer and wine.*

It's Tops

1801 MARKET ST, SAN FRANCISCO   📞   415/431-6395

CASTRO   🍴   *Diner*

For authenticity, forget about Mel's Drive-In (see review) or any of the other chains that try to re-create a '50s diner with brand-new neon and chrome. This place first opened in 1952 and is still decorated with vintage cigarette ads and black-and-white photos of old San Francisco; the waitresses even wear pink uniforms. Because of its age, it's managed to escape the cloying kitschiness of most diners. The coffee is good and weak and the breakfasts are big, greasy, and satisfying. Pancakes are fluffy and huge and come in eight varieties, including buckwheat and peanut butter and banana. The light, buttermilky waffles might be even better—especially when ordered with bacon crumbles. And you can have your fill of milk shakes, pie, and burgers at lunch and for late-night dinners (until 3AM Wednesday to Friday, or all night on Saturdays). In fact, this is a good place to go after a date: since the diner is wedged into a corner building, it's a tiny, angular space with lots of cozy, hidden booths. You can even treat your new honey to a love song from the tableside jukebox. *MC, V; no checks; breakfast, lunch every day; dinner Wed–Sat; beer and wine.*

Izalco

2904 24TH ST, SAN FRANCISCO 📞 415/206-9788
MISSION DISTRICT 🍽 *Central American*

Plastic tropical-fruit tablecloths and cherry-red vinyl seats create a bright atmosphere in this Salvadorean restaurant, where *telenovelas* play on the TV, music blasts from the radio (usually at the same time), and most patrons speak Spanish. The friendly staff starts you off by offering a host of different types of house-made aguas frescas, such as horchata or fruit cocktail, which is piled high with fresh fruit. After a few sips, start the eating with hot *pupusas,* the gooey tortilla-like pockets stuffed with melting cheese, or try fried yucca, similar to potato but with more texture and a sweet, nutty flavor and served with a smoky salsa. Entrees like grilled shrimp are big enough for two, served with a salad, rice, beans, and thick, handmade tortillas and salsa. This is also a great place to go at breakfast for a change from the usual omelet—perhaps for some fried plantains with eggs, refried beans, and sour cream. *MC, V; no checks; breakfast, lunch, dinner every day; no alcohol.*

Izumiya

1581 WEBSTER ST, SAN FRANCISCO 📞 415/441-6867
JAPANTOWN 🍽 *Japanese*

If you can't find something on Izumiya's menu that you like, then you just don't like Japanese food. They serve a little of everything here, from edamame (boiled, salted soybeans) to steamed fish to shrimp tempura to sushi. Bowls of soba (buckwheat noodles) make an economical lunch and are served lightning quick. Though the sushi is a bit more expensive than the other dishes on the menu, the nigiri items come with a fairly generous slab of fish draped over the rice. Unfortunately, the smell of food being fried in the kitchen doesn't mesh well with the more delicately flavored menu choices. And if you're looking for a refined atmosphere, keep looking; the groups of Japanese teenagers and swift service mean that the ambience is part boisterous, part businesslike. *MC, V; no checks; lunch, dinner Tues–Sun; beer and wine.* ♿

Jackson Fillmore

2506 FILLMORE ST, SAN FRANCISCO ☎ 415/346-5288
PACIFIC HEIGHTS ♔ *Italian*

If you like to make an entrance, go to Jackson Fillmore, the minuscule trattoria on Fillmore that's so small, everyone in the dining room can't help but stop eating and turn their heads to the door when somebody walks in. And then be prepared to wait. But that's part of the fun at this bright neighborhood restaurant, where chef-owner Jack Kreitzman is usually the one to greet you, with a smile and a suggestion for a great glass of wine. Once seated, you are quickly served a helping of the fresh-made bruschetta with a mouthwatering aroma of garlic. From ricotta ravioli to roast chicken with garlic (highly recommended) to portobello mushrooms, the recipes here are fairly straightforward and skillfully executed. Many entrees are $14–$17, so consider the pasta ($10–$13) if you're on a budget. This is a great place for a couple to dine, but larger groups can also be accommodated. *AE, MC, V; no checks; dinner every day; beer and wine.* ♿

Jade Villa

800 BROADWAY, OAKLAND ☎ 510/839-1688
DOWNTOWN OAKLAND ♔ *Chinese*

Ever since Lantern restaurant closed, the title of Oakland's top dim sum house has been transferred to Jade Villa, a behemoth of a restaurant that takes up nearly a quarter block in Oakland's Chinatown. During the lunch hour the place is packed with Chinese families sitting at large, round tables. The ornate dining room offers a tempting array of dinners, but the real reason you should come here is for the dim sum, served from 9AM to midafternoon. Sip a cup of aromatic tea as servers circulate through the room pushing carts laden with assorted delicacies. They'll pause by your table and lift the lids of tiered metal steamers to let you inspect the barbecued pork buns, stuffed dumplings, wedges of green pepper filled with shrimp, and lots of other tasty treats. You can afford to experiment here—two people can eat with abandon for about $25. *MC, V; breakfast, lunch, dinner every day; beer and wine.*

Jakarta

615 BALBOA ST, SAN FRANCISCO   📞   415/387-5225
RICHMOND DISTRICT   🍴   *Indonesian*

At the edge of the Balboa Street commercial district lies Jakarta, an Indonesian restaurant that is a serene spot to try out dishes that are just a bit more exotic than your average Thai, Chinese, or Vietnamese fare. Despite the too-close-together tables and railroad car-like connected rooms, the atmosphere here is peaceful, and the friendly, helpful service puts diners at ease. The restaurant's claim to fame is its hot and spicy sauce (which can be purchased for cooking at home), and it's shown off to perfection in dishes like *pepes*—tempeh or fish slathered in fiery spice paste, then wrapped in a banana leaf and grilled. For the fainter at heart, Jakarta also has some delectable coconut-milk curries, including one with fresh crab. Save room for the coconut dessert crepe or a compelling beverage of young coconut juice with rose water. The *rijsttafel* platter, the traditional Indonesian meal of a variety of foods and sauces served with rice, may not exactly be "cheap eats," but with nine separate items, you won't go away hungry. *MC, V; no checks; dinner Tues-Sun; beer and wine; jakarta@jakartarestaurant.com; www.jakartarestaurant.com.*

Joe's Cable Car

4320 MISSION ST, SAN FRANCISCO   📞   415/334-6699
EXCELSIOR   🍴   *Burgers*

Few would dispute that Joe's Cable Car serves the best hamburger in town, though unfortunately, it doesn't win the same gold star for atmosphere. Neither romantic hideaway nor bohemian stomping ground, this three-decades-and-running restaurant is decorated with lots of plastic and wrought iron, and the sun bounces freely off the beige Formica tabletops. Think Burger King crossed with a Mission taqueria—though without the noisy lines. All that, however, won't matter if you love your burgers, because ground beef has never tasted so good as it does between Joe's buns. In case you didn't already know, "Joe grinds his own fresh chuck daily." Yessir, and you'll read that phrase over and over the minute you step inside the place—on napkins, on the menu, and on the wall in big red letters. There's even a colorful mural of Joe himself working the grinder. When it comes time to bite down into one of Joe's 4-, 6-, or 8-ounce sandwiches, "fresh" is truly the operative word. This is a hamburger that's not about what you put on top—and there are lots of toppings to choose from—it's about the flavor of the meat itself. *MC, V; no checks; lunch, dinner every day; beer and wine.* &

Joe's Taco Lounge

393 MILLER AVE, MILL VALLEY ☎ 415/383-8164
MILL VALLEY ⊗ *Mexican*

Colorful and campy, with religious icons and hundreds of bottles of hot sauce lining the walls, Joe's has long been a Mill Valley favorite. The scene borders on the loud and chaotic—with clanging from the kitchen, babbling from babies, and spontaneous song from the cashier—but as long as you weren't expecting a romantic tête-à-tête, it's all fun. Grilled chicken tacos are a great choice here, made with shredded meat swimming in a peppery sauce on a layer of refried black beans. But, despite the restaurant's name, they do a lot more than tacos here. They also serve sandwiches like the Sloppy José, made of braised shredded pork mixed with a fiery chipotle barbecue sauce, and even pizzas and calzones with Mexican-style toppings, like the *pollo calzonita,* with barbecued chicken, refried beans, rice, cheese, and salsa. Counter seating (check out those glittery vinyl chairs) makes it a good spot for solo diners, but families can take advantage of crayons for the kiddies and a children's menu. *MC, V; no checks; lunch, dinner every day; beer and wine.* &

Juan's Place

941 CARLETON ST, BERKELEY ☎ 510/845-6904
WEST BERKELEY ⊗ *Mexican*

Covered wall-to-wall in bric-a-brac, from autographed black-and-white photos of '70s boxers to tiny ceramic sombreros, Juan's exudes a down-home charm that inspires the devotion of students, young working-class families, and the occasional biker. In the evening, a line often snakes from the cash register toward the door, with folks waiting for a Formica-topped table in one of the two dining areas. The day's sporting event plays on a TV in the barroom. All this popularity and good cheer (not to mention the jukebox, stocked with

Mexican Top 40 and an unforgettable rendition of "Happy Birthday") means that the decibel level can require raised voices. But if you've got a hankering for plain old Mexican food—rice and beans, enchiladas, fajitas, and burritos—no place in Berkeley can touch Juan's. Be warned that portions are generous (take advantage of the half-order option); the Super Burrito can easily feed two hungry adults. Whatever you choose, be sure to sample Juan's Slurpee-like wine margaritas, among the best in the Bay Area. *AE, DC, MC V; no checks; lunch, dinner every day; beer and wine.* ♿

Juban

1581 WEBSTER ST, SAN FRANCISCO 📞 415/776-5822
JAPANTOWN 🍴 *Japanese*

Your vegetarian friends will never speak to you again if you bring them here, as the only thing they'll find to eat is garnish. This is downtown Meatsville, and the menu lists no fewer than seven cuts of beef, including tongue, tripe, intestine, and liver, plus lamb, chicken, and some token offerings of seafood. Cook them to your liking yourself at the state-of-the-art table grills that perfectly eliminate all cooking odors. Sadly, the restaurant's flagship beef, the stunningly flavorful Wagyu loin (better known to many as Kobe beef) wasn't available on our last visit because, as the waitress explained to us, the entire herd of cattle had been tainted and destroyed. Just as well, it seems, because at almost $40, the delicacy is out of our price range anyway. Luckily, almost all the other dishes are extremely affordable—most meats are around $7 a plate. Welcome additions to supplement your meal include rice, any and all of the homemade Japanese pickles, or a satisfying bowl of the oxtail or daikon soup. It's a good place for groups or families, though the posh, Tokyo-sleek decor also lends itself easily to austere romantics or even businessfolks looking to close a deal. *AE, MC, V; no checks; lunch, dinner every day; beer and wine.* ♿

Just For You

1453 18TH ST, SAN FRANCISCO 📞 415/647-3033
POTRERO HILL 🍴 *Diner*

Though it may feel like a cozy, run-of-the-mill diner, this kitten has claws. The wait staff with attitude demands no whining, no cell phones, and no making out at the counter. And the tiny neighborhood lunch counter is intimate enough that transgressors will not escape unnoticed. All menu expectations are exceeded, however, with perfectly cooked eggs, yummy pancakes, succulent and spicy home fries, and fantastic grilled cheese. In addition, the menu travels the world, from superb Louisiana-influenced blue crab cakes with Creole mustard to excellent Mexican-style breakfasts with house-made chili and salsa, not to mention the fresh fruit, oatmeal, and granola ("This *is* California, after all," chides the menu). Excellent freshly baked bread, biscuits, and scones complement each hot plate. No one walks away hungry, disappointed, or unnoticed. *Cash only; breakfast, lunch every day; no alcohol.*

Kan Zaman

1793 HAIGHT ST, SAN FRANCISCO   📞   415/751-9656
UPPER HAIGHT   🍴   *Middle Eastern*

Glass-beaded curtains lead into Kan Zaman, a favorite destination for Upper Haight residents. Shed your shoes and gather around knee-high tables under a canopy tent—or snag the premier window seat—and recline on pillows while sampling the tasty, inexpensive hot and cold Middle Eastern meze (appetizers). Before long, you'll think you've been transported to (as Kan Zaman literally translates) a long time ago. Traditional menu items include hummus, baba ghanouj, *kibbee* (cracked wheat with spiced lamb), meat pies, and various kebabs. Sample platters offering tastes of a little bit of everything are ideal for large parties. Wine, beer, and spiced wine round out the offerings. *MC, V; no checks; lunch Sat–Sun, dinner every day; beer and wine.*   ♿

Kate's Kitchen

471 HAIGHT ST, SAN FRANCISCO   📞   415/626-3984
LOWER HAIGHT   🍴   *American*

Almost everyone who has been to Kate's adores it, and for many of us this hole-in-the-wall with a Southern slant is our favorite breakfast spot in the city. Warming our hands around a cup of hot, strong coffee, we vacillate between ordering a savory or sweet breakfast. Whether to order one of the fat omelets that comes with home fries and a side of lean, thick-cut bacon, or the French toast, served plain or heaped high with fresh fruit? Usually we come down on the side of the platter-size cornmeal pancakes, fluffy yet slightly crunchy with cornmeal, topped with goodies like sliced banana and walnut halves. Portions are so huge that even a Southerner suffering a nostalgia fit would have a hard time finishing off a side of hush puppies with honey butter or biscuits and gravy. If you're lucky enough to have time for a leisurely breakfast or lunch on a weekday, you can just waltz right in. On weekend mornings, expect a good 10 to 20 names ahead of yours when you sign up on the list kept on the door. *Cash only; breakfast, lunch every day; no alcohol.*

Katz Bagels

3147 16TH ST, SAN FRANCISCO   📞   415/552-9122
604 MISSION ST, SAN FRANCISCO   📞   415/512-1570
MISSION DISTRICT/FINANCIAL DISTRICT   🍴   *Bagels*

Though freshly baked bagels are the main draw here—and for good reason—come lunchtime Katz also serves up some excellent deli sandwiches that are worth coming back for. These include turkey, eggplant, chicken pesto, and hot pastrami, all generously garnished with fresh vegetables and served on over-size bagels. At the original 16th Street store, the huge flying bagel perched over the doorway is hard to miss; inside, however, the experience is much less sur-real. Both locations have a friendly, neighborhood feel, one that's enhanced by the numerous photos (shot by the owner) of local people adorning the walls. Mostly informal street portraits, they give you something to look at while wait-ing for your bagel to toast. Speaking of which, the bagels are fresh, not too soft, and just the right degree of chewy, and they come in a huge assortment of fla-vors. A variety of spreads are on hand—cream cheese, hummus, peanut butter—as well as specialty cream cheeses like vegetable, lox, and sun-dried tomato (a tangy complement to an onion or seeded bagel). Juices and sodas are in the cooler, and espresso drinks are available. The drip coffee's decent, too. *No credit cards; checks OK; breakfast, lunch every day; no alcohol.*

Khan Toke Thai House

5937 GEARY BLVD, SAN FRANCISCO   📞   415/668-6654
RICHMOND DISTRICT   🍴   *Thai*

There's something about the Khan Toke Thai House that inspires you to con-sider even the most mundane of dinner partners for a possible romantic inter-lude. Entering off busy Geary Boulevard, you are immersed in tranquillity as soon as the door shuts behind you. Lamplight flickers off polished teak carv-ings and the delicate scents of basil, ginger, and lemongrass hang in the air. A friendly Thai waiter asks you to remove your shoes before guiding you through the serene dining room. As you nestle down on cushions and tuck your feet into the deep well where the table sits, it's easy to feel as though you're the privileged guest of an affluent Thai friend. The only difference is that you'll still be asked to foot the bill. A beautifully tended herb garden in the back provides the aromas for such savory specialties as *choo chee goong,* prawns sautéed in coconut milk, curry, zucchini, and mushrooms. To really impress your date, order from the section of the menu devoted to curries featured in Thai literature. *AE, MC, V; no checks; dinner every day; beer and wine.*

Khun Phoa / Khun Phoa II

1068 18TH ST, SAN FRANCISCO 📞 415/771-3463
2367 MARKET ST 📞 415/431-3463
CASTRO 🍴 *Thai*

On one hand, Khun Phoa is just another decent neighborhood Thai place in a city with more than its share of just such establishments. Then again, there's a lot to be said for a homey restaurant with affordable prices, friendly atmosphere, and loads of tasty dishes to choose from. Imperial rolls, salads, curries, and rice plates are all good bets. Khun Phoa's version of the Thai staple *tom kha gai*–chicken-coconut milk soup spiced with chile, lemongrass, and galangal to create one of the most delectable flavor combinations in the world–is sweeter than average, but mighty fine nonetheless. A real standout, though, is the *sahai param,* a house-invented entree you won't find anywhere else, consisting of chicken, prawns, and vegetables tossed together under a beautiful peanut sauce. The room is small but cozy, the staff practically glow with friendliness, and the restaurant's two locations in the Castro near its famous 1920s-era movie palace make it an excellent choice for a premovie meal. *AE, MC, V; no checks; lunch, dinner every day; beer and wine.*

King of Thai Noodle House

639 CLEMENT ST, SAN FRANCISCO *(and branches)* 📞 415/752-5198
RICHMOND DISTRICT/SUNSET DISTRICT/UNION SQUARE 🍴 *Thai*

This cramped, busy, and sometimes boisterous establishment feels more like an American diner–complete with harried short-order cooks, a large TV that's always on, and a wait staff that takes no lip–than the sort of polite, sit-down Thai restaurants most San Franciscans are used to patronizing. But for those who have been to Thailand, the King of Thai will likely seem familiar. If you have to wait for a table, you can watch the cooks stir-fry seafood and vegetables, then deftly pour the boiling broth into soup bowls piled with thin rice noodles. Look for items you can't get at every neighborhood Thai restaurant, such as radish cakes, slightly sweet and delicately crisp, served on a bed of stir-fried bean with chile sauce. Seemingly over-the-top protein combinations, like ground chicken, shrimp, dried shrimp, squid, and tofu, come together over flat noodles in a piquant sauce garnished with nutty, caramelized garlic. Service is no-nonsense and grease is abundant, but the flavors are fresh and bright; this is one Thai restaurant that Thais actually go to. If the Richmond location is too booked, head to the sister restaurant, King of Thai Noodle Cafe, in the Sunset. Though they don't serve alcohol, you're welcome to bring your own. *Cash only; lunch, dinner every day; no alcohol.* &

Kirala

2100 WARD ST, BERKELEY   ☎   510/549-3486
SOUTH BERKELEY   🍴   *Japanese*

A no-reservations policy often means a long wait at Berkeley's favorite Japanese restaurant. Once you snag a seat in the plain-Jane dining area or at the sushi bar, however, get ready to taste some of the best Japanese food in town. The sushi and sashimi, so fresh you half expect it to swim away, are ready in a flash of a knife, the *gyoza* (Japanese pot stickers) and other appetizers are first-rate, and the skewers of seafood, vegetables, and meats emerging from the robata grill are cooked to perfection and seasoned with a delicate hand. Ask the sushi chefs or the servers what's best for sushi and sashimi that day. Sushi dinners often cost around $15, so consider noodle dishes, like the warming *nabeyaki udon* (with poached egg and shrimp tempura), if you're on a tight budget. An extensive sake bar—boasting more than 20 premium sakes from Japan—is a good place to enjoy a light meal. *AE, DC, MC, V; no checks; lunch Tues-Sat, dinner every day; beer and wine; www.kirala.citysearch.com.*

Kushi Tsuru

1737 POST ST, SAN FRANCISCO   ☎   415/922-9902
JAPANTOWN   🍴   *Japanese*

Next-door neighbor Mifune (see review) is so popular for its noodle dishes that many overlook this modest spot in the Japan Center. That's a shame, because local Japanese diners know that this place is a little quieter, a little more refined, and with service a bit more attentive than at the boisterous neighboring noodle house. A diverse menu ranges from sushi to *nabemono* (cooked in broth), *yakimono* (grilled), and *agemono* (deep-fried) dishes. Donburi dishes, like the chicken and egg donburi topped with green and yellow onions and a julienne of nori, are an especially good deal, and daily lunch specials, like Wednesday's deep-fried flounder and Friday's unagi donburi, are another bargain, at only $6.50. The high-backed booths and Japanese prints on the walls lend a quiet and serene atmosphere, though the hard, tiny cushions permanently affixed to the wooden booths do nothing to make them more comfortable. *MC, V; no checks; lunch, dinner every day; beer and wine.*

La Bayou

3278 ADELINE ST, BERKELEY 📞 510/594-9302
SOUTH BERKELEY 🍽 *Cajun/Creole*

Yellow walls, a purple ceiling, and Mardi Gras masks, hats, and beads hanging from the walls lend tiny La Bayou a festive atmosphere. This South Berkeley storefront attracts a crowd as diverse as the neighborhood—families of every ethnicity, young punks, and plenty of folks passing by on their way from the nearby BART station stop by for classic Cajun and Creole food. Choose from traditional offerings including nine varieties of po'boy sandwiches, jambalaya, dirty rice, and crawfish étouffée (crawfish in sauce with garlic, onions, and spices served over rice), plus numerous side dishes. In a nod to its California clientele, La Bayou serves dishes that are flavorful but not hot enough to scare off the spice-shy, and the restaurant even offers vegetarian specials along with its baked macaroni and cheese and Caesar salad, available every day. Order at the back counter and pull up a seat at one of the few tables, or choose from the to-go items in the deli case and have your order packed to take with you. *AE, MC, V; no checks; lunch and dinner Tues-Sat; no alcohol.*

La Boulange de Polk

2310 POLK ST, SAN FRANCISCO 📞 415/345-1107
RUSSIAN HILL 🍽 *Bakery*

You may be 6,000 miles from the Seine, but for heaven's sake, don't tell the patrons of this French bakery, where a patron was recently overheard saying "merci" to a Spanish-speaking staffer. It's an easy mistake to make. The outdoor tables, bright green facade, orange awning, and warm yellow interior—not to mention a few honest-to-goodness French employees—could transport anyone across the Atlantic. You'll even spot the obligatory French posters inside. As you wait to order—and the line stretches out the door on weekend mornings—try to decide among raisin brioche, *chausson aux pommes* (apple turnover), and an almond-encrusted croissant. Assorted madeleines, tarts, baguettes, and small and large bread rounds also provide temptation. You'll find the standard array of lattes, mochas, and coffees ($1.50 to $3.50, depending on the fanciness factor and the size), served in sunshine-yellow cups with matching saucers. More filling choices include savory tarts and delectable open-faced sandwiches ($7)—from smoked duck breast to pâté de campagne; all come with a green salad. You'll have trouble finding a seat on crowded weekends, but when you spot the jar of Nutella spread next to the cream and sugar, you may not mind standing in line. *MC, V; no checks; breakfast, lunch Tues-Sun; no alcohol.* ♿

Lalita Thai

96 MCALLISTER ST, SAN FRANCISCO ☎ 415/552-5744
TENDERLOIN 🍴 *Thai*

Lalita is not the cheapest Thai restaurant in the city, but it is one of the most innovative and attractive. Bright and airy, with a mural painted on one wall and fresh orchids at each table, the dining room is a welcome respite from the scruffy blocks outside. At a few popular tables you can even sit on pillows on the floor (with your feet in a well underneath). The menu is also a refreshing change of pace from your dime-a-dozen Thai restaurant. Witness the chicken and prawns with peanut sauce, a flurry of fried wonton wrappers atop a mound of chicken and prawns on a pile of leafy greens and baby corn, swimming in a rich sauce that tastes equally of peanuts and coconut milk. Service is deft, even when big groups of people working at nearby City Hall arrive for lunch. *AE, DC, DIS, JCB, MC, V; no checks; lunch Mon-Fri, dinner every day; full bar.* ♿

La Mediterranée

288 NOE ST, SAN FRANCISCO *(and branches)* ☎ 415/431-7210
CASTRO/PACIFIC HEIGHTS/SOUTH BERKELEY 🍴 *Middle Eastern*

Even on San Francisco's coldest and foggiest days, La Med, as many call it, seems as warm and cozy as the Middle East and Greece, the region whose cuisine it celebrates. Potted plants sprout from the walls, a stained-glass window hangs inside the front window, and a cushioned window seat makes your wait for a table more comfortable. Even the servers have sunny dispositions.

The *lule kebab* is a savory blend of lamb and spices, phyllo dough comes stuffed with shredded chicken, and most plates come with a dollop of hummus. The Mediterranean Meza for two or more allows you a taste of many of the best items on the menu, and desserts range from a decadent chocolate cheesecake to the more traditional baklava. *MC, V; no checks; lunch, dinner every day; beer, wine, and apéritifs.*

La Palma Mexicatessen

2884 24TH ST, SAN FRANCISCO 📞 415/647-1500
MISSION DISTRICT 🍴 *Mexican*

Both a store and a take-out spot, La Palma is one of the few places in San Francisco where you can get tortillas and tamales made with freshly ground corn flour, as opposed to the processed, dried kind. They're a revelation in flavor, with the sweet, smoky essence of corn and a nice granular texture. Watch workers pat tortillas together by hand and cook them on a large griddle, then take yourself home a steaming stack of the thick, sweet beauties for less than $2. For an unusual and particularly unhealthy snack, La Palma also makes its own *chicharrones,* or pork chitlins. There's nowhere to sit in the store, but locals line up until the 6PM closing for take-out items like tacos, burritos, and tamales, which are so perfectly spiced they don't even need a sauce. The store also carries inexpensive Mexican food products such as ground spices, cheeses, and dried beans. *MC, V; no checks; lunch, dinner every day; beer only.*

La Rondalla

901 VALENCIA ST, SAN FRANCISCO 📞 415/647-7474
MISSION DISTRICT 🍴 *Mexican*

Going to La Rondalla is kind of like taking a cruise down to Ensenada. Enter the door (or get off the boat) and next thing you know you're drunk on cheap margaritas and belting out mariachi tunes you didn't think you knew. This chaotic, perpetual party place has three main spaces: a crowded, tinsel-filled bar that has either a live mariachi band or the jukebox on full blast; an adjacent room full of groups celebrating a birthday; and a relatively quiet dining area that looks like an old-fashioned diner. The endless wait for a table might make you think that the kitchen has something to offer besides enchiladas and chiles rellenos smothered in sauce and cheese and bolstered by beans and rice. The hefty dishes, though, are little more than a vehicle for consuming copious amounts of tequila. But by the time you finally sit down, the La Rondalla spirit has grabbed hold and the food tastes just fine. This is one of the few restaurants in the city that stays open until 3AM every night (except Monday). *Cash only; lunch, dinner Tues-Sun; full bar.*

La Taqueria

2889 MISSION ST, SAN FRANCISCO 415/285-7117
MISSION DISTRICT *Mexican*

Where's the best burrito in the city? Ask anyone in the long lunchtime lines at La Taqueria and most would agree it's right here, behind the white stucco facade, wrought-iron gate, and small patio-style dining area of this longtime favorite Mission District establishment. The emphasis here is on burritos and tacos—filled with meat, beans, and salsa but no rice—though quesadillas and nachos are also available. The salsa is tangy and bright, and it beautifully complements the succulent meat and tender pinto beans. You can also add sour cream, chunks of whole avocado (recommended), and even extra meat if you want. Burritos are somewhat smaller than those at most Mission establishments, which means you won't wind up feeling bloated. If you're ordering tacos, one's a snack, two's a meal. And don't miss the fresh fruit drinks, which include *fresa* (strawberry), mango, and *tamarindo* (tamarind). Order food and drinks at the counter, hang on to your ticket, grab a seat, and wait for your number to be called. A bottle of tangy green hot sauce is on every table. *Cash only; lunch, dinner every day; beer only.*

La Vie

5830 GEARY BLVD, SAN FRANCISCO 415/668-8080
RICHMOND DISTRICT *Vietnamese/Southeast Asian*

This small storefront restaurant has little in the way of decoration besides a simple fish tank at the entry and musical instruments adorning the walls, but it offers a higher level of food and service than most of its competitors in the Richmond. If you like to eat family style, the waiters will ceremoniously bring out one dish at a time, turning a simple meal into a four-course feast. They also carefully explain how to eat some of the more traditional dishes by hand—such as the Vietnamese crepe, which should be broken into pieces, wrapped in lettuce leaf, and adorned with sweet and savory condiments. Careful attention also goes into the many dishes that are prepared tableside, such as Beef

Fondued Vinegar (with a lemongrass-infused broth) or Flaming Beef and Prawns with tomatoes, onion, and peanuts. Though most Vietnamese food is dominated by fish sauce and pork, the cooks offer a vegetarian menu of 14 items such as fresh spring rolls and eggplant with garlic sauce. *DC, DIS, MC, V; no checks; lunch, dinner every day; beer and wine.*

Le Charm

315 5TH ST, SAN FRANCISCO 📞 415/546-6128
SOUTH OF MARKET 🍴 *French*

Le Charm isn't as inexpensive as most of the spots in this book—the prix-fixe menu actually costs $24 per person at dinner—but this stylish, intimate French bistro offers some of the best values in French cuisine in the city. For your $24 you get three courses expertly prepared and cheerfully served. The appetizers might include fricassee d'escargot, roasted quail stuffed with mustard greens, or a perfect French onion soup. For the entree, your options might include duck confit, pan-roasted halibut, or the enormous leg of lamb. Desserts, which must be ordered in advance, are superb. The tarte Tatin and the chocolate roulade with coconut are showstoppers. At lunchtime prices are even lower, with entrees like salmon on a bed of mashed potatoes for less than $10. Outdoor seating is available, making this a great place to enjoy a sophisticated lunch on a warm summer afternoon. *AE, MC, V; no checks; lunch Mon-Fri, dinner Mon-Sat; full bar; lecharm@lecharm.com; www.lecharm.citysearch.com.* ♿

Le Cheval

1007 CLAY ST, OAKLAND 📞 510/763-8957
2600-A BANCROFT WAY, BERKELEY 📞 510/704-8018
DOWNTOWN OAKLAND/SOUTH BERKELEY 🍴 *Vietnamese*

Oakland has plenty of cheap Vietnamese restaurants serving steaming bowls of noodles in a spartan Formica wonderland. You won't confuse Le Cheval with any of them. Floor-to-ceiling windows, high ceilings, and white tablecloths distinguish this cavernous spot from its many competitors. But with everyone in the place shouting to be heard, the din in Le Cheval is impossible to ignore. The egg-carton acoustic material on the ceiling doesn't help, since it's about three miles away from the dining room floor—like trying to sound-dampen a stadium with velvet curtains. The menu runs the gamut of Vietnamese favorites, from raw marinated beef to shrimp in a clay pot. If you're bewildered by the epic-length menu, consider the vermicelli with toppings like pan-sautéed beef, each bite revealing a new flavor (peanut, cilantro, mint, peppers, and salty fish sauce). Be sure to sample some of the range of appetizers, which include imperial rolls, roast quail, and marinated beef in lemon. On weekdays the enormous crowds consists mostly of workers from the nearby office buildings taking a quick break. On weekends expect to see big Vietnamese families at the large tables with lazy Susans in the center. Service can be erratic: one day it's slow as molasses, then the next they're asking you for your order three times before you've even had a chance to open the menu. *AE, DIS, MC, V; no checks; lunch, dinner Mon–Sat, dinner Sun; full bar.* &

Left at Albuquerque

2140 UNION ST, SAN FRANCISCO   📞 415/749-6700
MARINA 🍴 *Mexican*

A well-dressed, young, and festive crowd packs into this noisy, dimly lit spot every evening for healthy Mexican food with a California twist. Earthy wild mushroom quesadillas are served with a smoky chipotle aioli and black beans, and the unique Inside-Out Enchiladas are stuffed with cheese and topped with chunks of beef or chicken. The signature Towering Tostada is an improbably high stack of cheese, black beans, grilled vegetables, and grilled steak or chicken. Margaritas and cocktails are $1 off during happy hour, when a very happy crowd indeed winds down after work. Some complain that this small chain, with branches in the South Bay and Southern California, is a little too slick, and it certainly doesn't have the down-home charm of Mission District Mexican joints, but halfway through a margarita and a bowl of guacamole, you're unlikely to mind. *AE, DC, MC, V; no checks; lunch, dinner every day; full bar; info@leftatalb.com; www.leftatalb.com.* &

Le Soleil

133 CLEMENT ST, SAN FRANCISCO   📞 415/668-4848
RICHMOND DISTRICT 🍴 *Vietnamese/Southeast Asian*

A cut above your typical hole-in-the-wall pho joint, Clement Street's favorite Vietnamese restaurant has a loyal following, which translates into lines that stretch out the door on weekends. The crowds come partly for Le Soleil's soothing and elegant atmosphere, with its pastel color scheme, seasonal decorations on the glass-topped tables, and huge tropical fish tank, but they stay for the delicious Vietnamese dishes. The popular Vietnamese crepe is a crispy-fried semicircle filled with chicken and shrimp (or mushrooms in the vegetarian version). To eat it, cut off pieces and roll them up in lettuce leaves with pickled garlic, basil leaves, and a piquant sauce. The seafood fire pot is cooked right at your table: you add seafood and vegetables to a hot pot of chicken broth, turning it into a rich stew. Another favorite is the savory Vietnamese grilled lemongrass chicken. Le Soleil even features a wine list that complements the food, with choices that pair well with the spicy flavors of Vietnamese food. *AE, DC, MC, V; no checks; lunch, dinner every day; beer and wine.* &

Lhasa Moon

2420 LOMBARD ST, SAN FRANCISCO   📞 415/674-9898
MARINA 🍴 *Tibetan*

If you can't hike the Himalayas, you can at least trek to the Marina district to experience the food of Tibet. This is San Francisco's only Tibetan restaurant and one of the few on the West Coast. The gracious co-owner Tsering Wangmo, Tibetan born and raised in a Tibetan refugee settlement in South India, revives the dishes she learned to cook from her mother. The menu is curious and amazing, with such dishes as *churul* (a pungent cheese and minced beef soup) and *phing alla* (a crepe filled with bean thread, vegetables, and mushrooms). A highlight is the *momo,* a dim sum–like array of juicy dumplings filled with anything from chopped beef to mint-flavored vegetables. Among the intriguing and flavorful main dishes, the *kongpo shaptak* (spicy cheese-flavored beef and chile peppers) and *jhasha shamdeh* (curry-marinated chicken in yogurt and herbs) are two standouts. Several vegetarian dishes are available as well. *AE, MC, V; no checks; lunch Thurs–Fri, dinner Tues–Sun; beer and wine; tseringwangmo58@hotmail.com; www.lhasamoon.citysearch.com.* &

Lichee Garden

1416 POWELL ST, SAN FRANCISCO   📞 415/397-2290
CHINATOWN 🍴 *Chinese*

If Goldilocks were to eat at Lichee Garden, chances are that she would proclaim it "just right." Unlike many Chinese restaurants serving dim sum, it's neither slick and Americanized for the benefit of all the tourists streaming through Chinatown, nor such a dive that it looks like some prison dining room. An almost exclusively Chinese clientele dines in the cavernous, clamorous restaurant–brightly lit, but softened with floral carpeting, potted plants, and large paintings on the walls. Large servings of dim sum go for a song. Whole shrimp stuffed in slippery rice noodles are uncommonly tender, and brown leaf wrappers hide a fist-size serving of sticky, glutinous rice surrounding a center of saucy shredded chicken. At dinnertime dim sum isn't served, but you can choose from an enormous menu, including both familiar choices (kung pao shrimp) and items you might eat on a dare (shredded duckling with jellyfish). Expect a crowd at both lunch and dinner (and especially for weekend brunch), but the staff keeps things moving briskly. *MC, V; no checks; breakfast, lunch, dinner every day; brunch Sat-Sun; beer and wine.* &

Little Thai Restaurant

2065 POLK ST, SAN FRANCISCO   📞 415/771-5544
RUSSIAN HILL 🍴 *Thai*

In you weren't able to figure out for yourself what kind of food is available at "Little Thai," the sign outside helpfully points out "specializing in Thai cuisine." And indeed, the dishes served here are the same as at most Thai restaurants in town, from chicken with lemongrass, chile pepper, and basil to the ubiquitous pad Thai. But this restaurant is uncommonly airy and pleasant, with a high ceiling and sun streaming in the windows. Servers are unusually solicitous, apt to ask if perhaps you didn't like that dish if you didn't polish it off. Highlights of the menu are the *pla muk pad phed*, a plate of not-too-chewy squid sautéed with chile pepper and bamboo shoots, and all the curry dishes, especially the green curry with vegetables and your choice of meat. *AE, DIS, MC, V; no checks; lunch Wed-Sun, dinner every day; beer and wine.*

Lois the Pie Queen

851 60TH ST, EMERYVILLE   📞 510/658-5616
WEST BERKELEY–EMERYVILLE 🍴 *Southern*

Lois herself may have passed on in 1993, but her spirit is kept alive at this friendly, family-owned diner that's been serving gut-busting Southern food for 50 years. What can you say about a place that puts fried chicken on the breakfast menu, or where one of the most popular combos, the Reggie Jackson special, consists of two pork chops, two eggs, hash browns or grits, and biscuits that taste like they're made with a stick of butter each? If you're like us, you'll say, "What a great idea!" Traditional Southern lunch items like grilled cheese sandwiches and deviled eggs leave you with a fighting chance to save room for one of the pies for which the place is justly famous—from sweet potato to peach cobbler to pecan. The small dining room is crowded and a bit chaotic on weekend mornings, but owner Chris Davis is there himself to make sure that everyone is taken care of. *Cash only; breakfast, lunch every day; no alcohol.*

Long Life Vegi House

2129 UNIVERSITY AVE, BERKELEY   📞 510/845-6072
DOWNTOWN BERKELEY 🍴 *Chinese*

Famed for its vegetarian "meats" in traditional Chinese dishes—think cashew chicken, kung pao beef, and sweet and sour pork made with wheat gluten and soy protein in various meaty disguises—this relaxed, unpretentious restaurant serves hordes of UC Berkeley students and plenty of long-former students. Standouts on the extensive menu include Monk-Style Vegetables (greens, mushrooms, carrots, and wheat gluten), Vegetable Fire Pot Soup (available in large or gigantic), and Long Life Vegi Chicken (battered faux chicken in a spicy garlic sauce). Half the menu features seafood selections, made of, well, seafood; Mu-Shu Prawns and Sizzling Rice Prawns are among the best bets. Long Life even offers your choice of white or brown rice. The food is good enough to distract from the lack of decor, save for a few plants and Chinese knickknacks. In fact, almost every year in the local papers this longtime Berkeley favorite wins honors as the best vegetarian spot in town. *AE, DIS, MC, V; no checks; lunch, dinner every day; beer and wine.*

Los Hermanos Mexican Food

2026 CHESTNUT ST, SAN FRANCISCO   📞 415/921-5790
MARINA 🍴 *Mexican*

The sign outside advertises that Los Hermanos has been here for 25 years—quite an achievement in this part of the Marina, where is seems every restaurant is a slick and soulless new chain. In contrast, this is a postage stamp–size joint where people just hunker down over a monster burrito. Combination plates like an enchilada and a chile relleno served with beans and rice are satisfying but not as popular as the burritos, which come in about 10 varieties, most spicy enough to make you glad that the sodas come in sizes large, huge, and ridiculous. A lot of people get their food to go rather than eat here—missing out on the charmless interior, five crowded-together tables, and plastic utensils. If this place were in the Mission, where there's another burrito joint on every corner, Los Hermanos might not be worth a second look. But for a cheap and tasty burrito in the city's most yuppified neighborhood, Los Hermanos really satisfies. *Cash only; lunch, dinner every day; no alcohol.*

L'Osteria del Forno

519 COLUMBUS AVE, SAN FRANCISCO   📞 415/982-1124
NORTH BEACH 🍴 *Italian*

Don't let the touristy Columbus Avenue location fool you: this tiny eight-table cafe attracts legions of locals who brave lousy parking for anything that comes out of the brick-lined oven, such as fantastic focaccia sandwiches, freshly made pizzas, and a wondrously succulent roast pork braised in milk (everyone's all-time favorite). Small baskets of warm focaccia bread and Italian wine served by the glass tide you over until the entree arrives. The kitchen is run by two charming Italian women, and the atmosphere is homey Italian bistro. Ergo, expect a warm welcome and authentic Italian food at low prices. Darn good espresso, too. *Cash only; lunch, dinner Wed–Mon; beer and wine; www.bstudio.com/l'osteria.* ♿

Lovejoy's Tea Room

1351 CHURCH ST, SAN FRANCISCO   📞 415/648-5895
NOE VALLEY 🍴 *Tearoom*

When San Francisco seems to have lost all civility, it's time for tea. At this cheerful spot with Victorian decor and old, mismatched china, the ritual seems soothing rather than snooty. Many stop by for a simple pot of English Breakfast and perhaps a currant scone slathered in clotted cream and strawberry preserves. Turn it all into a substantial meal by ordering the High Tea for Two: a pot of your favorite brew (try one of the fruit-flavored teas) accompanied by a two-tiered stand of finger sandwiches, salads, scones, and some sweet treat, such as a shortbread cookie. Purists will want to try the cucumber and cream cheese sandwiches, but another standout is the smoked finnan haddock. Heartier eaters can order the ploughman's lunch—cheese, chutney, bread, pickled onions, salad, and fruit. Lovejoy's closes at 6PM Tuesday to Sunday and is open until 9PM on Fridays. *MC, V; no checks; lunch Tues–Sun, dinner Fri; no alcohol.*

Lucky Creation

854 WASHINGTON ST, SAN FRANCISCO ☎ 415/989-0818
CHINATOWN 🍴 *Chinese*

Wheat gluten, the protein component of the grain, can be fashioned into a rainbow of different faux meats. And in Chinatown, Lucky Creation is the best place to sample Chinese cuisine with imitation chicken, pork, beef, and seafood ingredients. There are dishes like sweet lemon "chicken" and mu shu "pork"; there are several clay pots stuffed with "meat," tofu, noodles, and vegetables. Lucky Creation features other nonmeat protein ingredients too, like sweet-and-sour walnuts or tofu stuffed with mashed taro and doused with black bean sauce. This isn't one of those fancy Chinatown palaces–it has strictly local-dive nondecor and can even seem a bit shabby. It's tiny, too, with a few tables for four and a couple of bigger tables that you'll be asked to share if it's crowded. It's not for everyone, but for many vegetarians, the veggie-friendly, and the health-conscious, it's nirvana to have so many different (and delicious) choices. *Cash only; lunch, dinner Thurs–Tues; no alcohol.*

Luna Park

694 VALENCIA ST, SAN FRANCISCO ☎ 415/553-8584
MISSION DISTRICT 🍴 *California Cuisine*

This restaurant just barely makes it into the budget category, but the more expensive items are a bargain for their level of sophistication and quality ingredients, and if you stick to the larger appetizers, pastas, and salads you won't go wrong. A stroke of genius went into the goat cheese fondue, which arrives creamy and gooey in a little candle-warmed ramekin with slices of green apple and bread for dipping. Medium-size salads come in intriguing combinations like chopped romaine, radicchio, radish, and blue cheese. If you order the mussels from the appetizer menu–which cost $6.50 but are large enough for a main course–the accompanying *frites* (fries) come in a paper-lined silver cup. Entrees include a hefty lamb shank, which is braised to tenderness and served over brown-butter polenta with piquant greens and cranberry beans. Only a few things, like the bananas Foster, fall short: instead of being creamy and melting hot, the caramel sauce is cold, rock-hard, and probably a dental hazard. The restaurant is loud and simply decorated, with a rowdy central bar, green wood booths, red brick walls, and mural-size art. *AE, DIS, MC, V; no checks; lunch Mon–Fri, dinner every day; full bar.*

Maharani

1122 POST ST, SAN FRANCISCO ☎ 415/775-1988
1025 UNIVERSITY AVE, BERKELEY ☎ 510/848-7777
POLK GULCH/WEST BERKELEY 🍽 *Indian*

The decor might best be described as Pepto-Bismol eclectic at this Indian restaurant, where the walls are painted various shades of pink and mauve, and pink-fringed Victorian-style lamps dangle from the ceiling. Perhaps the unusual color scheme has something to do with the fact that the menu describes the restaurant, oddly, as "a tribute to the female of the human species." But if the wacky colors don't conjure up images of India, the food will: the spicy but not-too-hot tandoori chicken comes sizzling on a platter dressed with onions and fresh cabbage, and the onion kulcha is slightly crisp on the outside, moist with chunks of onion within. The staff is pleasant as punch, even when asked if chicken can be substituted for lamb in the lamb madras. The prices might be at the upper end of "bargain," but the food is flavorful and complex, the Indian music soothing, the service first-rate, and the number of Indian diners here assurance that Maharani is doing something right. *AE, DC, DIS, MC, V; no checks; lunch, dinner every day; beer and wine.* ♿

Malee

1450 LOMBARD ST, SAN FRANCISCO ☎ 415/345-9001
MARINA 🍽 *Thai/Vietnamese*

On an unlikely stretch of Lombard in the midst of a row of budget motels is an utterly charming restaurant whose menu runs the gamut from Hawaiian breakfasts to Vietnamese soups and noodles to Thai curries. It's an unusual and ambitious combination, but it works. Thai deep-fried calamari is tender and served with a tangy sauce, and Vietnamese rice noodle salads are a salty, minty, crunchy, refreshing treat. Plates like the Vietnamese *pupu* (appetizer) platter, with a variety of shrimp, veggie, and spring rolls, are perfect to share or even have as a main course. The restaurant is also surprisingly upscale for the price (most entrees are $6 to $10), with white linen tablecloths and extremely gracious service. A big-screen TV in the bar doesn't help the ambience, but the volume is kept mercifully low. *AE, DC, MC, V; no checks; breakfast, lunch, dinner every day; full bar.*

Mama's on Washington Square

1701 STOCKTON ST, SAN FRANCISCO ☎ 415/362-6421

NORTH BEACH 🍴 *American*

The line at Mama's is so long on weekends it just makes you want to cry, especially when the line takes a turn by the display cases that showcase the restaurant's most decadent items. Moist cranberry bread dusted with confectioners' sugar, home-baked brioche with a ribbon of nuts, raisin, and cinnamon running through it, and big slabs of carrot cake under a quarter-inch of frosting are enough to drive hungry folks right over the edge. After you've ordered you'll be seated in the country kitchen–style dining room, perhaps next to the china hutch along the wall. All the breakfast items are good, but here sweet triumphs over savory: perennial favorites include banana pancakes and chocolate cinnamon French toast. But egg dishes, like the Northern Italian omelet, with pancetta, mushrooms, garlic jack, fresh basil, and tomato, are nothing to sneeze at either. And although it's not always a good idea to order lunch at a breakfast place, the hamburger on focaccia here is very good. If you have a smoked salmon salad, it's that much easier to justify getting a slab of that carrot cake for dessert, or maybe one of those dense and chocolaty dessert bars tormenting the people waiting next to the register. *Cash only; breakfast, lunch Tues–Sun (also open Mon in summer); no alcohol; www.sfnorthbeach.com/mamas.html.*

Mama's Royal Cafe

4012 BROADWAY, OAKLAND ☎ 510/547-7600

NORTH OAKLAND 🍴 *American*

Diehard regulars don't even question the 40- to 60-minute wait required on weekends to get a seat at this 20-year-old Oakland landmark known simply as Mama's. A combination of good food served in large portions and a wildly eclectic decor (picture a '40s-style diner with pagoda door frames and vintage aprons hanging on the walls) attracts a crowd for some of the heartiest breakfasts in the East Bay. Unfortunately, the service can be suhloooow, and the waiters sometimes serve up a little attitude with your home fries. But who cares when the menu includes 31 types of plate-size omelets, served with sides like hub cap–sized scones. Somewhat more manageable are the fresh fruit crepes and burrito with chipotle tortillas. Order a "cowboy with spurs" and get a western omelet with fries; "wax" is sliced American cheese. Rumors abound of a ghost who haunts the third dining room, which allegedly was once a barber-shop where a local mobster was cut down midshave. *Cash only; breakfast, lunch every day; beer and wine.* ♿

Mandalay Restaurant

4348 CALIFORNIA ST, SAN FRANCISCO 📞 415/386-3896
RICHMOND DISTRICT 🍴 *Vietnamese/Southeast Asian*

This large, dark restaurant probably hasn't been redecorated—and perhaps not dusted—since it opened in the mid-'80s. But the prices haven't changed much either, and it's not like Burmese restaurants open every day in the Bay Area. Be sure to start with the *pak dok* (tea leaf) or the ginger salad. Both arrive on plates piled with colorful mounds of tea leaves, ginger, dried lentils, garlic chips, chiles, coconut, peanuts, and ground shrimp. The server ceremoniously mixes the ingredients at the table, and when you take a bite, all of the contrasting textures and flavors come together beautifully. The fish chowder, another Burmese specialty, is a dense soup heady with ginger and lemongrass, while the Rangoon smoked tea duck is full of deep, woodsy flavors. The influence of Burma's neighbors, such as India, China, and Thailand, can be seen in the satays, samosas, Singapore noodles, and mango salad that dot the menu. *MC, V; no checks; lunch, dinner every day; beer and wine.* ♿

Manora's Thai Cuisine

1600 FOLSOM ST, SAN FRANCISCO 📞 415/861-6224
SOUTH OF MARKET 🍴 *Thai*

There are dozens of Thai restaurants in the city, but this SoMa institution has always managed to stand out as one of the best. That explains the noisy atmosphere and the guaranteed wait during peak dining hours, but the food is so incredibly flavorful and reasonably priced that no one sweats these little things. Be sure to start the feast with the chicken satay, followed by the fresh stuffed mint rolls (divine). The menu has a vast array of Thai-style curries, tangy soups, meats, and vegetarian plates, but it's the seafood dishes that really shine, particularly the exotic deep-fried crab shell stuffed with fresh pork, shrimp, crab, herbs, vegetables, and spices. If you plan on going out after dinner, finish the meal with Manora's addictive sweet, caffeine-laden Thai iced tea or coffee. *MC, V; no checks; lunch Mon–Fri, dinner every day; full bar.* ♿

Marcello's Pizza

420 CASTRO ST, SAN FRANCISCO 📞 415/863-3900
CASTRO 🍴 *Pizza*

Every neighborhood has to have one: a late-night pizza-by-the-slice standby that's always there for you when you leave the party bombed and starving. In the Castro that place is Marcello's, which must make a small fortune serving a wide array of slices to a very eclectic crowd until 1AM Sunday through Thursday and until 2AM Friday and Saturday. Both thick- and thin-crust pizzas with a wide array of toppings are enticingly set behind the glass counter, and it usually takes only one big slice to do the trick. Chicken wings, calzones, salads, and sandwiches are also available, but most everyone sticks with the thick, gooey, God-this-tastes-good pizza. There are only about half a dozen stools in the cramped and narrow pizzeria, but the crowd moves quickly. *Cash only; lunch, dinner every day; beer and wine.* ♿

Marina Submarine

2299 UNION ST, SAN FRANCISCO 📞 415/921-3990
COW HOLLOW 🍴 *Soup/Salad/Sandwich*

Substance beats out style at this Union Street sandwich shop, where slow, sometimes brusque service is forgiven after a bite of a delicious, cheap sub. Sandwiches, served toasty warm, come in three sizes: five, seven, and ten inches. Prices for enduringly popular varieties—like turkey, avocado, and sprouts, hot pastrami, and the meatball special—hover around $3.60 for a five-inch sub, and $6.20 for a ten-inch. If you're brave and starving, consider the atomic sub, a fearsome combination of pastrami, turkey, corned beef, cheese, hot peppers, and special sauce (oil and vinegar to those in the know), all crammed into one roll. Fancy-mustard-lovers be warned: you'll have to make do with French's. Sides include potato chips, ice cream, chocolate chip cookies, and Snickers bars. Wash it all down with a fountain soda, or a cold one from the surprisingly decent beer selection. The decor—a handful of tables surrounded by beer signs mounted on red- and mustard-colored walls—isn't much. Take your order to go instead, or perch on the sidewalk and people-watch while you eat. *Cash only; lunch every day; beer only.* ♿

Mario's Bohemian Cigar Store

566 COLUMBUS AVE, SAN FRANCISCO 📞 415/362-0536

2209 POLK ST, SAN FRANCISCO 📞 415/776-8226

NORTH BEACH/RUSSIAN HILL 🍴 *Italian*

You can't consider yourself a San Franciscan unless you've had a focaccia sandwich at this classic century-old North Beach institution that, in a previous incarnation, really was a cigar store. The original Mario's is an adorable little low-key cafe in a prime location at the corner of Columbus and Union across from Washington Square. Both tourists and locals squeeze themselves into a seat at the well-worn bar or at a window-side table overlooking the park, order a cappuccino or a glass of wine, watch the foot traffic, and ponder the old black-and-white photos of longtime regulars. At night, musicians playing mellow jazz cram into the already-crowded space. There are several kinds of sandwiches to choose from, but the best are the hot meatball and the eggplant, both topped with melted Swiss cheese and cut into triangles for easy pickings. Note: The newer and somewhat larger Mario's on Polk Street is cozy enough but lacks the classic charm of the original. It does, however, have a few sidewalk seats. *Cash only; lunch, dinner every day; beer and wine.* ♿

Marnee Thai

2225 IRVING ST, SAN FRANCISCO 📞 415/665-9500

SUNSET DISTRICT 🍴 *Thai*

In surveys of the city's best Thai restaurants, Marnee Thai usually comes in second or third place—quite a showing for a restaurant in the Outer Sunset, a neighborhood of which many San Franciscans are only dimly aware as being that place at the end of a ride on the N Judah streetcar line. Despite walls and ceilings covered with palm fronds and bamboo in tropical-hut style, the dining room is not particularly atmospheric. And the service is efficient rather than gracious, with servers waving you toward a table when you enter and shouting your order back to the kitchen. But that kitchen turns out dishes that are a definite cut above. Pad Thai noodles are silky rather than sticky, dressed with a flavorful peanut sauce and served with a generous handful of the crispest bean sprouts. Potent *kang dang*, your choice of meat or seafood cooked with fiery red curry, coconut milk, and basil, is a favorite, though not for the timid. A small dining room means the wait at dinnertime can be considerable. *AE, MC, V; no checks; lunch, dinner Wed–Mon; beer and wine.*

Ma's Caribbean Cuisine and Roti Shop

1711 TELEGRAPH AVE, OAKLAND 📞 510/444-7684

DOWNTOWN OAKLAND 🍴 *Caribbean*

Ma's has a lot of things working against it: the dentist-office-pink tables have an awkward Taco Bell-esque feel because you can't separate the chairs from the table; the prominently displayed radio invariably blares nothing but staticky noise; and the Mardi Gras mask decor looks like it spent one too many sleepless nights in New Orleans. But none of these things can effectively counter the pleasure of sinking your teeth into a piping hot *roti* stuffed to the brim with collard greens, spinach, and curried potatoes. For the uninitiated, a *roti* is a soft dough wrapper that makes the perfect sheath to envelop such delicious specialties as homemade jerk chicken or tenderly roasted goat. And it's all thanks to Ma, who also goes by the name of Edna Martin and has imported a little slice of her native Trinidad into downtown Oakland. Two squeeze bottles of homemade golden sauces grace each table, and a healthy squirt of the spicy tamarind or the sweet hot concoction is enough to ignite anyone's taste buds. Ginger lovers should be sure to wash down their lunch with a glass of the spicy ginger beer—the liquid equivalent of sucking on the root itself. *Cash only; lunch Mon–Sat; no alcohol.*

Massawa Restaurant

1538 HAIGHT ST, SAN FRANCISCO 📞 415/621-4129

UPPER HAIGHT 🍴 *Ethiopian/Eritrean*

Platters of spongy injera flatbread topped with spiced chicken, lamb, beef, lentils, root vegetables, okra, mushrooms, and more are crowd-pleasers at this Haight Street favorite. For about $10 a head, diners can bathe their taste buds in a variety of selections; each comes with several side dishes, including *bersin* (lentils), *shiro* (curried chickpeas), cooked spinach, and a green salad tossed with a biting and uncomplementary Italian dressing. You'll leave satisfied and with money left in your wallet, but the monotony of the menu might not have you returning again tomorrow. Almost everything—meat, fowl, fish, and vegetable—is prepared in a similar ensemble of onion, clarified butter, house-made yogurt, and tomatoes. However, once in a while you'll crave the rich Massawa flavors that no other place in town can touch. *AE, MC, V; no checks; lunch, dinner every day; beer only.* ♿

Matsuya

3856 24TH ST, SAN FRANCISCO 📞 415/282-7989
NOE VALLEY 🍴 *Japanese*

This Noe Valley fixture attracts both locals and neighborhood outsiders with its low prices and intimate but funky ambience. There's a small sushi bar, a few tables, a little annex with room for one small table–and that's about it. Curtains hanging over the front door create the feel of an inner sanctum, which is accentuated by wood paneling on the walls. A tank of tropical fish looms above the single sushi chef, imbuing him with seafood authority. The chef works hard to keep up with all of the orders and is willing to create special concoctions if you ask him. His staff sometimes includes a wacky older waitress who enjoys teasing the customers into ordering more sake. Because the sushi is relatively inexpensive, it may not be the most incredible raw fish you've ever tasted, but the $12 prix-fixe dinners are a real value. They include sashimi, *sunomono* (fish and vegetables in vinegar), vegetables, pickles, and miso soup. Side dishes like seaweed or squid salad are delicious and only a few dollars extra. *MC, V; no checks; dinner Mon-Sat; beer and wine.*

Mel's Drive-In

1050 VAN NESS AVE, SAN FRANCISCO *(and branches)* 📞 415/292-6357
COW HOLLOW/POLK GULCH/RICHMOND DISTRICT/SOUTH OF MARKET 🍴 *Diner*

In 1947 Mel Weiss opened the first Mel's Drive-In in San Francisco, later immortalized in George Lucas's film *American Graffiti*. The 1950s are now celebrated in four San Francisco Mel's locations, where the chrome counters and Rock-Ola jukeboxes at each table look as if they'd be right at home in a *Happy Days* episode. From the Gene Autry and Andrews Sisters tunes on the jukeboxes, you might think that Mel's would be popular with the geriatric set. On the contrary, on most evenings local teenagers pack the place, flirting over milk shakes, while during the day tired tourists with kids take advantage of the plentiful high chairs, balloons, and kid-friendly menu. The food is fine but unexceptional, primarily diner favorites like burgers, meat loaf, roast beef sandwiches, hot dogs, and onion rings. Desserts, including old-fashioned fruit pies and hot fudge sundaes, are worth saving room for. *Cash only; breakfast, lunch, dinner every day; beer and wine; www.melsdrive-in.com.* ♿

Kid-Friendly Restaurants

They say that San Francisco is one of the best restaurant cities in the world—and it is. But many eateries in this big double-income-no-kids town are less than accommodating to the younger set. Being in a place full of glaring wait staff and huffing hipsters when your usually perfect two-year-old is having the mother of all meltdowns is not one of life's more pleasant experiences. Better you should search out an establishment where, at the first sign of trouble, a kind, gentle server rushes over with a cup of crayons, a balloon, or a basket of bread. In other words, a kid-friendly restaurant.

Finding child-friendly restaurants in an adult-oriented city like San Francisco can be tricky, but every neighborhood has its share of small, family-owned places serving good food at modest prices. Sometimes the menu is ethnic; sometimes it's good old American chow. Lots of them have high chairs and booster chairs, and some have separate children's menus. Here are some of our favorites:

Chava's Mexican Restaurant (3248 18TH ST; 415/552-9387)

Picky eaters can enjoy the cheese enchiladas or rice and beans; those with more adventurous palates can try the weekend special of menudo. The fresh-made tortillas are some of the best in town.

Chevy's Fresh Mex (VARIOUS LOCATIONS)

Some people pooh-pooh this chain of Mexican eateries, calling it cheesy and unauthentic. These people do not have children. Chevy's (which began in the Bay Area) is a place where both kids and parents can have a good time. While children play with balloons or watch in rapt attention as the tortillas come out of the Rube Goldberg–esque machine, parents drink frozen margaritas and eat perfectly adequate Mexican specialties.

Giorgio's Pizzeria (151 CLEMENT ST; 415/668-1266)

Most kids love pizza, and Giorgio's has some of the tastiest around. In addition, the hustle and bustle of this often-crowded spot can usually drown out any kvetching coming from your table. The comfy vinyl booths and tablecloths easily wipe clean.

Mel's Drive-In (3355 GEARY BLVD [and branches]; 415/387-2255)

Theme restaurants are great for kids. At Mel's they can flip through the jukeboxes at each table, look at the memorabilia from *American Graffiti* (which was set in the original Mel's Drive-In), and eat burgers and fries. Heaven.

In the Night Kitchen (101 4TH STREET, 4TH FLOOR; 415/369-6080)

Not surprisingly, the entertainment complex the Metreon is filled with restaurants that cater to the young and restless set. With its Maurice Sendak theme and menu of kiddie faves like peanut butter and jelly, mac and cheese, and Rice Krispie treats, In the Night Kitchen is more than just kid-friendly: it's a kids' restaurant that, with its artisan breads and heirloom veggies, is also adult-friendly.

Park Chow (1240 9TH AVE; 415/665-9912)

Low prices, a fireplace, and a menu of basics that ranges from pasta to burgers to salads are some of the reasons Park Chow is good for the kids. But the best reason may be its location: mere steps from Golden Gate Park.

Pho Hoa Hiep IV (239 CLEMENT ST [*and branches*]; 415/379-9008)

This is a Vietnamese spot that features one of the best beef noodle soups in the city. It's extra-inexpensive and, with high chairs and a kids' menu, it's a perfect place to introduce children to Vietnamese food.

Savor (3913 24TH ST; 415/282-0344)

If there's any neighborhood in need of a kid-friendly restaurant, it's Noe Valley (a.k.a. Stroller Valley). And Savor, with its homey atmosphere, home-baked goods, and super-cheap kids' menu, is a great place for the toddler set.

St. Francis Fountain & Candy (2801 24TH ST; 415/826-4200)

St. Francis doesn't have booster chairs or a kids' menu, but it does have a great old-fashioned soda fountain atmosphere. Step back in time with a grilled cheese sandwich and a milk shake and tell your kids what it was like in "the olden days."

Memphis Minnie's Smokehouse Bar-B-Que

576 HAIGHT ST, SAN FRANCISCO   415/864-7675

LOWER HAIGHT 🍽   *Barbecue*

The fire engine-red facade of Memphis Minnie's is tough to miss on this other-wise fairly drab block in the Lower Haight. When the restaurant recently reopened here after closing its doors in the Outer Mission, it was cause for cel-ebration for 'cue fans throughout the city. Inside, red-and-white-checked table-cloths, a corrugated metal counter, and recorded blues music set a Southern mood. On the menu: meat, meat, and more meat, with nary a vegetable in sight. An andouille sausage sandwich consists of generous slices of the spicy sausage on a crusty French roll and nothing else, served with one side dish like coleslaw, "potlikker" greens, or a satisfying macaroni and cheese topped with crispy bread crumbs. Dinner plates come with two sides, a slab of corn bread, and a prodigious plate of meat like Texas smoked brisket or St. Louis-style pork ribs ("tender, tasty morsels from our friend the pig"). A tip: You'll leave here smelling like a barbecue pit, so leave the dry-clean-only clothes at home. *AE, MC, V; no checks; lunch, dinner Tues–Sun; beer and wine.* ♿

Meriwa

728 PACIFIC AVE, SAN FRANCISCO   415/989-8818

CHINATOWN 🍽   *Chinese*

Partially hidden on the second floor of a mini-shopping mall, this dim sum hall gets few tourists but is extremely popular with local Chinese-American fami-lies. Though the entry could use a makeover, the main hall is grand and lush, decorated with carved wood panels and red banners. A few side rooms look down on busy Pacific Avenue. The food is a little on the greasy side but still delicious, and it's difficult to spend more than around $7 per person here. In addition to steamed dumplings and buns full of chicken, pork, shrimp, and vegetables, look for the particularly flaky egg custard tarts. Meriwa also makes a mean taro ball—mashed taro root that is stuffed with meat and vegetables and fried until delicate and lacy on top. If you come by on a quiet weekday, you might find groups of older men from the neighborhood chatting, reading the paper, and sharing a drink. *MC, V; no checks; breakfast, lunch every day; beer only.*

Metropol Café

168 SUTTER ST, SAN FRANCISCO   ☎ 415/732-7777
FINANCIAL DISTRICT 🍴 *Italian*

Everything is oh-so-European at this spot where Financial District workers go for a mini-splurge when they can't stand the thought of another tuna salad sandwich for lunch. As you walk in the door you're greeted by a smiling staffer in a white apron who will hand you a menu and help you make sense of the menu and ordering system (order at the counter and your meal will be brought out to you). It's not easy to choose from among the entrees, pizzas, innovative salads, and gourmet sandwiches. If all else fails consider one of the specials, perhaps a velvety carrot ginger soup, a tart, creamy cucumber salad with a sour cream and cilantro dressing, or an earthy portobello mushroom sandwich on fragrant rosemary bread. Ordering an entrée like oven-roasted salmon pushes the price over the top for this book, but items like the roasted pork loin sandwich are equally hearty and will leave a little money left over for a glass of wine or a slice of berry tart. The line to order can seem long and hectic, but the dining room, decorated with large flower arrangements and enormous, retro-style European posters, has a certain flair. *AE, DC, MC, V; no checks; lunch Mon-Sat, dinner Mon-Fri; beer and wine.* ♿

Mifune

1737 POST ST, SAN FRANCISCO   ☎ 415/922-0337
JAPANTOWN 🍴 *Japanese*

"It's OK to slurp your noodles," says a note on Mifune's menu. And that's a good thing, because you are likely to do just that at this spartan restaurant in the Japan Center. When a noodle fix is what you require, there is no better place than Mifune. Choose either an udon (broad, flat) or a soba (thin, buckwheat) base, then select from more than 50 toppings. Whether it's beef, chicken, tempura, or plain old miso, you won't be disappointed. The lunch special, with noodles, sushi, salad, and tea for less than $8, is a real bargain. You'll also find a few tempura and sushi selections, but don't waste your time. Noodles are the thing to order here. Just raise the bowl to your chin, shovel in the goodies with your chopsticks, and slurp, slurp, slurp! *AE, DC, DIS, MC, V; no checks; lunch, dinner Mon-Sat; beer and wine; info@mifune.com; www.mifune.com.* ♿

Milano Pizzeria

1330 9TH AVE, SAN FRANCISCO 📞 415/665-3773
SUNSET DISTRICT 🍴 *Pizza*

There's not a single thing hip or trendy about this pizza place near San Francisco's crossroads of cheap eats, the corner of 9th and Irving in the Sunset District. That's its appeal for many of the regulars, who ignore the dark rooms and drab decor for some of the city's tastiest pizzas. Don't look for Thai peanut pizza or cheeseless vegan varieties here. This is the place for a plain-Jane slice of pepperoni or mushroom, made with a crust that's simultaneously crisp and chewy. The pastas are merely okay; stick to the pizza or one of the Italian sandwiches, which are all pretty much like one another, but still messy and satisfying. Service is friendly but, since they make the pies from scratch, expect a considerable wait after you place your order. *Cash only; lunch, dinner every day; beer and wine.*

Miss Millie's

4123 24TH ST, SAN FRANCISCO 📞 415/285-5598
NOE VALLEY 🍴 *American*

When you want comfort in Noe Valley, stop by to see Miss Millie. The welcoming, 1930-ish diner first opened as a strictly vegetarian restaurant but has evolved into one of the best places in the area for brunch. The brunch menu is huge, with flavorful takes on the usual favorites. Try the lemon-ricotta pancakes with blueberry syrup or the spinach and goat-cheese omelet for something you won't soon forget. Dinners are also a treat: the roasted chicken risotto and the grilled red snapper are terrific. The menu is still heavily vegetarian, but the fare is so hearty that carnivores will feel right at home. And that's the whole point at Miss Millie's–to make everyone feel at home. *MC, V; no checks; dinner Tues-Sun, brunch Sat-Sun; beer and wine.* ♿

Moishe's Pippic

425 HAYES ST, SAN FRANCISCO 📞 415/431-2440
HAYES VALLEY 🍴 *Deli*

"Pippic" is Yiddish slang for "belly button," and Moishe's Pippic serves plenty of dishes to make a diner's belly burst. This is one of the few places that satisfy San Franciscans' cravings for an authentic Jewish deli. Here you can get all the kosher hot dogs, mammoth corn beef sandwiches, hot pastramis on rye, dill pickles, and bowls of matzo ball soup you'd rightfully expect to find on the East Coast. And while the food smacks of delicious authenticity, the staff of young Asians and African Americans reminds you of San Francisco's multicultural mix. The deli is never too busy, yet you'll be lucky to catch the place open: though people travel far and wide for even a glimpse of a real knish in this town, Moishe's is closed on Sundays and often locked up during regular business hours. *MC, V; no checks; breakfast, lunch Mon–Sat; no alcohol.*

Moki's Sushi and Pacific Grill

830 CORTLAND AVE, SAN FRANCISCO 📞 415/970-9336
BERNAL HEIGHTS 🍽 *Japanese*

Everyone in town has a favorite sushi spot, and everyone argues over which is the best. The folks in Bernal Heights have argued in favor of Moki's since the day it opened. Not only is the sushi very good, the rolls inventive and excellent, but this place also excels where the others try and fail—with selections from the grill. Try the Thai-style crab cakes in red curry sauce or the Vietnamese-style rice paper rolls stuffed with shrimp and avocado and you'll see what we mean. On the sushi side, the Ecstasy Roll is the specialty, with white and red tuna, avocado, *tobiko* (flying fish roe), and green onions. A friendly staff, cozy atmosphere, and that Bernal Heights perk—easy street parking—make Moki's worth a trip. *AE, DC, MC, V; no checks; dinner every day; beer and wine.* ♿

Molinari Delicatessen

373 COLUMBUS AVE, SAN FRANCISCO 📞 415/421-2337
NORTH BEACH 🍽 *Italian*

While Molinari is not a restaurant in the traditional sense, the food you can get there rivals some of the better sit-down places in the city. This Italian deli has a mere four plastic tables out front (perfect perches for watching the parade of tourists and locals streaming up and down North Beach's Columbus Avenue). Inside is a narrow space that is usually filled to the gills with the sandwich cognoscenti. Grab a number, then grab a roll. While you're waiting to be served, you can shop for imported Italian goods like olive oils, wines, cookies, cheeses, and more. When your number's called, order one of Molinari's deliciously overstuffed sandwiches, like Joe's Special—fresh mozzarella, sun-dried tomatoes, pesto, and roasted red peppers. Or devise one of your own: salami, provolone, prosciutto, mortadella—all the meats, cheeses, and spreads are fresh and high quality. Pick up some olives and a bottle of mineral water and picnic in nearby Washington Square Park. If you want to pick up something for dinner, be sure to show up before 6PM, when the store closes. *MC, V; checks OK; lunch, early dinner Mon-Sat; beer and wine.*

Phoraging for Pho

In Vietnamese neighborhoods around the Bay Area, you'll notice a lot of signs on restaurants with the simple word *pho*. A soup full of rich broth, tender meat, and thin rice noodles, pho is the ultimate meal in a bowl.

Traditionally a breakfast dish, pho is now served all day. Though it's ubiquitous in Vietnamese restaurants, it's best to go to the casual lunch spots—often with the word *pho* somewhere in their name—that specialize in this dish from Hanoi. In *Authentic Vietnamese Cooking,* author Corinne Trang notes that the soup has its roots with the Mongolians, and its name originates from the French word *feu,* as in *pot-au-feu,* meaning "pot on fire."

These linguistic origins will make sense when you order your first bowl of pho, which arrives steaming hot in an enormous bowl. In fact, thinly sliced raw or rare meat is used in *pho bo* (beef pho), since the broth is so hot that it finishes cooking the beef right as it's served. This wonderfully aromatic broth is the essential part of the dish—a rich, deep amber liquid that has been cooked slowly with heady spices like star anise and cinnamon.

Pho bo is the most popular variety of the dish, but you can find chicken and seafood versions of pho as well. Restaurants like Pho Hoa-Lao II in Oakland's Chinatown serve 18 different combinations of pho bo alone—if you're feeling adventurous, try combining your beef with meatballs, tendon, tripe, or other meaty delicacies.

When your bowl of pho arrives, your server will also present you with a plate of crisp bean sprouts, lime wedges, thinly sliced fresh chile pepper, and branches of fresh Thai basil and cilantro. On your table you'll find jars of plummy sweet hoisin sauce and red chili paste. The idea is to add a little of these elements at a time—a squeeze of lime, a few torn basil leaves, a squirt of hoisin—until the soup's many nuanced flavors are balanced just to your liking.

Mom Is Cooking

1166 GENEVA AVE, SAN FRANCISCO   ☏ 415/586-7000
EXCELSIOR 🍽 *Mexican*

Many San Franciscans cite this homespun eatery in the Excelsior—a mostly residential neighborhood directly south of the Mission District—as one of their favorite sit-down Mexican restaurants. And for good reason. It's been run for the last three decades by "Mom," a.k.a. Mexico City native Abigail Murillo, whose cooking keeps loyal fans coming back. Dig into a plate of chips and hot salsa—or sip on a sassy house-made margarita—as you peruse the huge menu, which is big enough to get lost in. Need help? The enchiladas with *carnitas* (roast pork) and *verde* (green chile) sauce are awesome, as is the chicken smothered in mole (a dark, thick, and burly sauce made with chiles, nuts, and unsweetened chocolate). The tamales are another specialty—dense and full of flavor. The tortillas are store-bought, and the service can be slow and sloppy, but in general the food's so good, these quickly become just minor annoyances. A hallway leads to a spacious room at the back that's good for private parties; beyond that is a backyard patio. *MC, V; lunch, dinner every day; full bar; www.momiscooking.citysearch.com.*

Mo's

1322 GRANT AVE, SAN FRANCISCO   ☏ 415/788-3779
772 FOLSOM ST, SAN FRANCISCO   ☏ 415/957-3779
NORTH BEACH/SOUTH OF MARKET 🍽 *Burgers*

When people start debating who makes the finest hamburger in the city, those who like their meat practically still mooing often come down on the side of Mo's, where they're not afraid to serve a blood-red burger. In fact, the menu here declares that "rare means cold inside, medium rare is bloody pink," and that they're "not responsible for well done burgers"—though they'll serve it to you any way you like. Unlike at many other burger places, here you can also get items like a roasted half chicken with veggies and mashed potatoes, and you can substitute beans or red cabbage for a side of fries. Grilled chicken sandwiches are saved from being dry with a generous dollop of spicy Thai curry sauce. Be that as it may, almost everyone is here for those seven ounces of center chuck broiled over volcanic rock, served with respectable fries in need of a generous sprinkle of salt and pepper. The original North Beach location is more atmospheric, even though the decor is fairly minimal, with photos of the

Three Stooges alluding to the restaurant's name. Solo diners eat at the counter on old-fashioned diner stools. *MC, V; no checks; breakfast Sat-Sun (North Beach location only), lunch, dinner every day; beer and wine.* ♿

Mr. Ralph's Café

30 NATOMA ST, SAN FRANCISCO ☎ 415/243-9330
SOUTH OF MARKET 🍴 *Soup/Salad/Sandwich*

Tucked away in a South of Market alley, Mr. Ralph's lures patrons in with its inviting green exterior, and keeps them coming back for the top-notch sandwiches, salads, and comfort foods like tangy three-bean vegetarian chili and macaroni and cheese. No other SoMa joint serves a better tuna melt–a generous portion of tuna salad topped with melted white cheddar on toasted wheat bread. Risk sounding silly by asking for the Honey Cluck-Cluck or order No. 17; either way, you're ordering the chicken and honey Dijon mustard sandwich with Swiss cheese served on a sweet baguette. Excellent sandwich alternatives include the salade niçoise, cobb salad, or Mediterranean lunch plate. In the unlikely event that you've saved room for dessert, you won't be disappointed with a peppermint chocolate cookie or a black bottom cupcake. Happy hour is mellow but fun, as are the mornings, with hot offerings like breakfast sandwiches and burritos, plus the usual pastries, bagels, and scones. Rotating works by local artists adorn the brick walls, and the wooden tables, chairs, and ceiling add to the cozy atmosphere. *Cash only; breakfast, lunch Mon-Fri; beer and wine.* ♿

Naan 'n' Curry

478 O'FARRELL ST, SAN FRANCISCO ☎ 415/775-1349
TENDERLOIN 🍴 *Indian*

If you find yourself in the Tenderloin late at night (at least up until midnight) and hungry, head straight to this dive, a long room with smoke-stained walls that echoes with Indian music. The late hours reflect the South Asian preference for late dining, though you might see Indians and Pakistanis in here any time of day. The food is truly delicious, served in huge portions and at unbelievably low prices. The *seekh kabab*, a ground beef skewer straight out of the clay oven, is a mere $1.50, and an order of tandoori chicken is less than $3. Order yourself a smoky, puffy onion naan and share a huge order of biryani (saffron rice with vegetables) among two or three friends and you're all set–the milky chai comes free. This place is definitely bare bones–you order at the counter and set your own table with less than pristine silverware–but the friendly staffers bring the dishes to your table. No alcohol is served, but feel free to bring your own. *Cash only; lunch, dinner every day; no alcohol.* &

Nan Yang

6048 COLLEGE AVE, OAKLAND 📞 510/655-3298
NORTH OAKLAND 🍴 *Vietnamese/Southeast Asian*

What the Bay Area knows about Burmese cuisine, it learned here. Familiar elements from Indian cooking, such as mango and curry, pepper the menu, and you'll notice nods to Chinese and Thai cuisine; you'll find a wide selection of vegetarian options. Offerings break down into categories including salads, appetizers, soups, curries, and noodles. Favorites include ginger salad, a refreshing and flavorful combination of cabbage, shredded pickled ginger, crunchy toasted split peas, fava beans, and coconut tossed in garlic oil and lemon juice; fried potato cakes; and the many varieties of garlic noodles, cooked to al dente perfection. Nan Yang is extremely popular among hip students and well-heeled families, and you'll often have to wait outside for a table. Cream-colored walls with metallic stripes and a marble bar combine with textiles and paintings of Myanmar (formerly Burma) to create a look that's trendy while remaining down-to-earth. Though the closely spaced tables and banquettes lining the walls are almost always full, and the noise bouncing off the brown slate floor can reach a dull roar, somehow the space never feels uncomfortably crowded or loud. *MC, V; no checks; lunch, dinner Tues-Sun; beer and wine.*

New Asia

772 PACIFIC AVE, SAN FRANCISCO 📞 415/391-6666
CHINATOWN 🍴 *Chinese*

This large Hong Kong-style dim sum hall is packed with families for weekend brunch–try coming here during Chinese holidays and you might find yourself heading to North Beach for pizza instead. But once you get a table, servers will almost immediately come by with carts full of delicious, freshly steamed *siu mai* (pork dumplings) or barbecued pork buns. Small plates all hover around $2, so it's worth trying some of the more unusual options like steamed chicken feet (they taste like chicken wings with less meat). You can also ask for more substantial noodle or rice dishes such as satisfying *chow fun* (flat rice noodles) with beef, Singapore-style fried vermicelli, or shrimp fried rice. The restaurant also opens for dinner, but this is really the place for an authentic Chinatown dim sum experience. *MC, V; no checks; breakfast, lunch, dinner every day, brunch Sat-Sun; beer and wine.*

New Eritrea Restaurant and Bar

907 IRVING ST, SAN FRANCISCO   📞   415/681-1288
SUNSET DISTRICT   🍴   *Ethiopian/Eritrean*

As usual at an Ethiopian restaurant, here you eat most items with your hands, scooping up meats and vegetables with pieces of the spongy flatbread called injera. Maybe that's why neighborhood families bring their broods here for an evening out, letting the kids indulge in their love of finger foods. Only here the finger foods are complex and sometimes spicy dishes like rare chopped beef tenderloin with *mitmita,* a fiery Eritrean spice, or a dip made from ground beans, onions, tomato, and fenugreek. A combination plate comes with *ziqni,* squares of beef simmered with red pepper sauce; *zebhi dorno,* chicken marinated with onions, tomatoes, and Eritrean spices; and our favorite, the *allicha begee,* squares of lamb and vegetables in a rich curry sauce. They all go down easily with a Harar beer, brewed in Harar, Ethiopia. The wall of mirrors and shiny bar running the length of the front room don't set much of a mood, but the back room is a tad cozier. *AE, MC, V; no checks; lunch, dinner every day; full bar.* ♿

Nicaragua

3015 MISSION ST, SAN FRANCISCO   📞   415/826-3672
MISSION DISTRICT   🍴   *Central American*

If the place feels empty when you arrive, don't be put off: Nicaragua attracts mostly Latino regulars from the surrounding neighborhood, some of whom take their meals to go. The food, in fact, is carefully prepared, fresh, and a pleasant change of pace from all the Mexican taquerias in this part of town. Inside, the fluorescent lighting is unpleasantly bright, but otherwise the atmosphere is warm and friendly. The staff do their best to answer questions about the food, like the Indio Viejo, a specialty whose menu description ("beef mixed with corn flour") doesn't do it justice. In actuality it's a flavorful (if salty) concoction of corn tortillas cooked with beef, and it's highly recommended. Ditto for the *chuleta de pescado en salsa*—fish that's been sautéed in a fabulous sauce of white wine and tomatoes. Dinner plates come with rice, a vinegar-laden coleslaw, and a cube of fried cheese. The menu includes several more beef, pork, and seafood dishes along with enchiladas, tamales, and various appetizers utilizing plantains (get the one with black beans and sour cream instead of pork or cheese). You can also dabble in Nicaraguan beverages like *pozol* (hominy and milk) or *tamarindo* (tamarind) and have a yucca fritter for dessert. *Cash only; lunch, dinner every day; beer and wine.*

Nippon (no-name) Sushi

314 CHURCH ST, SAN FRANCISCO   📞 NO PHONE
CASTRO 🍴 *Sushi*

The words "dive" and "sushi" aren't typically heard together, but perhaps they would be if there were more places like Nippon Sushi (still called "no-name" sushi by many, despite the tiny sign they put in the window several years ago). About eight battered tables and a counter are all you'll find in this tiny, bare-bones spot with a battered linoleum floor. But since you're not paying for ambience, this is just about the cheapest sushi you can find in the city. Orders of nigiri or rolls are about twice as big here as they are at most other sushi spots, and many hefty combo plates cost less than $10. We're not saying it's the best sushi in the city—but it's actually pretty good. Certainly they don't have any problems attracting customers: large crowds spill onto the sidewalk every evening. Nippon doesn't serve alcohol, but most people take advantage of the BYOB policy, popping over to the convenience store down the block for beer or wine. *Cash only; lunch, dinner Mon–Sat; no alcohol.*

Noah's Bagels

100 BUSH ST, SAN FRANCISCO   📞 415/433-9682
FINANCIAL DISTRICT/CASTRO/COW HOLLOW/DOWNTOWN OAKLAND/LAKE
MERRITT/MARINA/MISSION DISTRICT/NORTH BERKELEY/PACIFIC HEIGHTS/SOUTH
BERKELEY/SUNSET DISTRICT 🍴 *Bagels*

Noah's Bagels, with its black-and-white photos of New York City tacked on the walls, begs you to believe that its bagel shops will transport you to Brooklyn without the airfare. But let's face it: Noah's is a West Coast phenomenon and makes sacrilegiously flavored bagels such as banana nut and chocolate chip—oy vey! Still, as far as bagels go in the Bay Area, these are some of the best. And with a couple dozen shops in the Bay Area, you won't have to travel far to buy bagels and Jewish deli food. Bagel sandwiches, taller than the average mouth, make a nice change of pace for lunch. Pile on the smoked whitefish salad, lox and cream cheese, hummus, or flavored cream cheese, or go with meatier choices like corned beef, turkey, or pastrami-style turkey. Noah's will also pack bagels to go and breakfast platters to feed a crowd. The bottom line: What Noah's lacks in authenticity and homegrown flavor, it makes up for in reliability and convenience. *AE, MC, V; breakfast, lunch Mon–Sat (most branches also open Sun); no alcohol; www.noahs.com.*

North Beach Pizza

1499 GRANT AVE, SAN FRANCISCO *(and branches)* 📞 415/433-2444
NORTH BEACH/MISSION DISTRICT/SOUTH OF MARKET/UPPER HAIGHT/WEST
BERKELEY 🍴 *Pizza*

This North Beach stalwart started with a single location in the center of the neighborhood, and has since expanded to include several branches from San Mateo to Berkeley. The reason: damn fine pizza, with a crisp crust, a thick layer of cheese, and plenty of topping choices. Specialties include a clam and garlic pizza and the Coit Tower Special, topped with sausage, salami, pepperoni, and mushroom. The Caesar salad comes with a pungent, garlicky dressing (and a bit too much of it at that–ask for the dressing on the side). The atmosphere is extraordinarily warm and cozy, with big red booths and wooden walls. Expect a fair number of out-of-towners and families with children. Oh, and there's a variety of pastas on the menu, but there's a reason it's not called North Beach Ravioli–stick to the pies. *AE, DIS, DC, MC, V; no checks; lunch, dinner every day; beer and wine; www.northbeachpizza.com.*

O Chamé

1830 4TH ST, BERKELEY 📞 510/841-8783
WEST BERKELEY–EMERYVILLE 🍴 *Japanese*

Even jaded Berkeley food fanatics are bewitched by the fare in this exotic restaurant. Chef David Vardy spent years studying Buddhist-Taoist cooking in Taiwan, as well as Kansai and Kaiseki cuisine in Japan. (Kansai is the regional cuisine of Osaka; Kaiseki, created to complement the Japanese tea ceremony, consists of small dishes that can be consumed in a couple of bites.) Vardy developed an ardent local following when he opened the Daruma Teashop in North Berkeley in 1988, serving an intriguing assortment of teas, bento box lunches, and his popular teacakes–thin, sesame-based biscuits flavored with nuts or seeds. These and more elaborate works of culinary art may now be found at O Chamé, a soothing cafe crafted in the style of a rustic wayside inn from Japan's Meiji period. The à la carte menu changes often, but typical dishes include a very fresh vinegared wakame seaweed, cucumber, and crab salad and tofu dumplings with burdock and carrot. Though some entrees like the grilled river eel with endive and chayote can be pricey, ordering soba noodles with shiitake mushrooms and daikon will keep the bill in check. O Chamé also offers a range of delicately flavored teas and sakes, as well as good beers. *AE, DC, MC, V; no checks; lunch, dinner Mon-Sat; beer and wine.*

Oliveto Cafe and Restaurant

5655 COLLEGE AVE, OAKLAND   📞 510/547-5356
NORTH OAKLAND 🍴 *Italian*

While upstairs at Oliveto Restaurant a well-dressed crowd enjoys the air of an elegant Florentine trattoria, the rest of us pack into the boisterous Oliveto Cafe downstairs to sample chef/owner Paul Bertolli's inventive takes on rustic Italian cuisine. You may have to knock someone over the head to get a table, but so be it–the cuisine and the scene are worth the effort. You'll see chic singles sizing each other up over small, crisp pizzas and sophisticated salads like the *panzanella* with cherry tomatoes and fresh mozzarella. Flirt with your neighbor over awe-inspiring desserts such as the brioche bread pudding with apricot sauce, the divine rhubarb crisp with crème fraîche, or the dark chocolate torte with poached sour cherries and whipped cream. Excellent espressos, good wines by the glass, exotic beers, and sidewalk tables add to the appeal of this European-style cafe. *AE, DC, MC, V; no checks; cafe: breakfast, lunch, dinner every day; beer and wine.*

Pacific Restaurant

607 LARKIN ST, SAN FRANCISCO   📞 415/441-6722
TENDERLOIN 🍴 *Vietnamese*

Hugely popular with the Tenderloin Vietnamese community, this pho house is one of the best places in the city for the delicious Vietnamese noodle soup, served daily until 5PM. The broth is delicate and fragrant, the meat tender, and the fresh condiments piled high. The menu includes a huge array of other inexpensive Vietnamese dishes, such as fresh spring rolls stuffed with shrimp, cucumber, and lettuce, and pork shish kebab with thin rice noodles and vegetables. You might be joined by older men sitting down to the newspaper and a glass of iced coffee, suits from the nearby county courthouse taking a lunch break, and neighborhood families chatting and slurping noodles loudly. One room is decorated with a huge, whimsical mural depicting a Southeast Asian landscape, while the other has a strange display case full of miniature figurines. It's all a world away from the grimy streetscape outside, where transvestite hookers and drug dealers hawk their wares. *Cash only; breakfast, lunch every day until 5 PM; no alcohol.*

Pagolac

655 LARKIN ST, SAN FRANCISCO   📞 415/776-3234
TENDERLOIN 🍴 *Vietnamese*

If you're around the Tenderloin at night looking to dash quickly into one of Larkin Street's many Vietnamese restaurants, you might pass right by this nondescript place. But if you look beyond the dingy floors and tacky mirrors covering the walls, you'll notice that most of the patrons are local, the owners are friendly, and the food is fresh and good, from the pho served at breakfast to more substantial dinner dishes. The restaurant specializes in Seven-Flavor Beef, a seven-course meal ($13.95 per person, two-person minimum) of more-than-you-can-eat beef dishes ranging from carpaccio-like beef marinated in lemon juice to beef cooked tableside. Shrimp balls formed around juicy sugar cane come with lettuce, fresh vegetables, herbs, and noodles, all of which you wrap in rice paper and dip in a piquant fish sauce. The hard-to-find homemade sweetened soy milk is a must—this creamy, nutty beverage complements the food's sweet and sour flavors perfectly. *Cash only; breakfast, lunch, dinner Tues-Sat; beer and wine.*

Pakwan Pakistani Indian Restaurant

3180–82 16TH ST, SAN FRANCISCO   📞 415/255-2440
MISSION DISTRICT 🍴 *Indian*

Finding cheap Indian food isn't easy in San Francisco, so when Pakwan recently opened on an über-trendy stretch of 16th Street, it immediately started attracting young folks in the neighborhood who know a bargain when they see one. At both lunch and dinner, Pakwan is a busy place. Not that the Creamsicle-colored dining room is completely full; it just feels, well, hectic inside. But if you don't need a quiet, subdued dining experience, you'll get good Indian dishes for about half what they cost at most other spots. Enticing smells of tandoori lamb, chicken, and various kebabs greet you at the door; place your order at the counter, take a number, and it won't be long before those smells will be right under your nose. Many dishes will be familiar to

Indian-food veterans, while others, like the smoky-flavored *mirch salan* (a curry of roasted peppers and tamarind), are more unusual. The small and crunchy little vegetable fritters are disappointing, but in general the food—including the *bihari kabab*, extremely tender beef in a blend of spices and topped with slivers of onion—is excellent. Many dishes are quite spicy, so get ready to sweat a little, and be sure to order some rice or fresh-baked naan to ease the burn. *Cash only; lunch, dinner every day, brunch Sun; no alcohol.*

Panchita's Restaurant

3091 16TH ST, SAN FRANCISCO 📞 415/431-4232
MISSION DISTRICT 🍴 *Central American*

A vast array of great plates emerges from the enormous kitchen here, including rich soups, sweet plantain pies, and whole-corn tamales. The *pupusa*, a Salvadorean staple of handmade corn tortillas stuffed with pork, cheese, rice, or beans, is a great change of pace for burrito eaters, and you should absolutely order the steak. Get it on a plate with rice and beans and salad, or as part of a combination with fried shrimp, or stuffed into a burrito or taco, but to come here without sampling Panchita's scrumptious marinated meat would be a mistake. Few other places can match the quality or flavor of the beef here, especially at around $8 for a full meal. Fewer still have such a charming atmosphere—an ambience that's half 1950s kitsch (white molding and old dinette sets) and half old-time Mission hospitality. The hospitality, however, ends with the decor. The disgruntled teenage wait staff of one makes waiting tables a low priority; don't come here if you're expecting a quick bite. *MC, V; no checks; breakfast, lunch, dinner every day; beer and wine.*

Pancho's

3440 GEARY BLVD, SAN FRANCISCO 📞 415/387-8226
1639 POLK ST, SAN FRANCISCO 📞 415/474-2280
RICHMOND DISTRICT/POLK GULCH 🍴 *Mexican*

The Inner Richmond is awash in some of the best Asian food in the city. But sometimes you're just not in the mood for pad Thai, Vietnamese pho, or even Burmese curry. If what you're looking for is a satisfying burrito or a sky-high plate of nachos, Pancho's is where you'll find nirvana. There is a lot to like about Pancho's: most of the food is made to order, so although there's sometimes a bit more of a wait than at other burrito joints, the freshness factor is worth it. Pancho's is also one of the few taquerias in town where you can get beer-battered mahimahi tacos or grilled mahimahi burritos. There are even "small" burritos for the merely peckish. And don't miss the addictive guacamole and fresh house-made chips. It's all served up in a clean, well-lighted atmosphere featuring colorful tin signs on the wall advertising Mexican versions of Fresca and Wonder bread. The prices are certainly right as well—not even the rock shrimp fajitas will put much of a dent in your wallet. *MC, V; no checks; lunch, dinner every day; beer and wine.* ♿

Pancho Villa

3071 16TH ST, SAN FRANCISCO 📞 415/864-8840
MISSION DISTRICT 🍴 *Mexican*

Pancho Villa is one of the largest and most popular taquerias in the Mission. Nearly every night a line snakes onto the street from inside—there's even a security guard hired to keep watch and hold the door for arriving patrons (this is a scruffy block of 16th Street, after all). The interior is brightly lit and the walls are adorned with the work of local artists, which gives you something to stare at while you're waiting in line. Actually, you should probably focus on the large wall menu, because when it's your turn to order, you have to answer quickly. "What kind of meat?" "What kind of beans?" "Salsa?" If not outstanding, the food here is certainly good and fresh; the portions are large; and the choices for burrito and taco fillings alone are staggering. Try one made with snapper; or a "fajita burrito," stuffed with meat that's been simmered in a tangy pepper-and-onion sauce; or splurge on a steak-and-prawn burrito, the shrimp sautéed on the spot. *AE, MC, V; no checks; lunch, dinner every day; beer only.*

Papalote Mexican Grill

3409 VALENCIA ST, SAN FRANCISCO 📞 415/970-8815
MISSION DISTRICT 🍴 *Mexican*

The two brothers who own this small taco and burrito restaurant come with years of experience running restaurants in the family (their great aunt, Celia Lopez, started a local chain called Celia's in the 1960s), and they know how to bring a touch of style to the operation. Though the counter service is similar to that of other taquerias, the food is all made to order, whereas most places cook all the meat ahead of time, keeping it warm until it's ordered. The dining area is also a cut above, with brightly painted red walls, blue floors, and a shifting display of local art. The tacos aren't as authentic as the ones at dives along Mission Street, but they're tasty in their own right, served with fresh jicama salad and the addictive house salsa, a creamy roasted tomato concoction. In addition to carne asada, pollo asado, and grilled veggies, you can order your burrito stuffed with shrimp or fresh snapper. A range of draft beers, like Anderson Valley Brewing Company's Boont Amber, is the perfect complement to a quesadilla. Best of all, the owners are so friendly that even if it's your first visit, you'll leave feeling like an old friend. *AE, DC, MC, V; no checks; breakfast Sat–Sun, lunch, dinner every day; beer and wine.*

Park Chow

1240 9TH AVE, SAN FRANCISCO 📞 415/665-9912
SUNSET DISTRICT 🍽 *American*

There just aren't enough good things to say about Park Chow, one of our all-time favorite places to eat in the city. First of all, it's cheap (you get hefty servings of quality food for around $10 to $13); what's more, it's consistently good, the service is fast and friendly, the atmosphere is lively and fun, and you always leave feeling satisfied. Sample Park Chow's outstanding braised short ribs served with fresh greens and mashed potatoes, the giant portobello mushroom cap served with creamy polenta, or the linguine with calamari, mussels, clams, and shrimp. Burgers, chicken, salads, and a reasonably good wine-by-the-glass list are on the menu as well. While you're waiting for a table (they're always busy and don't take reservations), order a glass of wine from the bar and snuggle with your honey by the fireplace. On sunny days, request a table in the roof garden. Brunch is served until 2:30PM on weekends. If you're in the Castro, check out the sister restaurant, Chow (see review). *MC, V; no checks; lunch, dinner every day, brunch Sat–Sun; beer and wine.* ♿

Pasta Pomodoro

2027 CHESTNUT ST, SAN FRANCISCO *(and branches)* 📞 415/474-3400
MARINA/CASTRO/COW HOLLOW/JAPANTOWN/LAUREL HEIGHTS/LOWER
HAIGHT/NOE VALLEY/NORTH BEACH/NORTH OAKLAND/SUNSET DISTRICT
🍽 *Italian*

Since most people don't have much time to cook at home these days, Pasta Pomodoro fulfills a modern need: simple but well-prepared food in pleasant surroundings at a reasonable cost. Two can share a Caesar salad, then go for capellini with pomodoro sauce (tomatoes laced with garlic and basil) and an order of linguine with fresh clams and leave without blowing much more than $20. There are plenty of more creative options—like bell-shaped pasta with braised duck, pancetta, and portobello mushrooms—but this place is better when it doesn't attempt things that are too complicated. Because the local chain has set up shop in many of the Bay Area's most historic neighborhoods, including North Beach, the Haight, the Castro, and Oakland's Rockridge, some complain that it has a homogenizing influence. The restaurants do all have similar decor, with oversize Italian posters and red and black trim, but it's hard to complain about a place that will sell you a decent pasta with shrimp and asparagus for under $9. *MC, V; no checks; lunch, dinner every day; beer and wine; pasta@pastapomodoro.com; www.pastapomodoro.com.*

Pauline's Pizza

260 VALENCIA ST, SAN FRANCISCO 📞 415/552-2050
MISSION DISTRICT 🍴 *Pizza*

The pizza debate in San Francisco is a never-ending affair. It seems everyone is an expert, eager to offer his or her opinion on whose circle of dough with cheese on top is tops. Meanwhile, for years Pauline's has been quietly churning out what very well could be the best pizza in town. The bright yellow building on Valencia Street is as unassuming as the restaurant's reputation, but diners come from around the city to sit and enjoy the basic meal: pizza and salad. Don't bother looking for anything else, because you won't find it—and you won't want it. There's plenty to hold your interest on the toppings menu, from French goat cheese to spiced pork shoulder to house-spiced chicken. It all goes on Pauline's handmade thin-crust dough. The eclectic salads are prepared from certified organic, handpicked lettuces and vegetables, accented with herbs from the restaurant's own local gardens. Service here always comes with a welcoming smile. *MC, V; checks OK; dinner Tues–Sat; beer and wine.*

Phoenix Next Door

1786 SHATTUCK AVE, BERKELEY 📞 510/883-0783
NORTH BERKELEY 🍴 *Italian*

High ceilings, light-wood banquettes, terra-cotta tiles, and bucolic, window-framed landscapes give this intimate North Berkeley lunch spot an airy, loftlike feel. Phoenix Next Door opened as an adjunct to its neighbor Phoenix Pastificio, a specialty pasta shop providing noodles to some of the Bay Area's best restaurants and take-home fixings to those in the know. Phoenix patrons, who range from obviously well-off seniors to workers from nearby businesses taking a break from brown-bagging, choose from a brief, daily changing menu featuring gourmet pastas in innovative sauces, many available to take home next door. Favorites include goat cheese ravioli with kalamata olive pesto and smoked salmon ravioli with herbed cream sauce; the menu also features an organic salad and house-made vegetarian soup. Take a peek at the pastries and tortes, as attractive as they are tasty, on offer that day. *No credit cards; checks OK; lunch Mon–Sat; no alcohol; phoenixpasta@yahoo.com.* ♿

Pho Hoa Hiep IV

239 CLEMENT ST, SAN FRANCISCO *(and branches)* ☎ 415/379-9008
RICHMOND DISTRICT/SUNSET DISTRICT 🍴 *Vietnamese/Southeast Asian*

Pho Hoa may have plain-Jane decor and a too-brightly-lit atmosphere, but when you're facedown in a bowl of fabulous pho (for which you paid a mere pittance), you can overlook the drabbest of surroundings. Pho Hoa's beef noodle soup starts with a magical broth that is beefy and subtly flavored with star anise. The timid order theirs with rare steak, while the bold add flank, tendon, tripe, or brisket. It comes in three sizes: the "x-large," a bowl of truly impressive proportions, will set you back all of $5. Pho Hoa also offers chicken and seafood noodle soups, as well as nonsoup dishes like barbecued pork with noodles and imperial rolls. There's an interesting beverage list as well, featuring young coconut juice, durian shakes, and red bean drinks. Bring the little ones–Pho Hoa is one of the only Asian restaurants we've seen with separate menu items for kids. *Cash only; lunch, dinner every day; no alcohol.* ♿

Pho Tu Do

1000 CLEMENT ST, SAN FRANCISCO ☎ 415/221-7111
RICHMOND DISTRICT 🍴 *Vietnamese/Southeast Asian*

Pho, the Vietnamese bowl of noodles and soup, is an extremely satisfying meal, and Pho Tu Do is one of the best places in the city to enjoy a deep bowlful. Beef pho comes in your choice of rare beef, brisket, flank, and tendon with a deeply flavored broth and is served with a plateful of condiments–Asian basil leaves, bean sprouts, jalapeño peppers. It's the perfect dinner on a rainy winter evening. And while Pho Tu Do's beef pho can hold its own, the restaurant's chicken pho is truly out of this world. The rich broth is simmered for 24 hours, then loaded up with shredded light and dark meat chicken, along with sweet fried onions and a mass of rice noodles–it'll cure whatever ails you. Pho Tu Do also offers rice plates, including the bewitching five-spice barbecued chicken with rice. You can get your tapioca drink fix here, too. The only downside at Pho Tu Do is the paucity of options for vegetarians. *V; no checks; lunch, dinner every day; beer and wine.* &

Piazza D'Angelo

22 MILLER AVE, MILL VALLEY   📞 415/388-2000
MILL VALLEY 🍴 *Italian*

Piazza D'Angelo is one of Mill Valley's most popular restaurants, with large (often noisy) crowds of Marinites packing the pleasant, airy bar. They don't necessarily come for the food, mind you, but for the charged atmosphere. D'Angelo's Italian menu abounds with familiar though not always well-executed fare, including numerous pasta plates–spaghetti sautéed with kalamata olives, chile pepper, baby spinach, onions, sun-dried tomatoes, white wine, and pecorino cheese is one of the better choices–and several juicy entrees from the rotisserie. The calzones, stuffed with fresh ingredients like ricotta, spinach, caramelized onions, mozzarella, and sausage, are a reasonably priced choice, and the pizzas make a good lunch. Desserts are made fresh daily, and if there's a crème brûlée on the tray, don't let your server take it away. The extensive wine list features a respectable selection of California and Italian labels (about 150 bottles), including 10 wines poured by the glass. *AE, DC, MC, V; no checks; lunch Mon-Fri, dinner every day, brunch Sat-Sun; full bar.* &

Picante Cocina Mexicana

1328 6TH ST, BERKELEY   📞 510/525-3121
WEST BERKELEY 🍴 *Mexican*

Bright, bustling, and expansive, this West Berkeley mainstay is revered for its superfresh, tasty Mexican cuisine. The cheery, hacienda-like decor features ceramic-tile floors, colorful Mexican masks and textiles, and Diego Rivera prints; lively mosaic tiles offset the open kitchen and the tortilla-making station, where you can watch fresh corn tortillas come into being. Picante serves many of the same dishes you'll find at any Mexican restaurant–burritos, enchiladas, tostadas–but with handmade tortillas and chips, house-made roasted jalapeños, and menus for vegetarians, vegans, and kids, the food rises above the ordinary.

The grilled veggie burrito is a particularly good choice. Young families make up a good portion of Picante loyalists; it's loud enough that the little ones don't cause a disruption. Order at the counter and choose a table in the front area near the long bar or in the vast dining room, or head out back to the garden patio, surrounded by trumpet vine and Christmas lights, where a mosaic-tiled fountain babbles in the background. Heat lamps make the patio a viable option in the evening as well. *MC, V; checks OK; lunch, dinner every day, brunch Sat–Sun; beer and wine.* ♿

Piccadilly Fish and Chips

1348 POLK ST, SAN FRANCISCO 📞 415/771-6477
POLK GULCH 🍴 *Fish and Chips*

It seems that the affable old guy who single-handedly keeps this place running knows everyone who eats here and exactly what they're going to order. Admittedly, everyone orders pretty much the same thing: two pieces of fish and chips, three pieces of fish and chips, or four pieces of fish and chips. (You could order five, but we can't imagine how anyone could polish it off.) He fries it when you order it, so service is not lightning fast, but he knows that that's the only way to serve fish that's hot and crisp, perfect with a generous sprinkle of salt and vinegar. Not only are the fish and chips tops, the restaurant has a neighborly charm, from the antiquated cash register to the guy who will run out to the curb with your order when you can't find parking. *Cash only; lunch, dinner every day; no alcohol.*

Pizza Rustica

5422 COLLEGE AVE, OAKLAND 📞 510/654-1601
NORTH OAKLAND 🍴 *Pizza*

Housed in a salmon-colored postmodern building with blue Corinthian columns, this jazzy nouveau pizza joint has a cramped, noisy dining room with tiny, knee-bruising tables, bright pop art on the walls, and California pizzas made with a light, crunchy cornmeal crust or a traditional peasant-bread crust. The traditional Mediterranean-style pizzas are impeccable, but pizza adventurers should try one of the more exotic offerings: the Thai pizza is prepared with roasted chicken in a spicy ginger and peanut sauce, mozzarella, julienned carrots, scallions, daikon, peppers, and sesame seeds, and the Ambrosia features sundried tomatoes, artichoke hearts, roasted garlic, kalamata olives, and a mix of fontina, mozzarella, and Parmesan cheeses. *AE, MC, V; local checks only; lunch, dinner every day; beer and wine.* ♿

Bay Area Brewpubs

The cult of microbreweries and brewpubs exploded across the United States during the 1990s, with beer fans from coast to coast learning to discern their porters from their pilsners, their ESBs from their IPAs. And judging by the crowds that pack San Francisco's still-growing legion of brewpubs, the trend is still on the rise.

A brewpub is a bar where the majority of beer sold is made on the premises. These days brewpubs are usually accompanied by a restaurant that serves surprisingly elaborate—even upscale—food. Brewpubs are different from simple microbreweries or craft breweries, which bottle or keg their beer to be sold elsewhere. Brewpubs are a recent development in the United States because they only became legal in 1982. But ever since, beer aficionados have been excitedly exploring this vast new world of sturdy ales and lagers.

Although pubs in Europe celebrate their age and rustic qualities, many U.S. brewpubs have adopted a hip, urban, and often faux-industrial sheen. Call it the brewpub aesthetic: a large room with exposed brick and steel, brass trim that's polished to a Lemon Pledge shine, and servers in pressed white shirts who hand you a beer menu printed on colored card stock. Such a barroom may be the type to make Charles Bukowski turn in his grave, but on the other hand, it's clearly a look that mirrors the wholesome quality of the beers themselves. Ditto for the food, which in these establishments comes from a real kitchen and a real chef, not a plastic bag or a microwave oven behind the bar.

Below are some of our favorite local places for a quality beer-and-food experience. See also the review of Pyramid Brewery and Alehouse.

Beach Chalet (1000 GREAT HIGHWAY; 415/386-8439)

Poised at the outer edge of Golden Gate Park, this 1920s-era building is a worthy destination for its world-class ocean view and colorful Works Project Administration murals. Menu items like lobster-stuffed ravioli or rack of lamb might scare budget diners away, but don't run yet. The Niman Ranch burger is much more reasonable, and there are plenty of less-expensive appetizers—from nachos to grilled bruschetta—to go with your Churchyard Strong Ale or Playland Pale.

First Amendment (563 2ND ST; 415/369-0900)

The pizza, with its fresh tomatoes and deliciously chewy "beer mash crust," is as much of a draw at First Amendment as is crisp South Park

Blonde Ale or the creamy Shot Tower Stout. Stick to the tasty salads, sandwiches, and pastas and the prices won't seem unreasonable.

Jupiter (2181 SHATTUCK AVE, BERKELEY; 510/843-8277)

Though technically not a brewpub, Jupiter is still a worthy destination for craft-beer lovers with its extensive selection (about 20 taps) of regional brews. The pizzas are a fine accompaniment, too. Two floors of seating and a large backyard beer garden help handle the crowds of students.

Magnolia (1398 HAIGHT ST; 415/864-7468)

This friendly establishment is as down-home as San Francisco brewpubs come. The menu offers huge plates of fresh-made fries, sandwiches, and affordable entrees to go with house-made brews like Prescription Pale or the Stout of Circumstance. Magnolia specializes in cask-conditioned ales, which are naturally carbonated (no added carbon dioxide), less severely chilled than typical draft beers, and pulled from their kegs via a British-style hand pump.

San Francisco Brewing Company (155 COLUMBUS AVE; 415/434-3344)

For true Barbary Coast atmosphere, head for this longtime North Beach bar, located in a dark and moody saloon dating back to 1907. The atmosphere is thick with history—a far cry from the sterility of so many modern brewpubs. Try the well-balanced Emperor Norton lager with your burger (turkey, beef, garden), fried calamari, or curly fries.

ThirstyBear (661 HOWARD ST; 415/974-0905)

This spacious SoMa establishment is as much known for its tapas menu as it is for its house-made ales. Ordering full dinners will cost you plenty, but if you want snacks with your Meyer ESB or Brown Bear ale, try the cheap and tasty *patatas al ajillo* (garlic-seasoned potatoes) or the sautéed fish cheeks, a house specialty.

Toronado (547 HAIGHT ST; 415/863-2276)

While not a brewpub per se, the Toronado is certainly a craft brew mecca. The rotating beer selection is easily the Bay Area's most adventurous. Some 40 beers are available on tap, from Pacific Northwest favorites to hard-to-find Belgians and seasonal ales. When hunger strikes, the adjacent Rosamunde Sausage Grill (see review) has tasty, fresh-cooked sausages you can bring inside.

Pluto's

3258 SCOTT ST, SAN FRANCISCO 📞 415/775-8867
627 IRVING ST, SAN FRANCISCO 📞 415/753-8867
MARINA/SUNSET DISTRICT 🍴 *American*

American comfort food doesn't get much more comforting than Pluto's Caesar salads, herb-roasted Sonoma turkey, and "smashed spuds of the day," all served in portions big enough to share. Tender grilled meats get tucked between slices of focaccia to make hot, satisfying sandwiches, and side dishes include pan-cooked seasonal vegetables, garlic potato rings, and stuffing worthy of a Thanksgiving dinner. Perhaps that's why young and sporty Marina residents form mighty long lines almost every hour of the day at the Scott Street location, getting food to go or to eat in the tiny, high-ceilinged dining room with a slick, modern feel. It's clear that many of the patrons are frequent visitors and figured out the arcane ordering system long ago: after waiting in the line, pick up a slip that lists all your choices, then hand it to the appropriate server behind the counter when you order your food. At the end of the line, the cashier will use the slip to calculate your total, while you're tempted by the plate of homey cookies and dessert bars displayed near the cash register. *MC, V; no checks; lunch, dinner every day, brunch Sat–Sun; beer and wine.* ♿

Polker's American Café

2226 POLK ST, SAN FRANCISCO 📞 415/885-1000
RUSSIAN HILL 🍴 *American*

Though it's not much to look at (dimly lit and with yellow stucco walls), this comfortable spot is your best bet for burgers or breakfast in Russian Hill. Uncommonly good hamburgers come in variations like the Ortega burger (with avocado, feta, and green chiles), all accompanied by crisp, flavorful fries. Salads here are more than a mere afterthought: the Santa Fe chicken salad comes garnished with black beans, cheddar, and avocado, dressed in a tangy but not overpowering basil vinaigrette. Saturday and Sunday there's the predictable weekend morning line out the door of people waiting for breakfast fare like French toast, pancakes, and omelets and other egg dishes. The crowd is mostly the younger of the yuppies that call Russian Hill home. *MC, V; no checks; breakfast, lunch, dinner every day; beer and wine.* ♿

Pomelo

92 JUDAH ST, SAN FRANCISCO 📞 415/731-6175
SUNSET DISTRICT 🍴 *Eclectic*

This noodle house near UCSF is tiny—there are just a handful of tables and a few seats at the counter—but it dishes up fare that is truly global in scope. The menu items are named after cities, so you can start in Palermo with a tomato and basil bruschetta, then head to Phnom Penh for a rice noodle salad studded with tiger prawns and flavored with mint, lime, and sesame oil. Other toothsome destinations include Osaka and Tokyo for buckwheat noodles, Manila for rice noodles, and even Lima for quinoa pilaf topped with grilled tequila chicken. Don't miss the fresh-made fettucine of the Italian destinations. And while there are no dishes containing the oversized tangy citrus fruit that gives the restaurant its name, there is a salad that contains its cousin, the grapefruit. Though tiny, Pomelo is a cheerful spot with a bright yellow-green interior, friendly service, an open kitchen, and a big pomelo hanging over the door. *Cash only; lunch Mon-Fri, dinner every day; beer and wine; pomelo@pomelosf.com; www.pomelosf.com.*

Pork Store Café

1451 HAIGHT ST, SAN FRANCISCO 📞 415/864-6981
UPPER HAIGHT 🍴 *Southern*

So much pork, so little time. And this extremely casual Haight Street landmark is most definitely the place to enjoy it. Limited seating and ample demand—especially for weekend breakfasts—could make for a long wait, but it's worth it. You'll quickly forget your wait outdoors once you're seated and happily suckling on the house pièce de résistance, the two-pork chop platter with chunky, flavorful mashed potatoes, cooked fresh spinach, and biscuits savory enough to satisfy any Southerner—all for less than $8. The house-made applesauce that accompanies it just seals the deal. Those with smaller appetites should consider the year-round turkey dinner, fried chicken specials, and the well done but standard breakfast platters guaranteed to send any hangover back to bed. The pancakes are noteworthy, and they'll supply an enormous stack with a variety of fresh fruit for a mere $5. You'll squeal with delight at every bite. *AE, DC, MC, V; no checks; breakfast, lunch every day; no alcohol; porkstore@aol.com.* ♿

Powell's Place / Powell's Place #2

511 HAYES ST, SAN FRANCISCO 📞 415/863-1404

708 VALLEJO ST, SAN FRANCISCO 📞 415/434-2727

HAYES VALLEY/NORTH BEACH 🍴 *Southern*

Founded in 1977 by gospel singer Emmit Powell, the much-loved Powell's Place is a haven for fans of soul food. The original location has a large entryway and take-out counter and two individual dining rooms—one green, the other yellow, and both filled with interesting artwork and the sweet sounds of classic R&B. Powell's serves lots of Southern-style dishes—smothered pork chops, fried catfish, ribs, meat loaf—but the reason to come is the fried chicken. The pieces are hunky and fresh, the meat moist and tender under a tasty, crunchy crust. Order your pieces à la carte, and then pick a couple of sides to go with them—corn muffins, black-eyed peas, and greens are all recommended. Be warned, though, that many other items can be quite mediocre: on one visit the mashed potatoes, horror of horrors, tasted fresh out of a box, the gravy on the smothered (and quite leathery) chops was brown and boring, and the corn came straight from the can. As for the service? Lackluster to the point of comical. Still, the restaurant does have its charms, and if you stick to the chicken, you'll go home plenty full and happy. *AE, MC, V; breakfast, lunch, dinner every day; beer and wine; emmetap@aol.com; www.powellsplace.citysearch.com.*

Primo Patio Cafe

214 TOWNSEND ST, SAN FRANCISCO 📞 415/957-1129

SOUTH OF MARKET 🍴 *Caribbean*

Alas, Primo Patio's eponymous patio doesn't get a lot of sun much of the year. But thanks to the heat lamps and the spicy Caribbean tapas, you can dream of the tropics as you snack on ceviche and dine on grilled jerk chicken. One of our favorites is the big basket of "Snaps & Fries"–fried bits of flaky snapper, very lightly breaded and with a hint of heat—served with a tangled mass of spicy fries. Sandwiches like the jerk steak on a French roll or the roasted eggplant in a pita make a hearty lunch. In fact, portions of all the dishes are more than generous, and nothing on the menu is more than $8.50–not even the butterflied grilled lamb steak. The patio is packed on weekdays, especially at lunchtime, but considerably less so on weekends. Skip the hour-plus waits at the usual breakfast spots and come here for one of the egg dishes: the Barbados

Burrito, with scrambled eggs, sautéed shrimp, and jack cheese, served with black beans and cumin rice, is a real winner. *MC, V; no checks; breakfast, lunch, dinner every day; beer and wine; primo1@sirius.com.*

Puerto Alegre

546 VALENCIA ST, SAN FRANCISCO ☎ 415/255-8201
MISSION DISTRICT 🍴 *Mexican*

Every night is a fiesta at Puerto Allegre, where the margaritas flow freely and the roving mariachi bands play to enthusiastic, if slightly tipsy, audiences. Now, the Mexican food here is not going to win any prizes: they serve the usual burritos, enchiladas, and fajitas, some of which could use a wallop of spices. And the dark, cavernous dining room looks as if it hasn't been updated since the restaurant opened in 1970. But that doesn't keep the place from being packed every night of the week starting around 7PM. If you do as everyone else does and start off with a potent margarita and the free chips and salsa, you might fall under the restaurant's spell as well. If you're not in a margarita mood, the restaurant takes advantage of the shortage of breakfast spots in the neighborhood and serves dishes like huevos rancheros and eggs with chorizo on weekend mornings. *MC, V; no checks; breakfast, lunch, dinner Sat-Sun, lunch, dinner Mon-Fri; full bar.*

Pyramid Brewery and Alehouse

901 GILMAN ST, BERKELEY ☎ 510/528-9880
WEST BERKELEY 🍴 *Pub Grub*

Want a pint of fresh craft-brewed beer and a decent meal to go with it? Want a nice environment–a place you can even bring the kids? Plenty of people do want these things, which is why Pyramid has proven so popular since opening in 1997. The brewery is located in a block-long industrial building that Seattle-based Pyramid bought and renovated, and inside are not only a brewery and bottling plant but also a bright and spacious alehouse. The atmosphere can be a bit sterile, but on the whole Pyramid is an easygoing and friendly place for craft beer-loving folks of all kinds–including parents, who can keep an eye on their kids while kicking back with one of the nearly two dozen beers (made under the Pyramid and Thomas Kemper labels) or four craft-brewed sodas. The food–fairly typical brewpub fare, including pizza, burgers, steaks, fish and chips, chicken sandwiches, and pastas—isn't exactly adventurous or surprising, but that's okay. Like the beer, it's hearty and reliable, and you can't beat the extremely reasonable prices. *AE, MC, V; lunch, dinner every day; beer and wine; host@pyramidbrew.com; www.pyramidbrew.com/alehouses.php.* &

Q

225 CLEMENT ST, SAN FRANCISCO   📞 415/752-2298
RICHMOND DISTRICT 🍽 *Eclectic*

Wackily eclectic and not the least bit pretentious, this newcomer to the Richmond District dining scene has quickly made a name for itself serving delicious, great-value dishes to young, local hipsters. The quasi-industrial decor is funky rather than chic, with a corrugated metal ceiling, barstools covered in sparkly vinyl covers, and candleholders that look as if they came from the salvage yard. The good tunes on the stereo provide entertainment, as do the chefs grooving around the open kitchen—especially when partner and executive chef Andrew (Smilin' Andy) Gillen is manning the grill. Many menu items, almost none of which cost more than $10, have a Southern slant: in the "down-home favorites" category are beer-battered catfish, barbecued pork ribs, and some mighty fine fried chicken—three lightly breaded, perfectly crispy pieces piled on top of a mountain of mashed potatoes. But other items, like the California-influenced "slammin' salmon burger" with chile-lime aioli, the mahimahi and escolar quesadilla, or the vegan platter of grilled veggies, would leave Southerners scratching their heads. No matter what you order, expect heaping portions; two hungry people can easily share one appetizer and one main dish. *AE, DC, DIS, MC, V; no checks; lunch, dinner every day, brunch Sat–Sun; beer and wine.* &

R&G Lounge

631-B KEARNY ST, SAN FRANCISCO   📞 415/982-7877
CHINATOWN 🍽 *Chinese*

Situated in limbo between the edge of Chinatown and the edge of the Financial District, the R&G Lounge attracts a mixed crowd of tourists, businesspeople, and local Chinese residents. The restaurant's loyal following of diners come for the fresh Cantonese seafood dishes—especially the salt-and-pepper crab—and good prices. The main downstairs dining room has all the charm of a cafeteria, with glaring fluorescent lights and Formica tables; though it's harder to get a table in the formal upstairs dining room, the lighting there is a little easier on the eyes. The menu is half in English, half in Chinese, but not everything is on both menus, so ask your server for recommendations. Usually he or she will happily oblige, though service can get a bit rushed during peak times. *AE, MC, V; no checks; lunch, dinner every day; beer and wine.*

Red Tractor Cafe

5634 COLLEGE AVE, OAKLAND ☏ 510/595-3500
NORTH OAKLAND 🍴 *American*

The Red Tractor might remind you of an old New England farmhouse, and it's supposed to. Mason jars of pickled veggies line the wood walls, attesting to the comfort food on the menu. Step up to the counter and choose from "farm fresh" offerings such as meat loaf (and No Meat Loaf, made of polenta, wild rice, mushrooms, onions, jack, and smoked mozzarella), pot roast, chicken pot-pie, or macaroni and cheese, complete with side orders like homemade creamed spinach and mashed potatoes with gravy. Breakfast favorites include fluffy waffles with fruit, home fries, and biscuits with gravy. Besides the framed photos of different models of red tractors, the main decorative element here is paper place mats featuring–what else?–red tractors colored in by kids, university students, Rockridge-area yuppies, and everyone else who appreciates the Red Tractor's cheery service, reasonable prices, and hearty fare. *MC, V; no checks; breakfast Sat-Sun, lunch every day, dinner Mon-Fri; beer and wine; farmerandy@ redtractor.com, www.redtractor.com.* ♿

Rick and Ann's

2922 DOMINGO AVE, BERKELEY ☏ 510/649-8538
SOUTH BERKELEY 🍴 *American*

You'd have to get up mighty early to beat the brunch rush at Rick and Ann's, so you might have to resign yourself to sitting and reading the paper for an hour while you wait for a table. In a city overflowing with breakfast joints, you'd be hard-pressed to find anyone who didn't rave about the fresh-baked scones and hearty comfort food that's served up daily. And you'll find everyone from spandex-clad cyclists to well-coiffed society ladies vying for tables. So how do Rick and Ann continue to draw crowds after more than a decade of business? Basically, they make the food your mom would have made if only she'd been a better cook. Nothing starts a morning off better than the stick-to-your-ribs Down South, a tasty mix of cornmeal cakes, spicy turkey sausage, and scrambled eggs. And you'll never be able to go back to Kraft after sampling the rich and creamy macaroni and cheese. The simple-but-just-right country cooking theme continues to the decor, as you take a seat among wide farm tables inside or on the sunny outdoor patio. *AE, MC, V; no checks; breakfast, lunch, dinner every day; beer and wine.*

Roosevelt Tamale Parlor

2817 24TH ST, SAN FRANCISCO 📞 415/550-9213
MISSION DISTRICT 🍴 *Mexican*

It might seem daunting at first. This small, dark place has signs everywhere saying what you can't do: "No Credit Cards." "No Smoking" (as if). "Do Not Sit at a Table That Hasn't Been Cleaned Yet!" But this place has been around since 1922, and it looks like the management has figured out how they like things to be. It's hard to find the tamales on the menu, which is dominated by the usual taqueria standards as well as a handful of traditional items like *menudo*, ranchero steak, and *mole poblano*. But the tamales, which come in chicken and pork varieties, are good, big, and cheap, and accompanied by a smoky, thick red mole sauce. Don't worry: You'll be okay as long as you follow the rules. *Cash only; lunch, dinner Tues-Sun; beer only.*

Rosamunde Sausage Grill

545 HAIGHT ST, SAN FRANCISCO 📞 415/437-6851
LOWER HAIGHT 🍴 *Hot Dogs/Sausage*

If fresh-grilled gourmet sausages washed down with hearty craft-brewed beer sound like a good time, then Rosamunde Sausage Grill and the adjacent Toronado pub will more than satisfy. Rosamunde offers just over a dozen types of sausage–spicy Italian, smoked Hungarian, chicken with cherries, duck with hazelnuts–all on display in a glass case right inside the cozy storefront room. Make your selection and it's grilled to order on the spot, after which you can top it with sauerkraut, mustard, grilled onions, spicy peppers, or chili. The Nuernberger bratwurst is mild, the smoked lamb more full-bodied and pungent, and the andouille on the spicier side. The cooks know their craft, and each sausage is crispy outside and juicy within. Rosamunde has about nine stools and a counter along the window, but a better idea (especially since it serves no alcohol) is to take your meats next door to the Toronado, which offers 40 to 50 craft-brewed beers on tap. The pub can get crowded after dark, but it's worth bumping a few elbows to be able to choose from such world-class brews as Anderson Valley Brewing Company's Boont Amber, Germany's Franziskaner Hefeweizen, and Belgium's Delirium Tremens under one roof. Order your pints at the bar, and look for extra tables in the back room. *Cash only; lunch, dinner every day; no alcohol.*

Rose's Cafe

2298 UNION ST, SAN FRANCISCO 📞 415/775-2200
COW HOLLOW 🍽 *Italian*

Though it would be easy to spend 20 bucks or more on dinner here if you're not careful, the inventive and artistically presented food, charming neighborhood ambience, and good value make this offshoot of the more expensive Rose Pistola in North Beach a real winner. The dining room is somehow sunny and cozy at the same time, painted a warm yellow and decorated with bright chandeliers in primary colors. At lunch, when neighborhood regulars pack the place, favorite menu items include a salad with prosciutto and pears, as well as the unusual wafer-thin, plate-size slices of focaccia sandwiching melted crescenza cheese. At dinner, when people come from all over town, entrees like grilled salmon with lentils, radicchio, and tapenade are more popular. Wines, a surprising number available by the glass, come not only from Italy and California but from France, Australia, and beyond. If the weather is even remotely nice, request an outdoor table, separated from the sidewalk by large flower boxes. *AE, DC, DIS, MC, V; no checks; breakfast, lunch, dinner every day; beer and wine.* ♿

Saigon Saigon

1132–34 VALENCIA ST, SAN FRANCISCO 📞 415/206-9635
MISSION DISTRICT 🍽 *Vietnamese/Southeast Asian*

Large windows facing Valencia Street, unpretentious white-paper tablecloths, and simple yet tasteful decor set a scene at Saigon Saigon that's at once casual, uncluttered, and friendly. The restaurant has an inviting spirit that draws Mission District regulars—clean-cut dot-com employees and crusty poets alike—back to its tables again and again. Of course, that's thanks in no small part to its tasty, and quite affordable, meals. Water with fresh lemon and a cup of hot soup arrive automatically as you peruse the menu, which offers several dozen meat, seafood, and vegetarian dishes. Lunch is a great time to come, as the restaurant offers some excellent specials, many for less than $5. The sliced trout with mixed vegetables and ginger sauce is especially tasty, as is the rice vermicelli plate, which is served with your choice of meat or vegetables (or both). Saigon Saigon isn't trying to be trendy or hip, thank goodness; instead it offers a reliable menu and plenty of room to breathe. *AE, MC, V; no checks; lunch, dinner every day; beer and wine.* &

Saigon Sandwiches

560 LARKIN ST, SAN FRANCISCO   📞   415/474-5698

TENDERLOIN 🍴 *Vietnamese*

At lunchtime a long line of students from nearby Hastings law school and even the California Culinary Academy queue up for the crusty, crunchy, tangy, sweet, smoky sandwiches that are this spot's specialty. Each of the seven or so sandwiches, only $1.75 to $2.25 apiece, starts with thin, smoky slices of meat, like roast pork, liverwurst, or barbecue chicken. But the zing is in the generous garnish of vegetables: a julienne of carrots, sweet yellow onion, jalapeño pepper, and loads of leafy cilantro, all marinated in piquant fish sauce. There's not much else on the menu—just a pile of crab and lobster chips and Vietnamese bakery items like mung bean cakes tottering on the counter. The ladies behind the counter are gracious, but the spartan setup (one little table and a counter with three chairs) doesn't inspire many to stay; most get their sandwich to go. *Cash only; breakfast, lunch every day; no alcohol.*

Sam's Anchor Café

27 MAIN ST, TIBURON   📞   415/435-9767

TIBURON 🍴 *American*

It's another marvelous day in Marin. You want to relax with friends on a sun-drenched deck and relish views of San Francisco. Head for Sam's and a quintessential Marin experience. Just ask any of the locals who have flocked to this popular destination over the past eighty years. The wait for a table can be excruciatingly long (two hours or so) on sunny weekends, but half the fun comes from being part of the lively scene. This is probably the only restaurant in the Bay Area that promises a refund if a marauding seagull spoils a meal. There's also lots of indoor space if you're looking for peace and quiet. The classic bar is a great spot to eavesdrop, spin your own tale, or ask about Sam, a bootlegger and colorful character. Seafood is a popular choice, including cioppino and oysters

on the half shell, but many entrees hover around $15 and seem a bit overpriced—
even an omelet is almost $10. That's why you might want to order a burger on a
sourdough bun or a basket of fish and chips—the spectacular view is the same
whether you spend $15 or $50. *AE, DC, DIS, MC, V; no checks; lunch, dinner every day,
brunch Sat-Sun; full bar; sam@samscafe.com; www.samscafe.com.*

Sam's Log Cabin

945 SAN PABLO AVE, ALBANY   510/558-0494
ALBANY   *American*

There's no better place to wait in line for brunch on a sunny Sunday morning
than Sam's Log Cabin, where they invite you to kick back in lawn chairs in
their grassy backyard. You would think that a log cabin would stand out on this
urban stretch of San Pablo Avenue, where the restaurant is sandwiched
between auto body dealers and fast-food outlets. But amazingly, most locals are
ignorant of the charms of this family-run eatery. Inside, simple whitewashed
walls hung with vintage photos and old lanterns create an atmosphere that is
cute without being claustrophobic, not hip but homey. Dig into breakfast specialties like Swedish pancakes with fruit filling or favorites like griddle cakes.
Your coffee may come in a flowered mug that would make your grandma
proud, but the java is dark and strong, the eggs are organic, and they've got
three kinds of hot sauce. At lunchtime, you can fill up on simple classics like a
tuna melt or BLT. *Cash only; breakfast, lunch Tues-Sun; no alcohol.*

San Francisco Art Institute Cafe

800 CHESTNUT ST, SAN FRANCISCO   415/749-4567
RUSSIAN HILL   *Soup/Salad/Sandwich*

At this little spot atop the San Francisco Art Institute your $4 hamburger
comes with a million-dollar view. Though the cafe is little more than a convenient spot for students to congregate between classes, its location high on Russian Hill means drop-dead gorgeous views of Alcatraz Island and far beyond.
The food includes mostly standard fare—sandwiches, salads, and burgers—plus
daily specials. Many specials are fairly good, but others have a thrown-together
let's-see-what-we-can-do-with-leftovers quality (green beans on rice with gravy,
anyone?). The patrons are very young pierced and goateed types who attend
the school. The battered black-and-white tile floor, artwork on the walls, and
jazz recordings played by the counter staff set a very relaxed boho mood, with

nary a cell phone or business deal in sight. The hours vary according to the school year, but the cafe is generally closed on Saturday evenings, all day Sunday, and during school holidays. *Cash only; hours vary; no alcohol.* &

San Miguel

3520 20TH ST, SAN FRANCISCO   📞 415/826-0173
MISSION DISTRICT 🍴 *Central American*

With plants everywhere, gourds and baskets hanging from a corrugated tin ceiling, and a front counter full of fresh vegetables, this Guatemalan restaurant makes you feel like you're in an open-air market. You can reminisce about past trips to Central America while looking at the maps under glass at each table, and you might even get to practice some Spanish, because some of the friendly bussers don't bother with English unless you look really confused. The menu incorporates lots of Mexican dishes, such as a starter of *taquitos con guacamol*—small corn tortillas stuffed with chopped meat and fried, then topped with creamy guacamole, fresh tomato sauce, and slivers of red onion. Some of the entrees are huge, like the Plato San Miguel, with well-seasoned New York steak, hearty sausage, a huge wedge of fresh, soft cheese, refried black beans, fluffy rice, and delicious fried sweet plantains with sour cream. Scrape it all up with a pile of tortillas—this is definitely a dish to share. Many of the dishes are mild, but they're served with a very spicy habanero salsa if you need a little punch. You might not have time for dessert, like Guatemalan corn bread, because the restaurant closes at 7:30 or 8PM. *Cash only; lunch, early dinner Thurs-Tues; beer and wine.*

Sapporo-Ya

1581 WEBSTER ST, SAN FRANCISCO   📞 415/563-7400
JAPANTOWN 🍴 *Japanese*

Think of a neighborhood diner transplanted to Japan and you'll have an idea of Sapporo-Ya's ambience: slightly sticky tables, bowls of disposable chopsticks, and adequate, but not exactly gushing, service. All is forgiven, though, when the noodles hit the table. Ordering the ramen is a must, whether you opt for miso or shoyu broth, the thinly sliced pork or the vegetable tempura. The adventurous will want to try the *okonomiyaki,* a southern Japanese specialty consisting of an omelet thickened with rice powder and served with meat, vegetables, or seafood. Most dishes, at around $7, are a great value. Sapporo-Ya's prime

Japantown location makes it a best bet when you're headed to a movie at the nearby Kabuki theater. A word of warning: sodas are served in 6-ounce glasses, so if you're thirsty, you might want to wait and get a Coke after the meal. *AE, MC, V; no checks; lunch, dinner every day; wine only.* ♿

Saul's Restaurant and Delicatessen

1475 SHATTUCK AVE, BERKELEY 📞 510/848-3354
NORTH BERKELEY 🍴 *Deli*

Saul's brings the Big Apple to Berkeley, complete with black-and-white photos of old New York and a sign designating the dining room as Times Square. Settle into a red vinyl booth or fill your picnic basket at the counter, where you'll find respectable renditions of deli sandwiches such as pastrami, meat loaf, roast beef, and tongue (all served in two sizes: "Berkeley," or "modest," and "New York," or "emphatic"). Other choices include such stalwarts as matzo ball soup, latkes, and blintzes. Saul's devotees can sleep in and still make it for breakfast—from eggs and onions to fluffy challah French toast—served until 2AM on weekdays and 3AM on weekends. This North Berkeley favorite attracts neighborhood scholars—grad students writing in journals and professors poring over the newspaper—due in no small part to its proximity to Black Oak Books, North Berkeley's best bookstore. *MC, V; local checks only; breakfast, lunch, dinner every day; no alcohol; info@saulsdeli.com; www.saulsdeli.com.* ♿

Savor

3913 24TH ST, SAN FRANCISCO 📞 415/282-0344
NOE VALLEY 🍴 *Bakery*

Noe Valley locals pack into this place for the homey atmosphere, huge portions, and house-baked goods, especially on weekend mornings, when space on the shady back patio is at a premium. Besides omelets, there are special egg dishes like a New Orleans version of eggs Benedict with crab cakes and homemade biscuits. Served with hefty servings of crisp home fries and mixed greens, crepes are a good bet, though some combinations, like smoked tofu, shiitake mushrooms, ginger, and peanut sauce, take the whole fusion concept just a little too far. Nightly dinner specials like steamed mussels and roasted vegetable risotto take the menu out of the bargain category, but you can order the large salads, sandwiches, and the eggs and crepes all day. Rugs hanging on the walls and a fireplace create a cozy feel, and it's also the perfect place to bring kids. Not only is there a special $1.95 kids menu (unheard of in most San Francisco restaurants), the friendly wait staff will clean up what's left behind without blinking an eye. *MC, V; no checks; breakfast, lunch, dinner every day; beer and wine only.* ♿

Schnitzelhaus

294 9TH ST, SAN FRANCISCO ☏ 415/864-4038
SOUTH OF MARKET 🍴 *German/Eastern European*

If you like schnitzel, the German specialty of breaded and fried meat cutlets, you're in luck. Wiener schnitzel, Jägerschnitzel, Rahnschnitzel, and Kaiserschnitzel are only a few of your choices at this schnitzel wonderland that also serves a variety of German and Austrian dishes. The pine-paneled dining room, with its sloped ceiling, deer antler chandelier, and photos of German castles on the walls, is possibly the coziest spot South of Market, and the food is hearty and delicious. Though dinner prices are definitely on the high end for this book, lunch here is an extraordinary value. Lunch specials, like the big plate of *Paprika-Hühnchen mit Spätzle* (paprika chicken with noodles), come with a basket of bread with herbed butter, a salad or bowl of thick potato soup, and a side of sauerkraut—all for under $10. *DIS, MC, V; no checks; lunch Tues-Fri, dinner Tues-Sun; beer and wine; reservations@schnitzelhaus.com; www.schnitzelhaus.net.*

Sears Fine Food

439 POWELL ST, SAN FRANCISCO ☏ 415/986-1160
UNION SQUARE 🍴 *Diner*

Sears is your classic American coffee shop, where the decor and the staff haven't changed since the Nixon administration. Story has it that Sears first opened in 1938, when Ben the Clown decided to retire from the circus and open his own restaurant. His Swedish wife, Hilbur, chipped in her family's secret recipe (still a secret to this day) for Swedish pancakes (18 silver dollars to a serving), and there's been a line out the door every weekend morning ever since. Some might call it tacky, but there's something comforting about the matronly waitresses in their pink uniforms serving old-fashioned American food. If pancakes aren't your thing, try the crispy dark-brown waffles or sourdough French toast. The fresh fruit cup marinated in orange juice is also quite popular. Lunch is served as well, but it's the classic breakfast experience that makes Sears worth the wait. Too bad the coffee isn't any better. *Cash only; breakfast, lunch every day; no alcohol.* ♿

Shalimar

532 JONES ST, SAN FRANCISCO ☎ 415/928-0333
TENDERLOIN 🍴 *Indian*

If you're searching for authentic and ridiculously affordable Indian fare, Shalimar is for you. Despite its location on the edge of the Tenderloin, it's jam-packed each night with folks who love the dirt-cheap, so-spicy-it-makes-you-sweat Indian food. That's because when it comes to tandoori lamb and chicken and beef skewers, Shalimar does it with a skill that can only be learned from the homeland, and the flatbreads are delicious and served hot from the oven. Good thing the food is so delicious: sticky linoleum and glaring lights dominate the decor, and you stand in line at the counter to place your order. But what they save on interior design, they pass on to you—some items are less than $3! They don't serve alcohol, but you're free to bring your own. And you might very well want to pick up a beer at the store around the corner to wash down the fiery food. *Cash only; lunch, dinner every day; no alcohol.*

Slanted Door

584 VALENCIA ST, SAN FRANCISCO ☎ 415/861-8032
MISSION DISTRICT 🍴 *Vietnamese/Southeast Asian*

Thank goodness chef Charles Phan abandoned his original plan to build a crepe stand in San Francisco, because otherwise we never would have had the opportunity to sink our teeth into his superb green papaya salad or stir-fried caramelized shrimp, just a few of the reasons his restaurant is the darling of San Francisco foodies. When Phan and his large extended family discovered a vacant space on a slightly run-down stretch of Valencia Street, they ditched the crepe stand plan in late 1995 and transformed the high-ceilinged room into a bi-level restaurant specializing in country Vietnamese food. Phan's design talents—he's a former UC Berkeley architecture student—are evident from the moment you enter the stylish, narrow dining room and take a seat at one of his green-stained wood tables. But even more impressive is his unique fare, which attracts droves of people for lunch and dinner—reserve well in advance, especially for a weekend table. The dinner menu changes weekly to reflect the market's offerings, but look for the favored spring rolls stuffed with fresh shrimp and pork; crab and asparagus soup; caramelized shrimp; curried chicken cooked with yams; "shaking" beef sautéed with onion and garlic; any of the terrific clay pot dishes; and, of course, Phan's special Vietnamese crepes.

When business is booming the service gets slow, but if you order a pinot gris from the very good wine list, you won't mind so much. *MC, V; no checks; lunch, dinner Tues-Sun; beer and wine; eat@slanteddoor.com.*

Specialty's Cafe and Bakery

1 POST PLAZA, SAN FRANCISCO *(and branches)* 📞 415/678-2600
FINANCIAL DISTRICT/SOUTH OF MARKET 🍴 *Bakery*

The baked goods—breads, muffins, scones, and especially the thick, soft cookies—are the main reason people line up at each of the eight Specialty's locations every weekday morning and afternoon. No, this place isn't the best bakery in the world, but for a high-volume downtown establishment, they do a good job. And having your turkey, roast beef, or tuna sandwich encased in thick slabs of freshly made herb, potato-poppy seed, whole grain, or any of the many varieties of breads on the menu that day—and having it still warm at that—well, that leaves an impression. Some argue the bread is too soft and gummy; many more, however, find it chewy and flavorful. Standard sandwiches such as the turkey (made with processed turkey breast) lack excitement, while specialty creations like the Hot Hammer (hot ham and Swiss) are livelier and tastier. In the mornings the counter displays are filled with various muffins, rolls, and frosted breakfast breads—a sugar-infested yet quite tasty treat. And the cookies? Hard to beat a warm, chewy chocolate chip for a midafternoon snack. *Cash only; breakfast, lunch Mon-Fri; no alcohol; www.specialtys.com; specialtys@specialtys.com.*

Spettro

3355 LAKESHORE AVE, OAKLAND 📞 510/465-8320
LAKE MERRITT 🍴 *Italian*

A meal at Spettro is like a party in someone's dining room: you may not know everyone when you get there, but you might just end up making some new friends before the night is over. Brick walls and low-hanging Christmas lights give the place a warm, intimate feel, and the tables down the middle of the room are pushed together, which means you and your neighbors are practically at the same table. An eclectic crowd—from Oaktown hipsters to young families with little ones is tow—packs Spettro for its genuinely friendly service and funky cuisine, which ranges from Italian to Asian-influenced seafood and veggie choices. Standbys include Heather's Booberry Salad (greens with blueberry vinaigrette, candied walnuts, goat cheese, and blueberries) and pan-seared coconut-lime mussels. Pastas and meat entrees round out the offerings; be sure to check out the chalkboard for seasonal specials. And if you get stuck waiting outside for a table on a Friday or Saturday night, take consolation in free wine and pizza while you wait. *AE, DIS, MC, V; no checks; lunch Tues-Fri, dinner every day; beer and wine.* &

Squat and Gobble Cafe

237 FILLMORE ST, SAN FRANCISCO *(and branches)* 📞 415/487-0551
LOWER HAIGHT/CASTRO/UPPER HAIGHT ⍩ *American*

This is perhaps the most unappealingly named restaurant we've come across since discovering a crepe restaurant in France called Kramps. But as much as we'd like to hold that against the place, it's tough when you're sitting at one of the sidewalk tables eating a great big ham and cheese omelet with home fries on a Sunday morning. The menu ranges far and wide, from the usual brunch fare of waffles, omelets, and sweet and savory crepes to salads and sandwiches to pasta dinners like fettuccine alfredo and spaghetti marinara. As long as you avoid the most adventurous offerings, like pork chops or beef stroganoff, you're on safe ground, but breakfast is the real reason to come. The Lower Haight restaurant is cheerfully painted yellow, with colorful works by local artists on the walls, and the diners consist mostly of the tattooed, pink-haired, and dreadlocked set that call the neighborhood home. This location is just around the corner from Kate's Kitchen (see review), whose food is definitely a cut above. But on weekend mornings, when the wait at Kate's exceeds an hour, you can often get a table here in about 10 minutes–not the least of the restaurant's charms. *MC, V; no checks; breakfast, lunch, dinner every day; beer and wine.* &

St. Francis Fountain & Candy

2801 24TH ST, SAN FRANCISCO 📞 415/826-4200
MISSION DISTRICT ⍩ *Diner*

Now that every swanky new restaurant seems to have a retro theme, it's nice to see that the real deal still exists. And this ice cream parlor with wooden booths, a counter with stools, and powder-puff-pink walls trumpets the fact that it's been open since 1918 (in 1929, they sold a dish of maple nut ice cream for 15 cents). Lunch and dinner items are standard diner fare–frankfurters, hamburgers, grilled cheese sandwiches, and the so-passé-it's-kitschy cottage cheese and pineapple salad. But the real reason for visiting, of course, is the homemade ice cream, in flavors like rocky road and black raspberry marble. Triple-scoop milk shakes come as thick as you like and can be served as malteds; hot fudge sundaes are another traditional treat. A small selection of homemade candies, including dark chocolate–covered apricots, is displayed in the counter out front. *MC, V; lunch, dinner every day; no alcohol.* &

Suppenküche

601 HAYES ST, SAN FRANCISCO 📞 415/252-9289
HAYES VALLEY 🍴 *German/Eastern European*

Smack in the middle of the hip and trendy Hayes Valley is a little slice of Deutschland, a German wursthaus whose authenticity runs from the bratwurst to the beers to the volume level. Come hungry and thirsty; everything here is large and hearty. Favorites include the potato soup and the potato pancakes to start, then the Wiener schnitzel and the venison medallions in red-wine plum sauce. Brunches are very popular and include massive omelets with a plateful of potatoes and roast pork sausages in an egg scramble. But the biggest draw has to be the beer, served in giant-size steins and running the gamut from hefeweizen to pilsner to bock. It's all served on tap, and there are also a couple of Belgian and English brands just to keep things even. Though the prices are definitely on the high end for this book, budget-minded diners can find inexpensive items like a hearty cheese spätzle with onions or a lentil stew with bratwurst. And no matter what you order, expect to leave positively stuffed. *AE, MC, V; no checks; dinner every day, brunch Sat–Sun; beer and wine; peterk@ suppenkuche.com; www.suppenkuche.com.*

Swan Oyster Depot

1517 POLK ST, SAN FRANCISCO 📞 415/673-1101
POLK GULCH 🍴 *Seafood*

You won't find white linen tablecloths at this oyster bar—in fact, you won't even find any tables. Since 1912, patrons have balanced themselves on the single row of rickety stools lining the long, narrow marble counter cluttered with bowls of oyster crackers, fresh-cut lemons, napkin holders, Tabasco sauce, and other seasonings. On the opposite side stand the burly, wisecracking Sancimino brothers, some of the most congenial men in town, always ready and eager to serve. Lunch specialties include Boston clam chowder, sizable salads (crab, shrimp, prawn, or a combo), seafood cocktails, cracked

Dungeness crab, lobster, and smoked salmon and trout. A bowl of chowder and beer is a popular and inexpensive way to go. If you want to bring home some fish for supper, take a gander at all the fresh offerings in the display case: salmon, swordfish, red snapper, trout, shrimp, lingcod, and whatever else the boat brought in that day. *No credit cards; checks OK; lunch Mon-Sat (open 8AM-5:30PM); beer and wine.*

Sweden House Bakery & Cafe

35 MAIN ST, TIBURON   📞   415/435-9767
TIBURON   🍴   *Bakery*

Though the sunny seats on the deck overlooking the water are the most coveted (despite the dive-bombing birds out for your food), it's no hardship to sit inside the restaurant, where old rolling pins and copper cooking kettles decorate the country Scandinavian interior. Breakfast items include omelets, bagels and lox, and granola and fruit, but if you're here on a weekday–the only time it's served–consider the French toast, made with house-made Swedish limpa (sweet rye) bread and served with a dollop of sour cream, a side of syrup, and a sprinkle of powdered sugar. Sandwiches, like the open-faced avocado, bacon, and sprouts, are also available on the limpa bread, or on the heartier German six-grain. But a lot of people just stop by for the pastries–scones, napoleons, florentine cookies, pastel-colored princess tortes–to pack in their picnic baskets before heading to Angel Island. *AE, MC, V; no checks; breakfast, lunch every day; wine only.*   ♿

Sweet Heat

1725 HAIGHT ST, SAN FRANCISCO   📞   415/387-8845
UPPER HAIGHT   🍴   *Mexican*

Everything at this informal Mexican spot is a step above your average burrito dive–which is apparent from the moment that a waiter motions you to a table and arrives to take your order, rather than leaving you to stand in line. By the time he brings you a trio of salsas (a sweet tomatillo, smoky chipotle, and fiery mango) with your burrito or other dishes you've ordered, you'll wonder why you haven't come here before. The trademark starter of plantains and spinach, with a tamarind chipotle sauce, is a complex mix of savory, sweet, tart, and smoky tastes. Burritos, too, come in unusual varieties: beyond the typical grilled shrimp or beef choices you'll find a juicy achiote chicken burrito with pickled red onions. In fact, everything here is just so darn tasty that we're almost ready to forgive them that you have to pay for chips and salsa. *MC, V; no checks; lunch, dinner every day, brunch Sat–Sun; full bar.*

Taiwan

445 CLEMENT ST, SAN FRANCISCO 📞 415/387-1789
RICHMOND DISTRICT 🍴 *Chinese*

Big Asian families, hipster couples, groups of friends, and even solitary diners cram into Taiwan for big helpings of familiar Chinese foods, including lots of seafood and mu shu dishes. They like the atmosphere, too, which is several steps above hole-in-the-wall. Taiwan Restaurant also has a secret weapon: a slate of unusual dishes from Taiwan and Northern China, like the crispy and filling white turnip cakes and the unexpectedly delicious pork in red rice wine sauce. During the day, pedestrians have been known to stop in their tracks to drool over the display of Northern Chinese dim sum–like Chinese-style donuts and sweet bean cakes displayed in Taiwan's window. There are inexpensive lunch specials and plenty of options for vegetarians, too. *MC, V; no checks; lunch, dinner every day; beer and wine.* ♿

Taqueria Cancun

2288 MISSION ST, SAN FRANCISCO 📞 415/252-9560
1003 MARKET ST, SAN FRANCISCO 📞 415/864-6773
MISSION DISTRICT/SOUTH OF MARKET 🍴 *Mexican*

This taqueria has a huge loyal following seemingly in spite of itself. It does little to keep people coming back other than offer incredibly flavorful Mexican dishes à la carte and at bargain-basement prices. Its main location, on an unseemly stretch of Mission Street, makes for some unusual characters coming through the doors. But that's part of the Cancun's experience, second only to the incredible carne asada burritos and tacos and the hot, fresh-made salsas— best washed down with a cantaloupe-flavored agua fresca. A jukebox with mostly Mexican music keeps diners entertained while they're waiting for their number to be called. *Cash only; lunch, dinner every day; beer only.*

Taqueria El Balazo

1654 HAIGHT ST, SAN FRANCISCO 📞 415/864-8608
54 MINT ST, SAN FRANCISCO 📞 415/882-9575
UPPER HAIGHT/UNION SQUARE 🍴 *Mexican*

Like all the great burrito places in San Francisco, here you can stuff yourself silly with a meat and vegetable dish for around $5. What's different about El Balazo ("the gun" in Spanish) is the colorful, funky dining room and the vast variety of meals that have more pizzazz than your average carne asada. If you've gone cold to the usual meat, rice, and beans, try the chile relleno burrito, a piquant pasilla pepper stuffed with cheese and broiled in a tangy tomato sauce, then wrapped in a tortilla with rice and beans, or the yummy grilled chicken or vegetable tamales. The torta (sandwich), a crusty bun smeared with refried beans, then piled with avocado slices, steak or chicken, melted cheese, and tomato, is a great choice if you just can't look at another tortilla. A cabbage salad served with every meal makes a refreshing, citrusy accompaniment, as do the aguas frescas, light, sweet drinks of mango, cantaloupe, watermelon, or strawberry. The seafood is usually a disappointment, and the food and service can be inconsistent, so order what looks good. *Cash only; lunch, dinner every day; beer and wine.*

Taqueria La Cumbre

515 VALENCIA ST, SAN FRANCISCO 📞 415/863-8205
MISSION DISTRICT 🍴 *Mexican*

It may not serve the absolute best burritos in town, but La Cumbre is certainly a strong, reliable, and very affordable standby. Vegetarian items are available, but the real draw is the meat burritos and tacos: if you're hungry when you pass the door on busy Valencia Street, the smell of the fresh-grilled beef and chicken will suck you right in. Rice, beans, and salsa are included in the basic burrito setup. If you want extra toppings, make sure you have your terminology correct: a "deluxe" burrito adds cheese, sour cream, and guacamole; a "super" means extra meat and cheese; and a "super deluxe" packs it all in together (oh yes, it's big). Fearless carnivores who don't want to fool around can order the "all meat" burrito. Dinner plates are another option, offering meat, beans, rice, and salad spread out on a plate instead of wrapped up in a tortilla. Sit down at one of the tiny, teetering tables and dig in. *Cash only; lunch, dinner every day; beer only.*

Thai Cafe

3407 GEARY BLVD, SAN FRANCISCO   📞 415/386-4200
RICHMOND DISTRICT 🍴 *Thai*

On Geary Boulevard, the Thai Cafe's green and yellow neon sign and warm-looking interior beckons diners hungry for Thai food. Both this place and its sister restaurant, Clement Street's Vietnamese eatery Le Soleil (owned by the same people; see review), are known for reliably tasty dishes served in a nicer-than-average atmosphere. In the evening, Thai Cafe is generally bustling with both neighborhood folks and people on their way to a movie at the nearby Bridge Theater. At lunch, neighborhood workers and ladies who lunch enjoy the bargain specials served with a choice of entree, soup, fried shrimp roll, and a mound of rice. The menu offers reliable Thai favorites like hot-and-sour soup and pad Thai, as well as beef, pork, chicken, or seafood cooked in red, green, or yellow curries. Some of Thai Cafe's more unexpected dishes include roasted, marinated quail and duck with peanut sauce. Vegetarians can find something to order here, although the selection is not as broad as at other Thai restaurants. *MC, V; no checks; lunch, dinner every day; beer and wine.*

Thai House

151 NOE ST, SAN FRANCISCO   📞 415/863-0374
CASTRO 🍴 *Thai*

This is a neighborhood restaurant that people come from all over the city to enjoy. It's in a great location with an attractive and attentive staff, and despite each perfectly set table's starched white cloth napkins, a shorts-and-sneakers attitude prevails. Everything on the menu is good, so it's tough to go wrong. Whet your appetite with *som tum,* the shredded green papaya salad, or the *mieng kum,* tender bites of fresh spinach, ginger, onion, dried shrimp, toasted coconut, and peanut in a tamarind sauce. If you're looking for some guidance, classic Thai dishes like the *larb gai,* ground chicken and ground rice with chiles, lemon, onion, and basil, is perfection, as is the pad Thai. Sautéed beef with broccoli is flavorful, and the red snapper melts into an aromatic coconut curry that will make the hovering presence of those clamoring for your table on a busy night temporarily disappear. *MC, V; no checks; dinner every day; beer only.* ♿

Thep Phanom

400 WALLER ST, SAN FRANCISCO 📞 415/431-2526
LOWER HAIGHT 🍴 *Thai*

Winner of numerous awards, this cozy restaurant in a Victorian building is considered one of the best, if not *the* best, Thai restaurant in San Francisco. It's hard to chose from the lengthy list of appetizers, but one of the tastiest dishes on the menu is Paksa Vehok (Birds of Paradise), hot, peppery deep-fried quail offset with a sweet and sour dipping sauce. Or try *tod mun plah,* savory fried fish cakes with cucumber salad, or *yum nuer,* sliced top sirloin tossed with fresh mint, onions, chiles, and lemon dressing. For main courses, look for catfish in curry sauce with lemon leaves or sautéed pork with Japanese eggplant, fresh basil, and bean sauce. Each item is a few dollars more than what you find in most neighborhood Thai restaurants, but the excellent execution and use of fresh and exotic ingredients make it worth the extra cost. The only drawback is that the servers might try to hurry you through your meal to make way for the huge line of hungry customers waiting outside, so keep a firm grip on your plates until you're done. Unlike many Thai restaurants, Thep Phanom does take reservations, so call ahead for the shortest wait. *AE, DC, DIS, MC, V; no checks; lunch, dinner every day; beer and wine.*

Ti Couz

3108 16TH ST, SAN FRANCISCO 📞 415/252-7373
MISSION DISTRICT 🍴 *French*

When this popular Breton crepe restaurant doubled its size by opening an adjacent dining room, Ti Couz Too, fans were thankful that little else changed. The restaurant still has wooden plank floors, rustic wooden tables, and an all-around cozy feeling that makes you feel as if you really could be on the western coast of France. And though they added a few cocktails to the menu (the Couzmopolitan is their own take on the popular drink), purists still opt for the traditional hard cider, served Breton-style in small bowls. The savory crepes, made with buckwheat flour, come stuffed with fillings like ratatouille, ham and cheese, or even smoked salmon. Salads, like the *salade de marée* (seafood), packed with shrimp, scallops, seared tuna, eggs, olives, and capers, are enormous; a "small" portion easily serves two. The dessert crepes, though not inexpensive, are the reason many come here; "the Tod" comes stuffed with a chunky applesauce, dressed with caramel sauce, and topped with ice cream, while the "La Délice" is a decadent concoction with sliced bananas and the thick hazelnut chocolate paste Nutella. Despite the restaurant's expansion, waits can still be long, so put your name on the list and settle in. *MC, V; no checks; lunch, dinner every day, brunch Sat-Sun; full bar.* &

Tita's Hale 'Aina

3870 17TH ST, SAN FRANCISCO   415/626-2477
CASTRO   *Hawaiian*

If you're looking for tiki torches and sticky drinks served in coconuts, then this *hale 'aina* (restaurant) isn't for you. Vintage luau photography, the occasional ukulele hanging on the wall, and the soft strains of Hawaiian music are the only concessions to Hawaiian kitsch. Tita's instead prides itself on dishing up delicious comfort food in true island style. As testament to their authenticity, they've got Spam on the menu and a "Got Poi?" bumper sticker on the drink cooler. Mahimahi, coconut- and macadamia nut-encrusted chicken, and slow-cooked pork are signature dishes. Be sure to massage your stomach like old-time Hawaiian royalty to make room for Tita's homemade desserts, like the coconut pudding with a chocolate coconut crust. In keeping with the relaxed nature of the islands, speedy service is not the highlight of a visit here. So be prepared to kick back and enjoy the company of your fellow diners. And as for the umbrellaed drinks? They haven't even got a liquor license, so go for the guava juice instead. *MC, V; checks OK; breakfast Sat-Sun, lunch, dinner every day; no alcohol; titakoni@webtv.com; www.titashaleaine.com.*

Tokyo Go Go

3174 16TH ST, SAN FRANCISCO   415/864-2288
MISSION DISTRICT   *Japanese*

The owner of Ace Wasabi's in the Marina district figured the success he's had there could surely be duplicated in the Mission. So he opened Tokyo Go Go and gave it a retro-futuristic look, with quirky fixtures and smooth surfaces. His Marina loyalists followed, but they quickly gave way to residents of the area, who now populate this fun, lively spot. Fun is the order of the day here. The sushi is fresh and flavorful and you'll find all the standard selections. But the kitchen likes to cut loose, too, and if you are willing to experiment, you'll find some surprises. The Go Go Roll places cooked shrimp over a roll of cucumber that wraps a garlic crouton. The Tuscan Roll features salmon, cucumber, sun-dried tomatoes, basil, and capers rolled with rice in a cone of seaweed—hard to imagine, easy to eat. Or try the Flying Kamikaze: spicy tuna and asparagus topped with albacore tuna and ponzu sauce. The bar serves premium sakes in martini glasses garnished with cucumber slices—clearly not your typical sushi joint. *MC, V; no checks; dinner Tues–Sun; full bar; www.tokyogogo.citysearch.com.*

The Truth About Wasabi

Almost everyone is familiar with wasabi, that small green dollop with Play-Doh–like consistency that lends color and a sinus-clearing jolt to orders of sushi. But in reality, what most people call wasabi is nothing of the sort. The so-called wasabi served in almost all sushi restaurants is basically plain old horseradish with a squirt of blue and yellow food coloring. Why the deception? Economics. Wasabi is one of the most difficult and most expensive vegetables to grow. Fresh wasabi has to be carefully tended for two years before it reaches maturity and peak flavor, and it requires a constant source of extremely pure water for its cultivation. Oregon farmer Jim Tasley has made growing wasabi his business, and he attests that all this TLC comes at a price, often as much as $5 to $6 for a teaspoon-size serving. Tasley is the president of Pacific Farms, North America's largest producer of real wasabi—it even exports wasabi to Japan. You needn't travel so far, though: you can sample the real deal at **SUSHI KO** (1819 Larkspur Landing, Larkspur; 415/461-8400) and **ROBATA GRILL** (591 Redwood Highway, Mill Valley; 415/381-8400). These two restaurants, owned by Tasley, draw diners from near and far who are willing to pay a premium price for this culinary rarity.

But before you go drowning that wad of high-priced pleasure in a dish of soy sauce, take note: the traditional way to eat wasabi is to place the grated rhizome directly on the fish. Then you take the whole she-bang for a dive into your soy sauce. And you'll really look like a sashimi master if you grate the wasabi with a piece of jagged shark skin. Budding sushi chefs can also find fresh wasabi at **TOKYO FISH MARKET** (1220 San Pablo Ave, Berkeley; 510/524-7243) and **MARUWA FOODS** (1737 Post St, San Francisco; 415/563-1901). Or you can order it directly from **PACIFIC FARMS** (P.O. Box 223, Florence, Oregon, 97439; www.freshwasabi.com).

Tommaso's Ristorante Italiano

1042 KEARNY ST, SAN FRANCISCO   📞   415/398-9696
NORTH BEACH 🍴 *Italian*

It's just off the main Broadway strip, sandwiched between strip clubs, so it's something of a surprise that Tommaso's comes highly recommended for family dining. The restaurant, a small, cozy place with wooden booths and no windows, has endeared itself to locals by consistently turning out delicious traditional-style pizzas, available with any of 19 different toppings and baked in an oak-burning brick oven—all at rock-bottom prices. Although pizza is the main draw, the hearty Italian classics such as chicken cacciatore and a super-cheesy lasagne should not be overlooked. Order a bottle of chianti for the table and you're in business. Service is quick, efficient, and downright neighborly. A true San Francisco treasure. *AE, DC, MC, V; local checks only; dinner Tues–Sun; full bar; dario@tommasos.com; www.tommasos.com.*

Tommy's Joynt

1101 GEARY BLVD, SAN FRANCISCO   📞   415/775-4216
CIVIC CENTER 🍴 *American*

Roast beef, mashed potatoes and gravy, and a bottle of German beer: that's the kind of fare to expect at this 50-plus-year-old, hofbrau-style eatery. It ain't health food, but for those craving an inexpensive plate that's heavy on the meat and potatoes, grab a tray and get in line. You order at the counter, where big, mustachioed men in white aprons carve you fat slabs of roast beef, ham, and turkey, spoon out the potatoes, and serve up hearty bowls of buffalo stew. The patrons are a mix of neighborhood regulars—many of them weary-looking single men—along with hipsters on their way to a show at the nearby Great American Music Hall and tourists (Germans, Brits, Midwesterners) who are thrilled to find a no-frills, fill-you-up meat plate in the land of tofu and sprouts. You say you want local color? The building has an exterior you can't miss, and inside the walls and ceiling are packed with memorabilia. The bar has loads of imported bottled beer, but keep in mind that the bartender, while efficient, is probably more interested in the game on the tube than idle chatter with you. *Cash only; lunch, dinner every day; full bar.* ♿

Tommy's Mexican Restaurant

5929 GEARY BLVD 📞 415/387-4747
RICHMOND DISTRICT 🍴 *Mexican*

Red vinyl booths, red tablecloths, and colorful Mexican rugs hanging from the walls set a festive mood here. Or is it the tequila? Tommy's makes much of the fact that it serves the largest collection of 100 percent agave tequilas outside Mexico, and many come just to sample some of the dozens of tequilas, from unaged "silver" tequilas to *añejo* varieties, aged in barrels for a year or more. But the food is much more than something to dilute the effect of the tequila, and it's better than you'll find at other Mexican party spots like La Rondalla and Puerto Alegre (see review). The usual favorites—burritos, enchiladas, chiles rellenos—are all here, as well as more unusual Yucatecan specialties. The *pollo pibil*, a juicy chicken breast, roasted onion, and a whole roasted jalapeño, comes wrapped in a banana leaf and served with a slightly sweet, slightly smoky tomato sauce. Wash it all down with a pitcher of those margaritas: though you could spend $100 on a pitcher made with the rare stuff, the least expensive pitchers, for around $17, are still made with fresh-squeezed limes and are mighty tasty indeed. *AE, MC, V; no checks; lunch, dinner every day; full bar; julio@ tommystequila.com; www.tommystequila.com.*

Ton Kiang

5821 GEARY BLVD, SAN FRANCISCO 📞 415/752-4440
RICHMOND DISTRICT 🍴 *Chinese*

Critics call this one of the top Chinese restaurants in the Bay Area, comparing its dim sum offerings to the best in Hong Kong. Try to arrive before noon on weekends, when a crowd congregates on the sidewalk waiting to get in. Once you get a table, don't let the efficient servers hurry you, because the food should be savored. The dim sum is more creative and less greasy than at most restaurants. Pot stickers are excellent—the thin, delicate wrappers are crisp and golden on the outside and plump with savory fillings. Shrimp is paired with a dozen different ingredients, such as scallops, spinach, chives, crab, eggplant, mushrooms, cabbage, and pea shoots. The egg custard rice cakes are a scrumptious variation on the traditional tarts, with a chewy but light dough redolent of coconut milk surrounding the same luscious, yellow custard. Be warned, though, that the bill can easily add up to more than $15 per person if you're not careful. Counter to tradition, the restaurant also serves dim sum in the evening, along with a dinner menu offering a huge array of fresh seafood, vegetable, and clay pot dishes. *MC, V; no checks; lunch, dinner, brunch every day; beer and wine.*

Tortola

3640 SACRAMENTO ST, SAN FRANCISCO *(and branches)* 📞 415/929-8181
LAUREL HEIGHTS/FINANCIAL DISTRICT/SUNSET DISTRICT 🍴 *Mexican*

There's no chance of confusing this Mexican restaurant with the dozens of burrito shops in the Mission. From the tablecloths to the cloth napkins to the gussied-up ladies-who-lunch sitting next to you, everything is upscale at the flagship location of this restaurant in one of the city's poshest residential districts. And although some of the dinner items are rather expensive for inclusion in this book, the burritos are fresh and satisfying. The signature Santa Fe pork tamales, served uncharacteristically on a bed of lettuce, would be out of place in Mexico, but the fresh tomato salsa and lettuce are welcome additions to what is usually a pretty heavy dish. At lunchtime, a hamburger, turkey sandwich, and even salmon burger are added to the already eclectic menu. The other branches are "quick service" locations, geared toward office workers looking for takeout. *MC, V; no checks; lunch Tues–Fri, dinner Tues–Sun; beer, wine, and margaritas.* ♿

Tropix

3814 PIEDMONT AVE, OAKLAND 📞 510/653-2444
NORTH OAKLAND 🍴 *Caribbean*

The perfect antidote to a fog-filled day is a taste of the Caribbean at Tropix. Colorful murals, strings of gently swaying multihued lights, bamboo partitions, and walls painted in the warm tones of papaya and mango lend an island flavor to this cheery Oakland spot. On warm summer evenings, tuck a hyacinth behind your ear and dine outside on the sprawling backyard patio, strewn with cafe tables and shaded by umbrellas. It's the perfect venue for downing a couple of pitchers of *bul,* a tasty Jamaican blend of beer, sugar, ginger, and lime. On cooler nights, eat by candlelight in the airy dining room. After a platter of sizzling sweet fried plantains and a stomachful of spicy gumbo, you'll swear you've been swept away to a sunnier clime. Mango, curry, coconut, and jerk sauce work their way into most of the house specialties, and the spicy pineapple chutney is particularly addictive. One taste of the drunken chicken, a mouthwatering mix of rum, white wine, yogurt, and garlic poured over chicken and propped on a bed of mashed yams, will have you coming to the tropics on a regular basis. *AE, MC, V; checks OK; lunch, dinner every day; beer and wine; www.tropix.citysearch.com.*

Truly Mediterranean

1724 HAIGHT ST, SAN FRANCISCO   📞 415/751-7482
3109 16TH ST, SAN FRANCISCO   📞 415/252-7482
UPPER HAIGHT/MISSION DISTRICT   🍴 *Mediterranean*

Some people call them urban food logs–long, cylindrical items wrapped in tin foil that contain enough food to satisfy a hungry city dweller for around $5. Burritos usually dominate this category of food, but the Mediterranean version–wrapped in lavash instead of tortillas–is celebrated at this restaurant. The flatbread is rolled around succulent *shawerma* (marinated and broiled lamb or chicken), kebabs, or falafel balls and jazzed up with fresh parsley, tomatoes, seasoned onions, and tahini sauce. Vegetarian options–such as dolma-stuffed pita or a Mediterranean combo plate–are more bountiful than the meaty ones. Say yes to the spicy sauce, or the spiced potatoes (50 cents extra), which add a tasty dimension to any lavash roll. The Mission location seems to have more people working behind the counter than can fit in the seating area, but that's because they're making everything to order. *MC, V; no checks (Upper Haight location); cash only (Mission location); lunch, dinner every day; no alcohol.*

Tsing Tao

200 BROADWAY, OAKLAND   📞 510/465-8811
DOWNTOWN OAKLAND   🍴 *Chinese*

A favorite Sunday-night destination for local Chinese-American families, Tsing Tao delivers high-quality Cantonese cooking. It's a far cry from fancy (would you believe fluorescent pink walls dotted with cheap chandeliers?), but it's a definite step up in quality and service from many Oakland Chinatown restaurants. Avoid the standard dishes that seem aimed mostly at non-Chinese and ask about the chef's specials of the day–that's where you'll find the good (i.e., authentic) stuff. For the Chinese equivalent of Mom's meat loaf, try the steamed pork patty flavored with heavily salted fish, and pair it with the tender mustard-green hearts glazed with a rich broth. Another winning combo: stir-fried crab with scallions and ginger (ask the price first–it can be high here) and stir-fried baby pea shoots, a springtime delicacy. Prices vary wildly, from less than $7 for chicken in a clay pot to $25 for a shark's fin soup, but most menu items come in under $10. *AE, MC, V; no checks; lunch, dinner every day; full bar.*

Tu Lan

8 6TH ST, SAN FRANCISCO 📞 415/626-0927
SOUTH OF MARKET 🍴 *Vietnamese*

If you're a fan of out-of-the-way ethnic dives that serve top-notch food, have we got a gem for you. Located in one of the sketchiest and foulest-smelling parts of the city, Tu Lan is a greasy, grimy little Vietnamese diner that, unless you are hip to the secret, you would neither find nor frequent. Which makes it all the more bewildering that a drawing of Julia Child's unmistakable face graces the cover of the greasy menus, but apparently she's one of Tu Lan's biggest fans. And once you try the light, fresh imperial rolls served on a bed of rice noodles, lettuce, peanuts, and mint, you'll become one, too. Other recommended dishes include the lemon beef salad, the fried fish in ginger sauce, and the pork kebabs, though pointing at whatever looks good on the Formica counter works just as well. Note: The faint of heart may want to order to go, and definitely do not use the upstairs bathroom (that's a dare, of course). *Cash only; lunch, dinner Mon–Sat; beer and wine.*

Two Jacks Seafood

401 HAIGHT ST, SAN FRANCISCO 📞 415/431-6290
LOWER HAIGHT 🍴 *Seafood*

This is fast food that could send Long John Silver's back to shore. It's too large to be called a hole-in-the-wall, but this neighborhood mainstay just a few steps from the very busy intersection of Haight and Fillmore Streets is easy to miss. And contrary to the battered shingle out front that reads "Two Jacks Seafood, Fresh and Cooked Fish," you can't buy any raw fish to bring home and cook yourself. But once you've tasted the deep-fried fish platters and sandwiches here, you'll quickly learn you couldn't replicate those flavors at home anyway. Red snapper, rock cod, catfish, oysters, and prawns are just a few of the ten or so varieties of seafood fried to order, served on a sandwich or with a platter of french fries, potato salad, and coleslaw. The menu is simple, but the fish is perfectly flaky and crispy. Too bad the place is takeout only: despite the generous space inside Two Jacks, there isn't a table in sight. *Cash only; lunch, dinner Mon–Sat; no alcohol.*

Uzen

4515 COLLEGE AVE, OAKLAND ☎ 510/654-7753
NORTH OAKLAND 🍴 *Sushi*

If IKEA were to design a sushi joint, it might very well look like Uzen. The restaurant's designers have done an artful job of making a small room feel spacious. Simple, understated lamps illuminate the sushi bar and its knife-wielding masters, while floor-to-ceiling windows facing College Avenue and bare cream-colored walls give the narrow room an open, airy feel. Although you won't find the hugest selection of imported sake or gimmicky touches like pumping rock-and-roll music or clever sushi names, Uzen serves some of the freshest sushi in the East Bay, at extremely reasonable prices. You fill out your tableside sushi card for such reliable favorites as *unagi* (eel) and spicy tuna rolls, but delicious entrees like udon noodles and teriyaki dishes are also available for the faint-of-sushi-heart. Definitely save room for Uzen's version of *mochi*, yummy balls of ice cream wrapped in sweet rice cake, which make the perfect complement to your meal. It's not on the menu, but if you ask, you can usually get it. *MC, V; no checks; lunch Mon–Fri, dinner Mon–Sat; beer and wine.*

Vicolo

201 IVY ST, SAN FRANCISCO ☎ 415/863-2382
HAYES VALLEY 🍴 *Pizza*

A piece of pizza at Vicolo might cost you four bucks, but it's not your typical flat and greasy slice. For starters, the folks at Vicolo make their pizzas deep-dish style with cornmeal crusts. And instead of relying on standard toppings like pepperoni and sausage, they pack the pizzas with such combinations as Gorgonzola and mushrooms, eggplant and provolone, or sweet corn and smoked mozzarella. Order a side salad of mixed greens and marinated vegetables and a single slice will likely satisfy; extra-hungry eaters may want two, but beware that a double dose of Gorgonzola pizza can be overwhelming. You can also order calzones, lasagne, or even a whole pie, but be prepared to take some home. Though tucked away on a small alley, Vicolo is conveniently located near the symphony hall and opera house, which means it's usually packed before performances. After about 8PM, however, the crowd thins out considerably, and the spacious dining area can feel downright empty. *MC, V; lunch, dinner every day; beer and wine.* ♿

Vik's

726 ALLSTON WAY, BERKELEY   510/644-4412
WEST BERKELEY   *Indian*

It's hard to believe, but some of the best Indian food this side of the Ganges comes heaped on paper plates in a warehouse in a transitional West Berkeley neighborhood. While Vik's originally gained fame as a wholesale Indian food market, word has spread fast about its booming side business. They roll up the steel door just in time for lunch, to loyal patrons' delight. Take your spot in line, read the list of dishes scribbled on a dry-erase board, and order from an array of *chaat*–savory snacks that are India's version of tapas. Then grab a plastic spoon (the only utensil provided) and wait for your name to be called over the ridiculously loud speaker system. You won't find better samosas anywhere in the Bay Area, and there are always two delicious specials (one for carnivores, one for vegetarians) that come with a dollop of raita and a crisp chapati. If you can manage to finish one of the over-the-top rich pastries, you're guaranteed to slip into a satisfying food coma for the rest of the afternoon. Pumping Indian techno music often accompanies your search for a seat amid the folding tables crammed in the warehouse. And bring a jacket–it gets drafty. *MC, V; no checks; lunch, dinner Tues-Sun; no alcohol.*

Wa-Ha-Ka

1489 FOLSOM ST, SAN FRANCISCO   415/861-1410
SOUTH OF MARKET   *Mexican*

Within bar-hopping distance from SoMa hotspots like Butter, Paradise Lounge, and Slim's, this Oaxaca Mexican grill makes a lively starting point for a night on the town. Weeknights tend to be a bit quiet, but surrounding companies contribute to a bustling weekday lunch hour, and Friday nights are downright rowdy, especially when the infamous Mexican Bus pulls up with its cadre of women celebrating the bachelorette party of the week (Wa-Ha-Ka is on its raucous weekly route). Order at the counter, then pull up a colorfully painted wooden chair while you wait. All the basics appear on the menu, from burritos to quesadillas to nachos, plus more unusual items like Baja rolls ($4.50). Dubbed "Mexican sushi," these bite-sized nibbles contain cream cheese, lettuce, tomato, avocado, and grilled chicken, rolled inside a flour tortilla. Exposed brick walls, wooden tables, and yellow-and-white Corona flags make for a pleasant atmosphere. Alas, escalating rents forced two former locations on Polk and Union streets to close up shop. *AE, DC, DIS, MC, V; no checks; lunch, dinner Mon-Sat, dinner Sun; beer and wine.* ♿

Waypoint Pizza

15 MAIN ST, TIBURON ☏ 415/435-3440
TIBURON 🍴 *Pizza*

Even on sunny weekend days, when the neighboring restaurants with outdoor decks have two-hour waits for a table, the lack of outdoor seating here means there's rarely a wait for one of Waypoint Pizza's fine pies. Specialties include the shrimp pesto pizza, which comes studded with sun-dried tomatoes and scallions, and the somewhat less successful Thai Chicken, with bean sprouts and cilantro sprinkled over a bed of carrots and chicken flavored with peanut sauce. Salads like the Vineyard strike a nice balance of sweet, tart, and tangy, with a balsamic vinaigrette dressing a mixture of spinach, roasted red pepper, pine nuts, and grapes. The restaurant's designers tried to compensate for the lack of a view by enthusiastically embracing a New England seaside theme. A large model of a ship is the first thing you see upon entering, then picnic tables under an umbrella and Adirondack chairs in the window. Still, on the nicest of days you may want to get your pizza or "Between the Sheets" (calzone) to go and enjoy it while taking in the view of Angel Island from the lush lawn about half a block away. *AE, DC, MC, V; no checks; lunch, dinner Wed-Mon; beer and wine.* ♿

Yamo Thai Kitchen

3406 18TH ST, SAN FRANCISCO ☏ 415/553-8911
MISSION DISTRICT 🍴 *Thai*

Since there's only one small, red counter to sit at, it's easy to watch the cooks here whip up your food to order, yelling in a friendly way as they go. Large portions and extremely low prices distinguish this greasy spoon from more sedate Thai restaurants around town. One reason this place sheds all pretension is that it's located right in the seedy thick of the Mission at 18th and Mission streets. But the food is still great: a spicy, coconut milk-enriched red curry comes with your choice of meat and fragrant basil. For a change from *tom ka gai* (coconut milk-chicken soup), try the *guai tiew tom yum,* a noodle soup overflowing with pork, prawns, and fish cake. There are plenty of vegetarian dishes to chose from, but no beer—you have to bring your own. *San Francisco Bay Guardian* Cheap Eats columnist Dan Leone claims to eat here at least once a week or so–a very strong endorsement from someone who eats out for a living. *Cash only; lunch, dinner Mon-Sat; no alcohol.*

Yank Sing

49 STEVENSON ST, SAN FRANCISCO 📞 415/541-4949
1 RINCON CENTER, 101 SPEAR ST, SAN FRANCISCO 📞 415/957-9300
SOUTH OF MARKET 🍴 *Chinese*

If navigating your way around Chinatown in search of dim sum is a perplexing prospect, pull up a chair at Yank Sing. The restaurant's two branches cater equally to tourists and suited-up downtowners looking for fresh and flavorful Chinese food in a familiar (i.e., Americanized) environment. If the room is packed, don't despair; the wait isn't terribly long. The sleek and shiny environment might be a turnoff for some, but what Yank Sing lacks in deep Chinatown character it makes up for with its delicious food. The steamed shrimp dumplings are fabulous, and the pork buns, chicken satay, Peking duck, and pot stickers are always reliable. Be adventurous–portions are small, so it's an excellent opportunity to try something different. Order a plate of noodles and a salad of Chinese greens and you've got more than enough food to satisfy. For those craving dessert, the mango pudding tops things off beautifully. *AE, MC, V; no checks; lunch Mon-Fri, brunch Sun; beer and wine; www.yanksing.com.* ♿

Yukol Place

2380 LOMBARD ST, SAN FRANCISCO 📞 415/922-1599
MARINA 🍴 *Thai*

When people are making lists of their favorite Thai restaurants in the city, this sleeper rarely seems to make the list. All the better, as far as we're concerned, because when the wait's an hour long at popular spots like Khan Toke Thai House and Thep Phanom (see reviews) we can usually just waltz in here for uncommonly creative Thai dishes. Chef Yukol Nieltaweephong has a way with fish, perhaps steaming a whole fish in a banana leaf before serving it alongside a sauce tart with tamarind. And it seems a shame to order the standbys like pad Thai when the menu features a spicy duck salad bright with the flavors of lemon and mint. The decor is fairly nondescript, but the smiling service brightens the room considerably. *MC, V; no checks; dinner every day; beer and wine.*

Zachary's Chicago Pizza

5801 COLLEGE AVE, OAKLAND 📞 510/655-6385
1853 SOLANO AVE, BERKELEY 📞 510/525-5950
NORTH OAKLAND/NORTH BERKELEY 🍽️ *Pizza*

Zachary's has won polls for best pizza in the Bay Area so many times that it seems almost unfair to every other place that puts cheese and tomato sauce on a crust. The distinctive pies here are like no others in town: deep-dish concoctions stuffed with cheese, a blend of spices, and the ingredients of your choice, before being topped with an ultrachunky tomato sauce. Zachary's signature dish is the spinach and mushroom deep-dish pie, but thin-crust pizzas are available if you must. And daily specials take advantage of fresh produce; in season, try the pizza topped with fresh asparagus tips, red bell pepper, and a mix of mozzarella and Parmesan cheeses. Service is friendly if occasionally harried, and the restaurant is typically full of families and college students. The waits can be extremely long at dinnertime, and the pizzas take 20 to 40 minutes to cook once you order them, so you might want to consider picking up a half-baked pie to take home. *Cash only; lunch, dinner every day; beer and wine; www.zacharys.com.* ♿

Za Gourmet Pizza

1919 HYDE ST, SAN FRANCISCO 📞 415/771-3100
RUSSIAN HILL 🍽️ *Pizza*

Unlike your average pizza sold by the slice or the pie, the slices at Za are so civilized they beg to be ordered with a glass of beer or one of the two house wines. Every day the menu features about four types of pizza by the enormous slice: as well the usual cheese or pepperoni, your choices might include the very popular Potesto (roasted red potatoes, roasted garlic, and pesto) or Pesto Picasso (with pesto, clams, and fresh garlic). Even better is the Salvador Dali (roasted chicken and sun-dried tomatoes), though the Popeye the Greek (spinach and feta) doesn't have the punch of some of the other choices. If you want to order a whole pie, you can dream up your own creative combo with unusual ingredients like spicy Calabrese sausage, turkey Canadian bacon, artichoke hearts, and clams. The only other decision is whether to accompany your slice with one of the enormous garden or Caesar salads. The casual restaurant is uncommonly comfortable, with wooden plank floors and works by local artists on the walls. Service is superfriendly, both for newcomers and locals who are known to the staff by name. *AE, DIS, MC, V; no checks; lunch, dinner every day; beer and wine.*

Zante Pizza and Indian Cuisine

2489 MISSION ST, SAN FRANCISCO   📞   415/821-3949
3083 16TH ST, SAN FRANCISCO   📞   415/621-4189
MISSION DISTRICT   🍴   *Indian*

No, that's not a mistake: Zante serves both Indian food and pizza under the same roof. There probably aren't many restaurants on the planet where you can order onion *kulcha* (naan bread with onions), *gosht vindaloo* (lamb in spicy sauce), mango lassi (a sweet yogurt drink), and a pepperoni and mushroom pizza pie off the same menu. Crazy as it sounds, it works—so well that Zante, tucked away in an out-of-the-way Outer Mission location for well over a decade, has opened a second restaurant on busy 16th Street near Valencia. While the Indian food is plenty respectable and the pizza is fine, the chief reason to patronize Zante is for the one-of-a-kind item that brings the two culinary worlds together: Indian pizza. Instead of tomato sauce and cheese you get a combination of tandoori lamb and chicken, spinach, eggplant, garlic, ginger, and chicken tikka masala spread across a pizza crust. Imagine an order of naan topped with all sorts of spicy goodies and you get the idea. It's pretty greasy, but the uniqueness makes it worth trying. *AE, DC, DIS, MC, V; no checks; lunch, dinner every day; beer and wine.*

Zao Noodle Bar

2406 CALIFORNIA ST, SAN FRANCISCO *(and branches)*   📞   415/345-8088
PACIFIC HEIGHTS/CASTRO/MARINA/SUNSET DISTRICT   🍴   *Pan-Asian*

Signs in each of the Zao locations spout silly pseudo-philosophy like "A bowl of noodles is a snapshot of the Universe," and most menu entries conclude with enigmatic statements like "Make your acupuncturist happy" and "Must fill unfulfilled desire." None of this can obscure the fact that this is simply a comfortable place for a soothing, satisfying bowl of noodles cooked with a variety of Asian-influenced seasonings. Hot noodles might be served with prawns in a curry coconut sauce or swimming in a miso-basil broth. The popular Vietnamese rice noodles with seared pork are a riot of complementary flavors and textures: the heat of peppers, the salty tang of *nuoc cham* (fish sauce), the cool crunch of lettuce, and the bite of slivered vegetables dressed in a salty mixture at the bottom of the bowl. The restaurant is cozily done up, with wooden chairs and tables and colorful chopsticks displayed on each table. Service is solicitous, and the selection of beer, wine, sakes, and tea is quite good. *MC, V; no checks; lunch, dinner every day; beer and wine; www.zaonoodle.com.* &

Zarzuela

2000 HYDE ST, SAN FRANCISCO 📞 415/346-0800
RUSSIAN HILL 🍴 *Spanish*

It's almost as good as being there—really. Waiters with Spanish accents bring plate after plate of just-like-the-old-country tapas, and you feel like a member of an extended family. This excellent Spanish restaurant atop Russian Hill has been popular since day one. Drenched in soothing colors, it is an elegant, sophisticated spot for well-priced Spanish cuisine. Fresh bread and Spanish olives are whisked to your table as soon as you sit down, and sangria and a selection of Spanish wines are offered immediately. The waiters keep up a frenetic pace, but always slow down when they reach your table, making you feel like you have all evening to sample, sip, and savor. The small plates are prepared with fresh ingredients and a liberal use of seasonings that sets them apart from the usual tapas fare. Nibble on the favorite gambas al ajillo, shrimp bathed in olive oil and garlic, which arrives in a small iron skillet, or the cool, colorful seafood salad. The paella is excellent, arguably the best in town. And although it's easy to blow through a pitcher of sangria and $30 per person without thinking of it, diners on a budget can order a light supper and a glass of the fruity elixir for considerably less. *DC, MC, V; no checks; dinner Tues–Sat; full bar.* &

Zazie's

941 COLE ST, SAN FRANCISCO 📞 415/564-5332
UPPER HAIGHT 🍴 *French*

This elegant yet casual restaurant specializes in simple, honest cooking that owes more to the warm provinces of southern France than to snooty Parisian haute cuisine. The beverages alone make this a great place, from *chocolat chaud* (hot chocolate) and lattes served in sunny ceramic bowls to *citron pressé* (a make-it-yourself lemon and sugar drink), homemade juice spritzers, and fruity, bubbly, intoxicating French cider. Lunch is good, but breakfast and dinner are the strongest meals. Sunday brunch is a great excuse to linger over gingerbread pancakes served with warm pears, eggs with lamb sausage, and excellent house-made herb-roasted potatoes with whole cloves of roasted garlic. More substantial fare includes a magnificent buttery roasted trout, seasoned skirt steak, and fresh vegetable pastas. From time to time, they fill the tiny restaurant space with entertainment—such as an opera singer or a flautist—that perfectly accompanies the cuisine. *MC, V; no checks; breakfast, lunch, dinner every day, brunch Sun; beer and wine.*

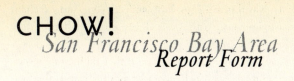

CHOW!
San Francisco Bay Area
Report Form

Based on my personal experience, I wish to nominate the following restaurant; or confirm/correct/disagree with the current review.

_____
_____
_____
_____

(Please include address and telephone number of establishment, if convenient.)

REPORT:

Please describe food, service, style, comfort, value, date of visit, and other aspects of your experience; continue on other side if necessary.

_____
_____
_____
_____
_____
_____

I am not concerned, directly or indirectly, with the management or ownership of this establishment.

Signed _____
Address _____
_____
Phone _____
Date _____

Please address to *Chow! San Francisco Bay Area* and send to:

Sasquatch Books
615 Second Avenue, Suite 260
Seattle, WA 98104

Feel free to email feedback as well: books@SasquatchBooks.com

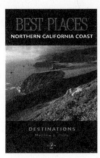